THE
ANGRY FILMMAKER
PRESENTS

ANOTHER
KELLEY BAKER
JAG

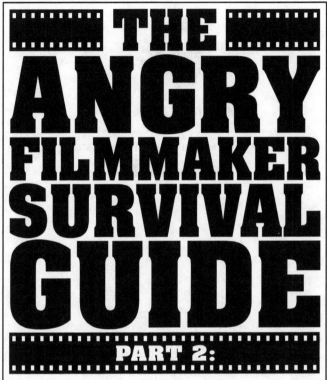

THE ANGRY FILMMAKER SURVIVAL GUIDE

PART 2:

Sound Conversations With (un)Sound People

KELLEY BAKER

(AKA: The Angry Filmmaker)

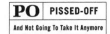

PO PISSED-OFF

And Not Going To Take It Anymore

ANGRY FILMMAKER

Angry Filmmaker, Inc.   PO Box 8322   Portland, OR 97207

AngryFilmmaker.com

To order additional copies go to http://www.angryfilmmaker.com

ISBN-13: 978-1466414563
ISBN-10: 1466414561

This book is printed on acid-free paper.
Printed in the United States of America

Wait a minute, wait a minute,
you ain't heard nothin' yet.
- Al Jolson, first synchronized dialogue in a motion picture

What makes it look like a movie is the sound.
- Karl Schaefer, Hollywood Producer

You can get away with bad pictures
but you can never get away with bad sound.
Don Coutts, Scottish TV/Film Director

To Kid
You keep me young and always learning.

For Kay
For giving me a lifetime of motivation..

ACKNOWLEDGEMENTS

I want to thank: Fiona Baker for being my light in the dark; Jim Baker, for always asking "Are you getting caught up?"; Margie Yap for continuing to be there; Will Akers for giving me good advice and a place to stay; Jay Tormohlen for putting up with my Photoshop ignorance; Bill Dever for pushing me to make it better; Brian David Johnson for stimulating conversation and being a fellow elitist; Jeff Pollard for great artwork and being a Shipmate; Professor Danger (Danny Boyd) for being a brother; Enie Vaisbaud for her constant support; and Dianna Stirpe for her good ideas.

I also want to thank Mary Baker, Leslie and Jamie Baker, John Ray, Jon Gann, Wayne Woods, Concha Solano, Debby Dietrich, Paul Lewis, Janet McIntyre, Michelle Mower, Matt Meyer, Joe Heyen, Don Campbell, Cari Callis, Prema Thiagarajah & the Nashville Film Institute, Josh Cross, Kim Blair, Alexander 23, Tim McHugh, Dana Driskel, Saul Zaentz, Steve Shurtz, Scott Roberts, Paul Sabal, Richard Mozer, Ricardo Moore, David Comer, Jonathan Stark, Kianna Cambria, Chris Hansen (not that one!), Paul Diener, Andy Wiskes, David Parker, Harris Mattarazzo, Nic Brown, Fiona Young-Brown, Daniel Braddock, and Mel Sloan.

And all of the casts and crews I have worked with over the years as well as, all of the talented people who have taught me what "Great" sound is. Thank you.

Thank you for putting up with all of my questions:

Tom Johnson
Gary Rydstrom
Harry B. Miller III
Jim LeBrecht
David A. Cohen
Dan Olmsted
Dianna Stirpe
Michael "Gonzo" Gandsey
Peter Kurland
Ron Eng
Jana Vance
Glen Trew
Tomlinson Holman
Gregor Hutchison
Jane Tattersall
Milly Iatrou
Bob Hackl
Lee Haxall
Ken Karman
Reka Yellek

A Huge Thank You

Brian David Johnson
Suzie Wright
Margie Yap
Dianna Stirpe
David Comer
Erica Tika Pelishek
Jenette Purcell
Becca Pollard
Kianna Cambria

Without their support this book
would never have made it to the printers.
Thank you all. Your copy is in the mail.

FOREWORD

Listen: It's All About the Sound Stupid.

Brian David Johnson

I have something to tell you that might surprise you. The book you are holding in your hands is not about sound. Now I know it's called *The Angry Filmmaker Survival Guide Part Two: Sound Conversations with (un)Sound People* but as you are reading this introduction I'm going to assume you haven't read the book yet. I have. It's a really good book. You should buy it if you haven't already. But I feel I have to tell you it's not about sound. It's not about sound design, location sound or even dialogue editing. Oh sure, there are sections in the book about these things. There are some really insightful conversations about sound. These conversations also happen to be about the business of filmmaking (both Hollywood and Independent), the art of filmmaking, the craft, the love of movies, and even the personal stories of passionate talented people who give movies a voice. But this book is not about sound. This book is about filmmaking. It is a book for filmmakers about sound and so much more.

Let me tell you a little bit about myself. I am a futurist. I work at the Intel Corporation, the people who make the microchips that go into your computer and that run the Internet. It's my job at Intel to create a vision for how people will want to act and interact with computers ten to fifteen years from now. Now, this might sound like science fiction but it's not. It's incredibly pragmatic. You see it takes five to ten years for us to design, develop and manufacture the chips. It's very important to Intel's business that we have an understanding today of what people will want to do with computers in ten years.

Now you might be asking yourself: *Why is a futurist writing an introduction this book?* Good question. There are three reasons for that. First, I'm a huge fan of the Angry Filmmaker, Kelley Baker. I'm a fan of his movies, a fan of his writing but most of all I'm impressed by his massive impact on the world of filmmaking.

Over the past few years I've started to see Kelley Baker, as a kind of bridge between two eras of filmmaking. He knows his stuff. He literally has cut audio and film with a razor blade. He is a man who respects the past but embraces the future. If you want to see what the future of storytelling looks like then check out Kelley Baker. He has educated and inspired an entire generation of storytellers to take back control of their stories. He's also taught them the craft to make those stories more polished and engaging.

The Angry Filmmaker has moved filmmaking into the 21st Century. Let's be clear, most movie making is still firmly planted in the last century but you can't fault them - they are still making a lot of money doing it the old way. But give it time - things have already started to change with digital production and distribution to multiple screens via the Internet. If you think about it this way, Kelley Baker really is living in the future. He's the future of filmmaking.

The second reason I'm here is that storytelling is extremely important for the futurecasting work I do. It's not enough to have a vision for the future; you also need to be able to communicate that vision. And you can't just do it one way. I don't think it's enough just to get up on a stage or tell the press, "I think the future is going to be like this. . . " Not good enough. I believe you need to show people what the future might look like. I think it's important to spin out stories about the future, multiple narratives of the futures that we might live in. Everyone needs to be an active participant in the future and stories are the best way I've found to do this.

Why is telling stories about the future important? Well, I'll tell you. The future is not some fixed point just over the horizon that we are all helplessly hurdling towards. No. We are not powerless. The future is not written. The future is made every day by the actions of people. That is why I have always believed that everyone should be an active participant in the future. If we are all making it and we are all going to live in it then why not do something about it. And stories are one of the best ways to spark those conversations and make us ask ourselves: what is the world we want to live in? What is the future we want to avoid? These are powerful questions and if we can get enough people talking about them then we can actually change the future for the better.

So that's the second reason why I'm here kicking off this Kelley Baker jag - if you want to learn how to tell a good story listen to the Angry Filmmaker. His films, guides, lectures, and web site are one of the best resources I know of to get you off your butt and tell compelling stories. I used his approach to filmmaking and storytelling in a book of mine called: *Science Fiction Prototyping: Designing the Future with Science Fiction*. The book is about how to use science fiction based on science fact to create stories, films, and comics as a development tool for science and technology; literally using stories based on real science to create better products and envision better science. It's that vision part that's really important.

As we all know and Kelley will tell you, a really good story is about people. A really good science fiction story is also about people. It's not about the technology or the science. It's about the affect of the science and technology on the people and the world around them. Science fiction prototypes use stories, films, and comics as a way to play around and experiment with emerging science to envision how it might affect real people. This way both scientists and regular folks can imagine the future they would like to live in and also use these stories as a way to talk about the future we might want to avoid. You really can use science fiction to design a better future.

In the science fiction prototyping book there is a chapter about film. I use a healthy bit of advice from the first *Angry Filmmaker Survival Guide*. If you haven't read that book, I couldn't recommend it more. Since its publication the science fiction prototyping book has been picked up and taught by both engineer and media programs at universities and schools all over the world. Kelley Baker's reach and influence continues to grow!

The third and final reason I'm standing here between you and this book is because I have learned firsthand as a futurist and a storyteller that sound is incredibly important. The book you are holding in your hands is magnificent. Kelley has pulled together a staggering list of experts who have had a hand in some of the greatest movies of our time. Led by the author, they give us insights into the craft and art of sound. The stories of how they got into the business alone are a reason to spend a good long time with this book.

For the last decade I've been talking to people about the future of entertainment and the Internet. It's pretty clear to me that we are moving towards a future where we will be surrounded by screens. The cinema, TVs, laptops, tablets, smart phones even cars and digital signs. All of these screens are now a way for filmmakers to tell stories. As filmmakers you have more opportunity to reach people, to connect with them, tell them your story, engage them in an experience that could move from the TV to the smart phone to the car. Why not? One of the things I know for sure from over a decade of research all over the world is that people love to be entertained. They love TV, movies, and stories. They need them. As humans we have a deep cultural connection to stories. Basically what I'm telling you is that if you are a filmmaker and you can connect with people you're still going to have an audience in the future.

Now with this in mind there's something you must know. Even if you are showing your story on a smart phone or a laptop it must have good sound. It's essential. Even if the picture is the size of postage stamp and the digital compression makes it look lousy it has to have good sound. People will tolerate bad visuals; they physically cannot take bad sound. It's not that they *won't* watch your story - they literally *can't* watch it.

But it doesn't stop there. As a part of my futurecasting work I interview people all over the world. I feel really fortunate that I get to go to interesting places and interview interesting people. Let me tell you one quick story about the importance of sound that I've experienced. I was in Mumbai, India, earlier this year. I had gained backstage access to a Bollywood musical comedy show. I wanted to talk to the director and crew about the future of entertainment Mumbai-style. Let me tell you, Bollywood knows how to put on a show!

The place was packed with people. They had twenty-four automated cameras all around a shimmering set. The stage was covered with nine foot tall horse heads and go-go dancers in glittering silver costumes. The walls were draped in rich scarlet velvet, gathered in deep folds around massive clown heads with immense balls on their noses. The audience was filled with men in short-sleeved white shirts (it was over ninety degrees) and women in traditional Hindi dress. I went further backstage, along the giant electrical cables and army of production people. I even made it back into the dark control room where the director and the producers were generous enough to tell me their vision for the future of entertainment and storytelling. The director just smiled at me when I asked and pointed to his smartphone and the producer's laptop. The future is all about screens! It was an experience you could only have in Bollywood.

Pretty cool right? Well, I can never show this footage. Why? Why wouldn't it be awesome to show this amazing spectacle? Well, it looks great but the sound is awful. I literally can't show it because the sound is unusable.

Although I do have a background in media and filmmaking, much of what I film these days are short videos and interview that I post on the Internet. They are like small snippets of a TV show but not the traditional Hollywood or TV world. But after reading the book I realized that that didn't matter. Actually it's more important. If you are making short videos or blogs or interviews for this screen future that you will show on all those 15 billion screens out there, you have to have good audio. If the audio is terrible, then no one will watch it.

In the future the tools for filmmakers will only get better. They will enable you to tell your story for less money, with less people and it might even take less time (but don't scrimp on that too much). Technology has allowed a whole generation of filmmakers to do just that - tell stories regardless of where they are shown. But take it from me, the thing you have to remember is that being a good filmmaker means being good at sound. Some of the best advice you'll get about sound can be found in the pages of this book.

I've already started using what I learned.

It's been an honor for me to kick off this next Angry Filmmaker Jag. Buckle up. Let's get this thing started!

Brian David Johnson
Futurist
On a 777 bound for Berlin, Germany

PREFACE

Why Does the Sound in Your Film Suck?

Kelley Baker

I have been approached many times by (so called) filmmakers and students and our conversations go something like this:

```
INT. ANYWHERE - DAY

FILMMAKER (so-called) or STUDENT approaches KELLEY BAKER.

                    FILMMAKER
          I just shot my new film with the...

INSERT

The latest, coolest camera available.

                                        BACK TO SCENE

                    ME
          What kind of mics did you use?

                    FILMMAKER
          I don't know.

                    ME
          So your film is going to look great
          but sound like shit...

                    FILMMAKER
          It doesn't matter, we're going to
          replace the dialogue anyway.

                    ME
          So the acting is going to suck too?

                    FILMMAKER
          The dialogue is always replaced in
          films.
```

```
                    ME
     Where did you hear this?

                 FILMMAKER
     On the internet.

                    ME
               (rolling eyes,
                walking away)
     Then it must be true...
```

FADE TO BLACK

But it's not true! Every now and again a lot of dialogue on a particular movie might be replaced but that's the exception, not the rule. It's usually on big, loud, special effect laden pictures and it really doesn't matter in those films because the dialogue is pretty lame anyway. It's just filler in between FX sequences. Ask Michael Bay.

I am well known for being a sound designer, but I don't consider myself one. I am a filmmaker who spent quite a few years making my living doing sound for other filmmakers. The reason I was hired is that I approach sound as a filmmaker, not a sound geek. I have no idea about the specs on a lot of audio gear and I don't care. I do know how to place a microphone to get the best quality recordings on set, and when it comes to Pro Tools I can get it to do what I want.

Filmmakers neglect sound because they can't see it. It's easy to look through the lens and say that something looks good. It's harder to think about multiple layers of sound coming together to capture an emotional feel. We are visual creatures but sound is where the emotion lives. Some pictures are worth a thousand words, but sound conveys a feeling, an emotion, it can transport you to a different time and place. We all remember what songs were playing during certain important times in our lives, even if the images start to dim.

When I hear people say we can fix the sound in post, I realize I am in the presence of an amateur. I understand that it's harder to fix picture in post if you screw it up. Yes we can fix the sound, but it'll never be as good as what you could have, or should have captured on the set. You're missing out on the actor's performance and a lot of the nuisances. Many actors are great with ADR (Automatic Dialogue Replacement) but many are not.

To make a truly great film you need to think beyond pictures to the emotional content of what you're trying to convey.

I believe the three most important things in any movie are story, acting, and sound. If your audience can't understand the dialogue, you don't have a movie.

To quote my friend Jon Gann, founder and artistic director of the DC Shorts Film Festival, "If one audience member says, "What did she say?" you've just lost the entire audience."

Audiences will forgive bad camera work, horrible lighting, they will even forgive out of focus shots, think BLAIR WITCH PROJECT, but they won't forgive, *bad sound!*

Every few years some little film gets a big Hollywood distributor on board (EL MARIACHI, BLAIR WITCH PROJECT, PARANORMAL ACTIVITY, and others) and we're told how the filmmakers made these films for eight dollars and a handful of magic beans or some crap like that. What you're not told is that in many instances what you see in the theater has had extensive sound work done before it's released. The studios will drop $200,000 or more to re-do the audio so that audiences can understand what's going on, and then they market it as this little film that was made for peanuts. The studios understand the importance of good sound.

In Hitchcock's PSYCHO, we get no audio clues that Janet Leigh is about to be attacked in the shower and that scene (as dated as it is now) scared more audiences and generated more buzz then any film before or since, because Hitchcock broke the rules. In JAWS, we hear the music and know someone is going to get attacked, the music keeps us on edge.

When I was a kid and saw the film, THEM about giant ants terrorizing the countryside it scared the hell out of me. Until we finally saw the ants that is. The special effects were cheesy so for most of the film we heard the creepy sound of the ants and saw the destruction. It worked great.

Think about that when you are taking the easy way out and laying in scary music. Why not forgo the music, give us some simple, subtle atmospheric effects, and put the audience on edge that way. Or completely shock them by not giving them any clues.

Take a look at TOUCH OF EVIL and you'll see Orson Welles working with "worldizing" music in that opening shot, something that Walter Murch thought he was pioneering fifteen years later! Listen to the sound on THE CONVERSATION, ONCE UPON A TIME IN THE WEST, or DAS BOOT and you will see innovative filmmakers taking sound to a new level.

I find it fascinating that so many filmmakers can talk all day about cameras but rarely can name more than one brand of microphone, let alone a location mixer or audio recorder.

Why is this? Is sound that scary?

That's why this book came about.

There is no excuse for someone who wants to make films not to understand the entire process. Personally, I'm a filmmaker that takes a lot of pride in my craft and my art. I know about the different positions that make up a film crew and I've done just about everything on a film set at some point over the last thirty years.

If you don't utilize all of the possibilities with sound you aren't much of a filmmaker.

You need to think about sound, plan for it and surround yourself with professionals just like you do when it comes to the camera crew. You aren't going to hire a DP off of Craigslist, why are you looking for sound people there?

Sound is one of the most important parts of your film, if you don't believe me, maybe you'll believe the people I have assembled in this book. They are the professionals and creative as hell! They have to be because they spend a lot of time fixing other people's mistakes. Like yours.

So read on and maybe you'll learn why the sound in your movie sucks, and how you can do better next time.

What the Hell do I do First?

Pre-production - Check your locations for sound, while you are scouting them for picture. Where is your location and are there going to be potential sound problems. That location next to the railroad tracks might look great but there are freight trains moving back and forth twenty-three hours a day and your sound will probably be unusable.

Hire a Location Recordist & Boom Operator, give them a location list and have a discussion about what you want/expect from them.

This is a great time to talk to a sound designer or supervising sound editor and listen to their input as to what they hear in your story and ways to achieve great audio while you are shooting.

Bring on a post-production supervisor when you hire your editor so that all of the steps of the post-production process can be thought out and any potential problems can be spotted and discussed before they become actual problems.

Production - Listen to your sound department and make sure they have the equipment and time, within reason of course, they need so that you can get the best audio possible.

Have your picture editor and post-production supervisor co-ordinate with the location audio people the manner in which the editor receives the audio dailies. If the location people are having a problem getting certain things that will enhance the audio those things need to be brought up and discussed. Make sure that the editor has a good mixed track they can edit with and make sure that all of the elements on a multi-track recording are labeled and easily available to picture editorial.

When possible do wild lines on the set if you think there might be audio issues. Most of the time wild lines from the set work better than ADR to replace a line within a scene that has a bump, cloth rustle, generator noise, or a million other things that occur on location.

Post-production - hiring a picture editor with a strong sound background is always a plus. If that can't happen, bring in your sound designer or supervising sound editor as soon as possible and have them contribute temporary sound effects and ideas at this stage. Many filmmakers fall in love with sound effects or music that has just been thrown in to a rough edit and it can be extremely hard to replace those temp effects or music with the good stuff later on.

Bring on the music people and have them start to feed temp music. This will help the picture editor do a better cut. I have seen too many montages cut to temp music that have to be totally re-cut when the real music with a totally different beat shows up, costing time and frustration among the different crews.

Have discussions with your sound crew to spot trouble areas and plan for ADR and Group ADR.

When the picture editor finally starts turning over "locked picture" reels to the sound editors - do your best not to keep making changes. Yes, we work on computers, but even the simplest changes can take hours to conform on all of the sound reels.

When the sound crew comes on to your movie this is what happens.

Dialogue is spotted for problems and decisions are made that will relate to the overall track.

ADR is spotted, scheduled, recorded, and edited.

Group ADR is spotted, many times written, scheduled, recorded, and edited.

Sound Effects are spotted, recorded or pulled from libraries, and edited.

Foley is spotted, cued for the Foley Artists, recorded, and edited.

Music is composed, recorded, and edited.

Pre-mixes are where all of the different sound elements are mixed down to make them more manageable during the final mix. In many instances you might have twelve to twenty-four separate dialogue tracks, anywhere from ten to sixty separate sound effects tracks, twelve to twenty-four channels of music, and sixteen to twenty-four tracks of Foley. You'll also have ADR and Group ADR tracks to contend with as well.

Once all of these pre-mixes are finished it's time to do the final mix and that is where all of it finally comes together.

I prefer to do my final mix on to what are called "stems". These are separate dialogue, music, and effects tracks. When you are making the final version in stereo, or 5.1 or whatever, you can set all your faders on zero and play the stems to make your two or six channel final version. This helps if you need to make different versions of a mix, or maybe you forgot to clear that piece of music and now you need to replace it.

By mixing to stems you can just change out a single element without having to re-mix the entire film.

You're done! Hopefully.

CHAPTER 1

Location! Location! Location!

Production Recordist

For whatever reason people think anyone can learn how to use a recorder or hold a boom mic. It's not that easy.

If you use a production mixer and a boom operator with lots of experience you're going to save time and money and your film is going to sound better.

What does an experienced sound crew bring you? How about good microphone placement, the knowledge of when to boom and when to rely on wireless mics, and the proper way of wiring an actor for best results? When do you put up sound blankets or pads under chairs? Sure those footsteps sound cool in that hallway but what's going to happen when you try and cut them together from different angles?

Production is a crazy and intense time on the set, there is no doubt about that. The mistakes you make here are going to live with you throughout the life of your movie. As a filmmaker I see things that bother me in every one of my films that I wish I could have fixed. Many of those things occurred on the set.

When I'm directing I wear Comteks, (wireless head phones) so I can hear what is being recorded at the same time it's being laid down. The dialogue recording is so important to me that I want to be able to fix things before they become a problem.

If fifty percent of your film is the sound, why aren't you more careful about whom you hire as your production sound mixer and your boom operator?

Peter Kurland

"I'm capturing a performance, and that performance is only going to happen one time the way they want it, in the environment, with everybody in the mood."

Peter Kurland has had a career most of us would envy. He has worked with the Coen Brothers since 1984, first as a boom operator on BLOOD SIMPLE and THE BIG LEBOWSKI, among others and then as the location sound recordist on films like TRUE GRIT, NO COUNTRY FOR OLD MEN, and BURN AFTER READING. He has worked on THE WILD, WILD WEST and MEN IN BLACK for director Barry Sonnefeld, WALK THE LINE, and television episodes for PUSHING UP DAISIES and NOTES FROM THE UNDERBELLY.

If you want to know more about Peter Kurland check out: http://www.imdb.com/name/nm0004212/

He has come across almost every type of problem there is in location sound recording and has come through it all with his sense of humor intact. I spoke with him while he was in-between jobs.

KB: How did you get involved with sound and location recording in particular?

PK: I was involved with sound as a theater person in high school. Then I got hired on a TV movie and ended up in the sound department for no particular reason, except that I said I had some knowledge in that area.

Really, the honest truth of what happened is that they wanted to punish the sound mixer on that TV movie. He insisted on having an assistant, so they tried to get someone who didn't know anything. They asked me if I knew anything about movie sound and I said no, they asked me if I knew what a Nagra was, and I said no, and then they hired me.

KB: That's a dubious beginning, isn't it?

PK: Yes. But it worked out very well.

KB: Were there any particular films that were a big influence on you when you started?

PK: I can't say that I was inspired by watching a movie. I can say that the first feature film I worked on, which was BLOOD SIMPLE, was a huge influence mostly because the people who I worked for on that movie I'm still working for now, twenty-six years later.

KB: Do you find that common in the business?

PK: I think it's common if you work with people and they like you and you like them. What's unusual about this is that they are still making movies twenty-six years later. The challenging part is that a director or producer can make one movie a year, or one movie every two years, and they're employed on that for the whole time, whereas a sound guy might be employed for three months on that movie. The hard part is trying to always work with the same people, but also being able to pay your mortgage. You can't take the rest of the time off, and if you work for somebody else, then maybe you won't be available for the people you want to work with regularly. There are a lot of sound mixers I know who always work with the same clients, but every once in awhile it doesn't work out and they can't. I don't want to go down that road so I end up turning down a fair amount of work just so I don't overlap.

KB: Can you tell me exactly what a production sound recordist does?

PK: The day-to-day job is pretty simple. You're recording the sound in sync with the action on the set of a movie, wherever that movie is, and you're doing that in conjunction with other people in your department: a boom operator whose job it is to make sure the microphone or microphones are in the right place, a utility person who's helping to make that happen. The sound mixer is responsible for combining that sound, recording it, and sending it in to post-production for later processing. That's the day-to-day part of the work.

When somebody hires me to do a job, I break down the script to find out what the special sound requirements are, if there's playback, if there are communications issues, or if there are difficult locations. I have to find a practical or electronic solution for those challenges, and then find a way to do those things fitting within the budget and the schedule of the movie.

There are other elements. Every time you arrive at a new location, which can be three times a day, or once every three weeks, you have to find the issues about that location (noisy backgrounds, airplane landing patterns, etc) and find solutions for those as well.

KB: How much control do you have over what you do? You've got this long relationship with the Coen Brothers - how much interaction do you normally have with them?

PK: I have interaction all day long, because at any given moment, none of us have any control over certain parts of the environment. If we're shooting outside and an airplane goes over or something like that, they depend on me to tell them whether the recording is useable in the movie. It's not for me to say whether we do another take because they may know that they don't care if it's usable or that they can fix it, but they want to know from me whether it is.

There is some interaction in the beginning of the project where they need to know whether certain locations are useable for sound. For example, we were shooting in New York City and they had a location that looked perfect to them but was right on a major highway. They wanted to know from me whether it was possible to record dialogue there because there was a lot of dialogue. I basically said no and we ended up shooting part of the scene there and part of the scene three blocks away where it didn't compromise their idea of what the location should look like, but it made the sound useable.

KB: What is your biggest challenge when it comes to location recording?

PK: The mean answer is the biggest challenge is always the director. If the director doesn't care about sound or they don't know how to get good sound or they don't think about it, that's a challenge because it makes everything difficult. Everybody's going to look to them for these decisions and I don't have any control over that.

That isn't much of a factor for me because I only work with a handful of directors. The ones I work with all the time are very sound conscious and even though they don't make all of their decisions based on sound, they're at least reasonable about it.

Outside of that, the big challenge is the recording environment. It's very easy to record good sound in the studio where there are no issues to deal with, and if there's machinery and what-have-you, like for special effects, then no one expects to get good sound. The challenge is when you're working outside and there are airplanes or traffic or wind, those are all really difficult things to deal with . . . as well as just the human environmental challenges of working in extreme cold, heat, in sand, or whatever.

KB: Why do you think good sound is important?

PK: It's a significant part of the movie-going experience. Clearly there were movies before there was sound and there's also radio and recordings where there is no picture, but when you actually go to the movie theater, sound is a huge portion of the experience. That's the reason why completed sound has to be good.

The reason why production sound has to be good is that basically I'm capturing a performance, and that performance is only going to happen one time, the way they want it, in the environment, with everybody in the mood. To recreate that later on a looping stage - it's never the same. The voices don't sound the same, the performance isn't the same, the experience isn't the same. The reason why it's important for me to do my job correctly is so I can preserve those performances.

KB: Of the films you work on, how much do you think they replace by the time they get into mixing?

PK: I always ask. On a Coen picture, the vast majority of the sound that I record is used. That's not to say that 100% of the sounds in the movie are my recordings. They also add dialogue that wasn't written at the time that the movie was shot or they may use dialogue from alternate takes. But they use just about everything that I record.

In terms of the percentage of dialogue in their movies that's my original recordings, I would say 95% or better. I would say with the other directors I work with, I like to think it's always better than 90%. I've done a lot of big effects-type movies where there is a higher expectation that more of the sound will be lost. I've done a lot of big-event movies with Barry Sonnenfeld, and he's very sound-aware, he wants to have the original performance and so we find a way to make it work and we're able to use basically 90% to 95% of the original dialogue.

That's not always the case and it's not always the fault of the production mixer or even the director. If you choose to make a movie that takes place on a highway at 80 mph in an open convertible you're probably going to have to loop parts of that. But given a tiny bit of time, a lot of experience, and a reasonable approach, I think it's possible to get useable sound, particularly dialogue, the vast majority of the time.

KB: And speaking of approach, do you approach a big film - like WILD, WILD WEST, differently than you would one of the smaller independent films that you've worked on?

PK: One of the restraining factors is how much time they're going to have and how much money they're going to have in post-production. The challenge with a student film or an ultra-low budget movie is that they're not going to do a lot to the sound when it's done. It's ironic that in extreme low-budget filmmaking they pay the least attention to the sound department, and that's where they don't have the money to fix it in post. If you're doing a movie like WILD, WILD WEST, they've got weeks and weeks with the actors and with technology to make that movie sound the way they want to. That's actually easier for me, whereas on an independent film you really want to get it right the first time.

The Coens represent an interesting combination because even on their ultra-low budget movies, Skip Lievsay, their supervising sound editor and mixer, will go to a lot of trouble to make the sound really good so I know if there are problems he'll be able to fix them. I try to make as few problems as possible for him, particularly on the low-budget stuff.

KB: Do you communicate a lot with the supervising sound editor on films?

PK: With Skip I do. We talk in advance about new technology that might be used on the set. We talk about some mundane issues of data management, how the stuff has to be recorded, how they'll use it, how many tracks are useful for him - those kinds of things.

During the course of production if there's a specific issue we might talk about what the best way to go about it is, or what I can do to help him. Obviously we don't have daily conversations but we talk regularly.

On some other movies, like WALK THE LINE for example, I really liked the post-production guys and they did an excellent job, but they weren't hired until three months after I was done on the movie so there was no way to communicate with them.

KB: Do you think that that's more normal?

PK: On a lower-budget movie, other than the Coen Brothers, I think it's normal that they don't have the post-production people in mind yet. I know with Joel and Ethan, Skip has done every one of their movies. I know Skip is going to be there so it's easy to keep that communication. Barry also has post-production sound people with whom he works on a regular basis. I will be in touch with them in advance, and I also try to go to at least part of the final mix on all the movies that I do.

It's very interesting to find out what they can use and what they can't. I can explain during the sound editing process what I have recorded that might be a solution to a problem they're having. I'm recording on multi-track often, sometimes there's going to be thousands of hours of material that's been recorded for the movie, and they wouldn't find something unless the person who was there recording it can say that it's buried in here in this particular sound or alternate dialogue, or here's some wild tracks I did.

KB: I always feel that sound gets absolutely no respect until post-production, then sound is expected to come in and fix everything. Do you think that is true?

PK: In my career it's not, in some people's careers it is. I know I've been on sets where the director of photography, for example, has said, "I don't care about sound." He didn't say it that way, he actually said, (with accent) "I don't give a shit about sound." Often that's true with directors. They're very concerned about time, particularly first-time directors who haven't been through the experience of post-production. They don't realize what a pain it is to loop and they don't realize how much less they'll like the performance when it's looped. They'll say, "Let's not worry about it, we'll fix it later." Experienced directors often really care, and they'll be very helpful.

And compromises have to be made. If I say we can't shoot here because it's in the flight path of the airport, that's not my call if that's the only location that's available and if it's all been set up, there's nothing anybody can do about it.

I remember there was a scene in THE MAN WHO WASN'T THERE. There was a police action where there was a helicopter rounding somebody up and they were doing circles around the neighborhood once every thirty seconds. And it's a two-minute dialogue scene so you know it's going to be interrupted at least three times. Since I was working with Joel and Ethan, they appreciate that, what they'll let me do is help them find timing for starting the scenes and set it up so that where the sound is no good will be different in every take so that by the time they're done they know they'll have a full performance that they can cut together.

KB: Over the years you've done so many things with the Coen Brothers. Can you talk about how they approach sound in their films?

PK: Well, I can't speak on their behalf. During awards season on NO COUNTRY FOR OLD MEN, we gave all these seminars where Joel and Ethan were there and I was there with Skip and we actually got to talk about this stuff, which normally we don't. Essentially if you read one of their scripts, sound is a big element. They often have music in mind, they have sound effects in mind, some of their scenes have a sound-scape that's the most important element for them. So they have thought about the movie in the sound dimension from its very inception.

I don't know how to put this - oftentimes, that will mean that my work doesn't have to be included. In SERIOUS MAN, there were thirty pages of a montage that they knew in advance was going to play under a particular soundtrack, they knew effects weren't going to be used so as far as they were concerned, they didn't care if I was there to record sound or not.

I have this professional obligation always to try to record everything just in case they change their minds. So in the case of SERIOUS MAN we went to a lot of locations where Joel and Ethan kept saying, "There's no reason for you to be here, there's no reason to record anything," and sometimes we would anyway. The comeuppance in that movie was that there's one particular character who is in this montage, they knew they'd never use his voice. They knew he'd never speak so they didn't have to hire a SAG actor, so I wasn't actually allowed to record him. That made that decision.

They know well in advance what they want in the sound. They've got a vision for it just like the picture and if I wasn't achieving that for them we'd find a way to make that happen. Sometimes it's a post- thing and sometimes it's a production thing.

They're very concerned about sound with this idea that they are working towards a particular goal. There are other directors who are extremely concerned about sound, maybe not with such a preplanned idea of what the sound is going to be like but knowing they want to get the elements. Barry Sonnenfeld is one of those people. He is extremely interested in recording clean sound and getting everything, so that when he gets to post-production he can make those choices. So he's very concerned about sound but in a different way.

There are other directors who are equally concerned about getting good sound but don't want to do anything to accomplish it. They'll say "Get this perfect, but here's the thing, we're going to be shooting this on top of a moving bulldozer and we have to shoot this in the rain and the wind, but everything has to be perfect."

KB: What is the worst sound challenge you've ever had to deal with?

PK: The most challenging thing was very early in my career, recording my first TV pilot. It became clear from the get-go that there was going to be no post-production, and what I recorded was the final sound. I remember making a couple of compromises, one major mistake, and being horrified when I saw the thing. They just cut it together and they aired it just the way it was. That was a little scary and I imagine that's the case for most people who are making ultra-low budget or student films, the huge challenge is that you know you don't get another shot at it.

KB: Do you approach working in TV differently from how you approach features?

PK: Yes. As mean as it is to say, when you know that the final product is going to be played through a two-inch speaker, maybe you don't have to worry so much about background noise. That's one element.

When you do a TV show there is no time, you're trying to record ten to twenty pages of dialogue a day. You're not going to ask for an extra take because one of your fader moves wasn't perfect. The standard has to be different. On a feature film where I might wait until the last possible minute to make a decision to put a radio mic on somebody because I know it's not going to sound good. In the TV world you might put radios on everyone from the very beginning just in case you might need them, because everybody's aware that you can't take the five minutes if you have to change your plan. So that part's very different.

KB: What do you prefer, boom or wireless?

PK: Definitely boom. I like the boom for a lot of reasons. There's a weird technical reason I like it, which is that it's more natural to the ear to get the time delay from when the person speaks until when you see their lips move. That's a huge variable now with HDTV. With radio mics the timing of it is wrong and it just seems weirdly disconnected. You have to imagine that even with the best radio mic you're going to get the perspective of your head on somebody's chest. That's just not what you expect to hear.

There's also something very natural-sounding about combining the voices of the people in the room, the background ambiance, as opposed to having to combine them later on. Electronically they're being combined in the air like they would be naturally and it just sounds more natural to me. And I'm not a huge fan of completely recording things in perspective unless that's the aesthetic you want. It sounds better when the shot is slightly wide and if the microphone sounds slightly wide, and when the shot is very close you want a very present sound and when you record with radio microphones everything is always extremely present and it's very hard in post-production to try to make it sound natural again.

KB: With all of these new digital cameras and all this digital equipment now, do they make your job easier or harder?

PK: Some of these new cameras make it harder because everybody tries to use them in a sort of all-purpose way. There's a big temptation to record sound with them even though they all, even the best ones, record sound very badly. Synchronizing is very difficult with them because they all have a time code system, that's supposed to make it all automatic but in actuality all those things add a huge technical complexity on the set, and they don't necessarily make things better.

There's a very practical challenge, when you're not running film nobody cares whether they cut or not. You could roll for hours which makes it really hard on the boom operator for one, and it makes it hard for everybody because you never get a chance to re-group. Whatever you're doing, you're stuck with that particular set of microphones or placement until they're done with maybe five or six takes in a row. You can use HD cameras the same way people use film cameras, you can shoot exactly the same way, but people don't.

KB: Why do you think that is?

PK: I don't think anybody ever liked the idea of the film magazine running out after ten minutes. I think people never liked the restriction of knowing that every second you're shooting you have ten dollars' worth of film and processing running through the camera. So when they're given the opportunity to be free from that, they don't want to still be bound to that just because it makes it easier for the boom guy. Everybody else's career changed as a result of that, and our technology has to come around. My boom operator, for example, invented an accessory that makes it easier for him to boom long scenes without the camera cutting. All that stuff is pretty easy it's just taking awhile for the rest of us to catch up.

KB: You have some specific thoughts on a lot of these digital cameras, because you just said briefly that none of them record very well. Can you elaborate on that?

PK: I don't know when your book's going to come out so I don't want to be way off-base, but for example the RED camera, which is very popular right now. It wasn't until they got to Build Sixteen that they solved a major problem with the sound recording capabilities of the camera in terms of noise and whatnot and even then the hardware was a little bit non-standard, which makes it very hard to interface anything else to it. I know they've addressed some of those issues, but when you're recording to a separate recorder you've got the ability to listen to things back, you can adjust your headphone volume easily, you can watch the meters very carefully. When you're trying to do that kind of recording to a camera they've got all this other stuff in there that takes precedent so the headphone amps are going to be cheesier, the microphone input is going to be cheesier, the meters are not going to be designed for the use of the sound guy, they're going to be designed to make it easier for the cameraperson and all of it makes it a challenge.

KB: I was talking to a friend of mine who also does location recording and he made the comment that a lot of people that are working on the new cameras, half of them don't even know how to program the sound, have you found that at all to be true?

PK: Oh yeah, it's hard. I have a sound mixer colleague in Israel who's an expert on all things video camera so I will always go to him when I have to work with a new camera and say, "Hey, I have to work with the Panavision Genesis camera, what's going to be different about that?" and he'll know.

Right now in the industry there are only a handful of different professional sound-recording machines that are used. Literally there are probably four of them now. There are hundreds of different models of HD cameras and every one of them has twenty-seven layers of menus and they all have a different input rating, the meters are calibrated differently, the microphone powering is different, the displays are different - down to the place on every meter there's a mark where zero is. It's different for a Sony camera, a Panasonic camera, a RED camera, they're all different.

As a sound guy you have to have some kind of encyclopedic knowledge if you want to use the camera to record sound. If all you want to do is record time code for example, even that is incredibly challenging because it's different on every camera.

I did a shoot last year that was a pre-production shoot for a movie. And we shot on all these high-def cameras and we kept asking about their time code capabilities can we put time code in, can we take it out, and they kept saying it was no problem. It turns out on that particular camera which shall go unnamed, you can do all that stuff on a firewire cable. So you can connect the cameras to each other, you could even connect the cameras to computers and decks, but you can't get time code back and forth to a sound recorder. Each one of these things presents it's own challenge. And they all have a different opinion about what is in sync and that's another huge problem.

KB: You just said cameras and formats are changing all the time but there's really only four different audio machines out there. Do you think audio is keeping up with cameras?

PK: The percentage of video production that's done with a

separate sound recorder, I actually don't know what it is but I'm going to guess it's 1%. All the TV news stuff, all low-budget video shoots, corporate work, none of those people are going to have a separate recording device. So the market for recording devices even amongst professional filmmakers is very small in the sound department as compared to video. Because that market is small it doesn't make sense for a company to totally retool.

For a while it was hard to keep up because new technology was being invented and change was very fast as it was with computers because essentially we're going from analog systems to digital systems and tape-based systems to non-linear file-based systems.

Now it's a little bit easier because a huge number of the improvements that are being made are software improvements so you don't have to go buy a whole new thing every time they make technological advances. And because it's software you need a small team of people writing it, it's easy to disperse, there's no retooling time, so even a small electronics company can make huge changes. There's no question that any given electronics manufacturer can make a new HD camera every six months. Often faster than that and new audio recorders come out every few years at best. The technology changes so fast in something as simple as, every computer for a while had one set of connectors, then everyone had firewire and now computers don't have firewire anymore? So something as simple as that creates this huge hardware challenge.

KB: And as location sound recordist you're expected to keep up with all of the new audio gear.

PK: I probably spend an hour a day, or better in my off time keeping up with new technology. When a lot of change is happening it's multiple hours a day. It's a lot to keep up with, you have to continually upgrade your equipment, hardware and software and learn the new techniques. As you were saying, when the camera technology changes you've got to find a way to be able to interface with that when you need to.

KB: I want to make you a director for a minute. . .

PK: I want to get the pay increase.

KB: We'll try to get you that, no promises! What should filmmakers look for in a good location sound recordist?

PK: It's very hard for me to make that decision from a directors perspective, because I know what I think is valuable in a sound mixer. I would say, like with anybody you're working with in the feature film business, the number one criteria is somebody you can get along with, communicate with and somebody who can work in your style. If Albert Einstein decided to get into the location recording business he might have an entirely new concept of how it's supposed to be done but if you can't get along with the guy, you don't want him on the set. That's number one.

Number two is you want somebody who's compatible with your philosophy on filmmaking. In the case of Joel and Ethan, and Barry as well, they want to have great sound but they don't want to lose a lot of production time as a result. They're willing to make compromises where they need to be made, and they don't want to make them where they're not useful. So to find somebody who agrees with the break point in that, where it all falls into place, that's a huge factor.

KB: What's the most important thing students and young filmmakers need to know about sound?

PK: The number one thing they have to think about is how hard it will be for them to improve their sound in post-production, and based on that, how much time they should devote to resolving sound issues. That's also includes finding a sound person who has knowledge or experience, or who's willing to learn what is necessary in order to get good sound for them.

Instead of thinking that I have to find someone who can do this and, "My brother Fred can come over for the day. He doesn't know anything about sound but he can learn to use the recorder." That's going to cost them.

I think over the course of a day the thing that makes the most difference in sound is the boom operator. The boom operator has so much more influence on how things sound than the sound mixer does. So if you decide not to have a boom operator or you decide to get a friend who you feel can hold the microphone for a long time because they work out, that's not going to help you.

I think a lot of it has to go into having respect for the craft and what good sound will do for you on location. And once you get there, then you can start to deal with other issues, like do you want a location with a lot of background noise? Do you want to set up shots that are impossible to get good sound on? Do you want to get this shot in another way? Are you going to light with the idea in mind of being able to use a boom or are you just going to do whatever is fastest and most convenient and make it difficult for the boom operator? As a director it will be harder for you to know all those factors than it would be for you to take a few minutes to try to get somebody decent to help you with the sound, and let them use their knowledge and experience to help you.

KB: What would you tell a film student who wanted to specialize in sound, how should they go about it?

PK: The number one piece of advice is, if you're interested in doing movie-type work what you want to do is to end up on the set of a movie, in any job. If that means you're a PA and you're stopping traffic, or you're carrying boxes back and forth to the production office, you want to take that job because you want to get experience on the set and see what it's like. Nobody wants to hire somebody to work on the set who hasn't done it before, because there are so many issues of set etiquette. A person who knows anything about the set is head and shoulders above someone who knows a skill but doesn't know how to be on the set.

It used to be that a great way in was to take a job at a rental house, where you would learn the equipment and meet the people who use it because they'd come in. So many friends of mine in the sound world started that way. It's not as easy now because fewer people rent.

Another thing to do is to try to meet people who do this and find out from them what opportunities are available. You used to be able to have people come visit on the set or have somebody intern for a little while. Now because of insurance restrictions on studio features, the process to get an unpaid intern is three months long and requirements are so strict. I've managed to do it twice, and it ended up taking six to eight weeks each time to get the proper studio permissions. You have to be matriculated in school and earning credit, you've got to get the college to give you credits. It's really hard to do that now.

I just got a guy this morning he wants to get into the sound business. He's really interested in helping out and he's willing to work for free. I have no way to help him, short of saying, call the production office and see if they need any PAs. Even the PA jobs are pretty competitive.

KB: Can you think of any films that you think students and other filmmakers should see?

PK: In terms of sound I'm very biased in saying NO COUNTRY FOR OLD MEN. Not just because of my part in it, but because of the choices Skip made. It's a fascinating movie that shows where music can be useful and when it's not. The sound effects in that movie and the ambiance take the place of the music track in a way. I'm not saying I'm anti-music - it helps you have perspective on why traditions are the way they are and how they can be altered. I definitely recommend that one.

I think BLOOD SIMPLE is another one. They had no money, they had no time and a lot of what makes that work is the way the music is factored in, the way the effects are factored in, their use of dialogue - it's really amazing for first-time filmmakers.

KB: I was pleasantly surprised with NO COUNTRY FOR OLD MEN. I'm not a music hater but films today have too much music in them and a lot of it's not even motivated.

PK: With some filmmakers where the music is a huge part of the story-telling or it completely sets the mood or it's a huge element of the style, I'm all for it. There are some filmmakers for whom that's everything. Obviously, ALMOST FAMOUS, not just because the musicians are in the movie but the whole idea of the soundtrack, it alters everything.

There are some movies that are extremely effects-driven. THE MAN WHO WASN'T THERE, is notable because the main character in that movie never speaks. We would laugh about it every day, Billy Bob would come in and say, "I'm not saying anything today!" He didn't speak for three months of production. The last couple of days we took him off to a room and recorded all his voiceover. Virtually all his dialogue in the movie was voiceover and it worked great for the film.

KB: You've been doing this now for over twenty-five years. Do you still like what you do?

PK: I do. I really like the people I work with. I really enjoy being involved in making movies, I've always been a movie buff, and to be part of that is really great.

As I get older some of the things are physically harder. I was commenting to my wife this morning, on how early in my career I worked on a movie with a guy who was a sound mixer, and a multiple Academy Award winner, he was 68 years old. He came to work every day, he dealt with basically the same physical challenges I deal with now. He was a lot older than I am and he was fine with it. My wife's response was, "Yeah, he had a heart attack, in the middle of the movie he had to go have triple bypass surgery."

So there are things that make it harder. I'm about to go do a movie where the physical environment is very difficult. It's going to be high altitudes, extremely cold, and as much as I've enjoyed going to different places all over the world that I wouldn't get to go to otherwise, I'm very envious of the guys in the post-production studios in their Aeron chairs in their air-conditioned environments - and they can have lunch brought in!

KB: (Laughs) Yeah, I always told people I got into post because I didn't like being wet and cold. Now that I'm directing I don't mind the weather at all.

PK: We could have a whole conversation just about that! Directors, and I can't necessarily put Joel and Ethan and Barry into this category, but directors as a general rule, they are so fired up about the work they are doing, they have a very limited amount of time to achieve their vision, that the physical environment just doesn't occur to them that much I think. I had that experience this summer where I had people who never wanted to stop shooting. They were happy to shoot sixteen to eighteen hours a day. I've talked to Joel and Ethan about this. They're in production for two months and in post-production for twelve months. They don't care how hard the production phase is they look forward to it, So it's a whole different perspective as a director, as a crew member, and I try to be respectful of the director and the producer, the actors and the experience they're having versus my experience. I only hope in some small corner of their mind that they're empathetic with my experience as well.

KB: As much as I love shooting and I love being on the set, I try to keep everything to ten-hour days, because I work with very tiny budgets. So my whole thing is all about respecting the cast and the crew and their time, being organized.

PK: I think it's very possible to make a movie in eight-hour days. I think depending on your rental situation with your equipment, how long you have it and your actor availability, you're actually ultimately paying less per hour filmmaking on an eight-hour day than you are on a twelve- or fourteen-hour day, it's just more complicated to arrange it.

There are plenty of directors in the feature film world who shoot eight hours a day, Sidney Lumet, Woody Allen, Clint Eastwood shoots short days, and with Joel and Ethan we're lucky to still have work to do after lunch! The tradeoff with them is they are incredibly efficient, so you cram just as much high quality shooting time in that six or eight hours as you would on another film in eighteen hours. The experience is much, much more intense, much more draining, but when you're done, you're done and you have a lot more time to recover.

KB: I see too many people come to the set unprepared, they're so excited to get to the set that they don't do their homework.

PK: If I had to give advice to a young filmmaker and I don't think I've ever formed a sentence that made me sound as old as that. It would be do as much as you can, in advance, working by yourself, to figure out exactly what you want and how you want to do it because that's the way you're going to achieve it. I know everybody wants to have choices on set, they want people to have choices in the course of production, they don't want to commit to things because something organic might happen in the course of filmmaking. And that's true, it often does. But for every one organic moment that you feel is a huge improvement over what your plan was, there were a hundred compromises that have been made just getting the material shot because you didn't have enough time because you didn't plan everything.

Joel and Ethan very carefully storyboard and we end up following the storyboards closely, and that matches what their intention was to begin with. They are not dogmatic about it. If something happens and it's different, then they work around that.

If you start with a blank slate everyday, the amount of effort it would take for even the most articulate director to explain to fifty different collaborators what we are trying to accomplish in that scene, I don't know how you could do it and not work eighteen hours a day.

Michael "Gonzo" Gandsey

"I still pretend to get room tone. It's totally cool to make all those bastards on the set hold still for a minute or so. There's no reason for it, it's just our policy."

Gonzo and I go back quite a few years. What I appreciate about him is that he has done location recording, live sound mixing for concerts, sound editing, and sound re-recording (mixing). He is one of the few people I know that has done all of this and does it well.

I have traveled with him extensively and when problems come up he is absolutely cool under pressure. I have never seen him lose it. He slowly and methodically figures out the problems and then solves them. I love having him on the set, I know he is going to get the best and cleanest dialogue recordings he can because he might have to edit them as well. His attention to detail is a great thing and his sense of humor keeps everyone loose.

Gonzo has also done location recording for: IMAGINARY CRIMES, THE HUNTED, WELCOME TO THE CLUB, THE GAS CAFE, episodes for NOVA and THE AMERICAN EXPERIENCE, and more commercials and corporate pieces than I can remember. His sound editing credits include: BIRDDOG, GOOD WILL HUNTING, PSYCHO (the remake), FINDING FORRESTER, and FAR FROM HEAVEN.

If you want to know more about Michael "Gonzo" Gandsey check out: http://www.imdb.com/name/nm0304204/

KB: How did you get involved with sound, and location recording in particular?

MG: When I was a little kid, my Aunt Mary had a reel-to-reel tape recorder, which I used to record her snoring. From there, I was on to other bodily sounds.

When I was in college, my dad had a connection with IATSE in Hollywood. I started taking calls on weekends doing sound work. I was mixing live sound, going to college and doing studio work. It seemed like I could make a pretty good living at this. I thought to myself, what's this college stuff for? I quit college after three years and mixed music for the early part of my career. In the early 90s a friend of mine started a film production company in Portland, Oregon. I took a few trips up - and said hey, this seems like a beautiful place to live - so I made the move.

I made several trips up here in the summer. My background was music mixing - studio and live. It was later in my career that I got into sound for picture.

KB: What exactly does a production sound mixer do?

MG: The production sound mixer is mainly responsible for recording the best possible dialogue tracks.

If it's an interior, you record the dialogue and ambiances for the scene. If it's exterior, you would include backgrounds specific to the location. The idea being that the post production team has elements available to build the scene. There are times when the location sound mixer also records specific sounds - such as a certain vehicle, birds, traffic, rivers, etc.

KB: What makes a good location recordist?

MG: A good location recordist is always thinking ahead to the next couple of shots. Able to change directions quickly and adapt to a variety of conditions. Grace under pressure. Plan on one or all the other departments screwing you at any given time.

KB: What's your biggest challenge when it comes to location recording?

MG: The "Let's F - k the Sound Department" vibe. That, and lack of communication about everything that effects sound.

KB: Do they ever discuss the scenes, the obstacles, everything with you ahead of time?

MG: Rarely.

KB: Why do you think sound is at the bottom of the pecking order?

MG: Because filmmaking is a visual medium, at least that's what the camera crews say and there are more of them than us.

Everyone is jealous of the sound mixer as well. It's because the chicks dig us. It's true- all the female actors hang out at the sound lounge. We are true renaissance men.

KB: But then it seems like, once people get into post-production they realize that they've screwed up. So the next time they do a show, one would think they would have learned, right?

MG: Same as it ever was. It only hurts for a little while.

KB: Do you think they swear at you guys later in the editing room, do you think they're saying, "They didn't get me the right stuff or any good stuff." when actually it had nothing to do with you?

MG: No respect from either end! I've actually gotten calls from post production halfway through a film, demanding things.

KB: What's so important about recording sound on location? Why don't people just ADR everything in the end?

MG: It's impossible to duplicate the emotion of a scene in ADR.

KB: You're talking about performance, right?

MG: We have all seen films that have massive amounts of ADR and the performance isn't there and the feeling isn't there.

KB: If you had an opportunity to sit down with a director ahead of time, what would you tell them as far as what you need and what they should be thinking about when it comes to sound?

MG: I need to sign-off on locations. I'd like some input regarding wardrobe. A small change in clothing can make a huge difference. I was a sound editor on Todd Hayne's film, FAR FROM HEAVEN, there was a scene in which Julianne Moore was wearing a hoop skirt under her dress, and was walking down a staircase while delivering lines- horrible for sound. This could have been easily corrected.

KB: Why is it that you always hear that phrase, "We're waiting on sound," what's that all about?

MG: Since we've been screwed by everyone all day on the production, the gaffer, the grips, and the camera department - once things have quieted down enough to roll, that's when we find our problems.

KB: And that's when the camera crew starts yelling.

MG: You don't really know until that moment, and that's when you usually find the problems. And everyone is like, "We've been working for the last hour, what have you been doing?"

KB: You're one of the few people I know who does both location work and post-production sound. What have you learned in post- that you took with you back out on the location and vice versa?

MG: Let's start on set where it all begins, to thinking ahead to post-production. It's a fact - location sound doesn't get any respect. Everyone on production is out to get you. Watch your back at all times. Be realistic. The production wants to keep moving, they have a twelve to sixteen hour day ahead of them. Pick your battles. If some stray sound makes it into the dialogue track, decide whether or not it's a big deal or not. If not, move on. Performance rules.

From the post-production side, it's the realization that the location mixer is really under the gun - and you can't always get what you want. The location mixer is truly doing an amazing job given the circumstances.

KB: Are there differences when you do live music recording as compared with location sound for movies?

MG: With a movie, you can usually always get another take. Live is live, there's no second take.

KB: Do you find the live music people harder to work with than the movie people?

MG: Recording music is all about the sound - and the people understand that. Movie people are visual. Sound takes a back seat to the picture.

KB: They don't expect you to do your best job on a film set?

MG: They do. Except they don't respect you. As long as you're moving fast and don't slow things down then everybody seems to be happy on the set.

KB: And it doesn't matter if the recording's not very good.

MG: It does to me and it does to the director and the actors. I've never heard anyone on a film set after a playback say, "Wow! That sounded great!"

KB: You've done dramatic pieces, television and documentaries. Does your approach vary from project to project?

MG: Yeah, in a lot of ways it does. The core of it stays the same, which is to produce the best tracks possible given the conditions. But in most feature films the scenes are shot with a single camera, in most dramatic television it's multiple cameras, so it's a way different approach to what microphones you can use. You really have to be on your toes for TV because they'll be rolling on the wide when you're not ready to go with the right kind of microphones. You think it's going to be a close-up, but because they can shoot with multiple cameras it's a whole different approach to how they do things and the speed they move.

KB: If the shoot is more complicated, multiple cameras and stuff, are you more likely to meet with the producer or director ahead of time so you know about this a head of time or do they spring it on you?

MG: Usually they spring it on me. It's just the nature of the beast. It's all about the bottom line. You have to get through a bunch of pages in a day, so the likelihood that they're going to consult with me is slim.

KB: Do the directors leave those decisions up to you or are they standing behind you saying boom or wireless?

MG: They're not really concerned with what you use as long as you get it right. There's certainly not a lot of discussion as far as a preference, as far as what to use in a situation.

KB: Do you have a preference, boom or wireless?

MG: Boom. You can hear the difference. Much more open and natural.

Obviously, the shot dictates what the mic of choice will be. If it's a wide shot with dialogue, the boom may not be the right choice.

KB: What do you think students need to know most about sound?

MG: On location, don't complicate things. If in doubt about which mic to use, go for the boom. Buy the best you can afford - you can hear the difference.

KB: What about with post-production? What do you think most students need to know about post-production sound?

MG: Sound can evoke images, images cannot evoke a sound. Sound is powerful stuff. Close you eyes and listen. The simpler the better when it comes to post-production sound. The less manipulation you do, things will sound better. Sometimes it's better to take things away than to keep adding because if you keep adding, all you end up getting is brown.

KB: On location, what's the most common sound problem that you encounter?

MG: Interiors - Refrigerators and the AC/heat system. I've also noticed that buildings are getting noisier and noisier. It seems to be the way the air handling works. Exteriors - sirens, airplanes, cars and elk. (Laughs).

KB: (Laughs). Are you referring to my use of elk sounds on most of the films we've done together? What's the worst sound problem that you've ever encountered on location and how did you deal with it?

MG: I was the location sound mixer on Kelley Baker's film, THE GAS CAFE. The film takes place in a diner, that was literally ten feet from a railroad track. We had to shoot at night as well, when the restaurant was closed for business. All the streets were quiet, but little did we know that the railroad was moving freight all night in front of this restaurant. Literally, you could reach out through the front door and touch the trains as they went by. The director simply shut down production whenever we had a train.

KB: I heard that guy was pretty good!

MG: He's good, yeah. You can shoot with the trains, but then you have trains in your film, so is it a movie about trains, or is it a movie about something else? You know some things you can't fix, but this was one of those cases where we shot around it.

KB: With budgets changing all the time and getting smaller what is the biggest change that you've seen in how sound is done, thinking about budget stuff.

MG: Time compression. You get less planning and less time to correct problems.

KB: With all of these new digital cameras do they make your job easier or harder?

MG: Easier. Everything I do now is double system. Take the Canon 5 and 7D. Any sound you record onto these cameras sounds like crap, so by default I record double system.

KB: I talked with some on certain digital cameras location recordists about equipment and a couple of them went off. One person said it may give you a cool picture but he tells people all the time if you're going to shoot with one of these cameras, run out to the music store and get a $200 recorder because the sound you get with that is so much better than what you'll get with some of these cameras.

MG: I consider any audio sent to a video camera a scratch track. HD records video and sound separately, and I've had problems in the past. You can playback picture and have it look fine, and the sound can be toast.

KB: Cameras and digital formats are changing all the time, is the same thing happening in audio?

MG: Things change, things get better. From the 44.1khz/16 bit DAT recorder to hard disk recorders that can record at 24-bit and high sampling rates. 24-bit depth gives you this huge amount of dynamic range on location. It's about double the range of DAT tapes; you can get a lot more information on the track, it's a richer sound. A company called Zaxcom makes a wireless mic system with a recorder built into the transmitter. Even if an actor is out of range, the on-board recorder has captured the audio. Brilliant.

KB: Can you think of any films that had outstanding sound and why you think it did?

MG: APOCALYPSE NOW - all the sound elements worked for me. Especially the helicopters! THE CONVERSATION - The sound really put you into Gene Hackman's head. THE LORD

OF THE RINGS Trilogy - A huge fan of the books, all of the sounds were just right.

KB: If you are looking for a sound mixer, what are the things you want to know about that person and their work

MG: You want to know if they're on parole for anything. You don't want to lose your sound mixer in the middle of the show.

Somebody that's the perfect mix between an artist and technician - and being able to deal with any situation that comes up.

KB: A lot of students ask me how can they get into sound, what would you tell them?

MG: Find somebody that will let you haul gear and hang out and watch how it all works. Be persistent. Don't be afraid to make a mistake. If you think this is for you, find a college that suits you and study.

KB: Do you still like what you do after thirty years?

MG: It's really not like a job. I dig it.

KB: Can you think of anything else pertaining to sound that you think students who want to become filmmakers should know?

MG: Yeah, forget about getting room tone! The most useable ambiance is just before a take, and directly after.

However, I still pretend to get room tone. It's totally cool to make all those bastards on the set hold still for a minute or so. As they say, there's no reason for it, it's just our policy.

KB: That's going in the book.

Glen Trew

"With TV I like to say, we walk on the set and throw in the towel."

In addition to running his company Trew Audio, Glen Trew has been recording audio for over thirty years and there's not much he hasn't seen or recorded. He was the production recordist on films like RED STATE, COUNTRY STRONG, JERSY GIRL and HANNAH MONTANA: THE MOVIE. All of these films had challenges when it comes to production audio and Glen has the experience to tackle anything that comes his way.

To find out more about Glen Trew check out his imdb page:

http://www.imdb.com/name/nm0872490/

KB: How did you get involved with audio?

GT: I think with me it started with an interest in sounds, I really enjoyed listening to the strangest things, leaves rustling, people whispering, air conditioning fans, mostly very subtle sounds. I never thought too much about it, but I was always keying into them and enjoyed listening to them.

Then an interest in music followed, and that turned into a profession playing the French horn. I put myself though college playing the French horn professionally in symphony orchestras, then recording sessions, small ensembles, woodwind quintets, brass quintets, and brass choirs. And all along the way I had a keen interest in mechanical and electronic devices. Understanding how they worked, building my own, I was always involved in that kind of thing as well. So really, what

I do now is a complete blend of those three things. Listening to sound, music, and fabricating and operating mechanical and electronic devices.

KB: You're a business owner, and a production sound mixer. Did you start out as a boom operator or were you able to just jump right in?

GT: I started by doing live sound. Basically PA mixing for traveling pop and rock & roll bands, that sort of thing. I guess you could say my first legitimate job in sound was doing sound for a theme park in Nashville called Opryland, USA. It was Broadway type shows with a little bit of country flavor. That was a dream job for someone my age. I think I was nineteen or twenty, mixing thirty-two microphones from a cast of singers and dancers and a live orchestra. Compared to the construction jobs that I had done the previous summers, this was like a dream.

KB: What exactly does a production sound mixer do?

GT: The production sound mixer is in charge of the production sound. We are not on location to be told how to do it, and we aren't hired to be told what to do. We're hired to get it done. And that's something that a lot of people don't realize. Generally on a major production the director isn't interested in how you do things they just want to go about their business directing, and expect the sound to be done correctly. Once you get past that, what we do primarily is record dialogue, the actors speaking. We do other things too, like sound effects, ambiances, and wild tracks. But mainly it's recording the actors speaking while the camera shoots them.

KB: If you have problems on the set, how much control do you have as far as trying to get the sound?

GT: Really we have zero control. As far as having authority on controlling things, sound will always take what is left over from the picture. The picture has to be the primary consideration because it's the most difficult if not impossible to fix later on. Part of the art of what we do is making the best out of the situation we are given. It involves some technique but mostly it involves experience in a creative way to make that happen.

KB: I know from experience, the camera crew can spend hours lighting and getting everything set. Typically, how much time do you get to set up?

GT: We get almost no time to ourselves. We do our preparation while the camera crew and the lighting crew are doing theirs. And if the sound department isn't ready when everybody else is and you have shown a pattern of not being ready when everyone else is, you'll be replaced. It's that simple. So part of what we do is try to be prepared, anticipate what's needed and work to get everything situated in the background, so nobody waits on us.

Of course every now and then there is something that comes up that is beyond our control that might cause us to need something. Then they might wait for us, but not always. Sometimes they say, "We can't wait, the sun is coming up and we're losing darkness . . . just get a guide track (a track for the actor reference later when replacing the original recording)."

As far as what we have authority to control, we have none. If an issue comes up and we need more time that what was given, we can make our case and talk about why more time is needed, explain what it is and how we need to go about doing this. Sometimes it is agreed that perhaps it can make the production better so we're given a little more time. Sometimes we may need more equipment that goes above our budget, you can make your case for that.

It's generally a battle, especially on a high-end production. Even though you may be arguing with the producer about it you are expected to voice your opinion. Because if this comes up a couple months later in post-production and they're all sitting in their chairs and it's either, "Now we understand why he wanted those things." or, "Dang, why didn't the production mixer explain better what he needed because then we wouldn't be in this predicament."

KB: I tell students the three most important things in any movie are story, acting, and sound. And yet I find most students think that 90% of the dialogue that is recorded on set is replaced in ADR.

GT: That is not true, at least not as a rule. There are some shows that are maybe 90% ADR, shows with a lot of special effects for instance. There is dialogue while mechanical things are going on maybe its robots or a wind machine. Maybe it involves the stunt coordinator giving instructions to the crew, while dialogue is going on. So in those cases we know all we're getting is a guide track for the actors to replace later. But that's really the exception. Most of the shows I work on probably use 95% production tracks. Some more, some less, but that's usually the case, especially for dialogue-driven productions.

KB: Any idea where this 90% replacement thing comes from?

GT: In my experience it comes from people who want an excuse to not give sound a chance to do their job. I have heard it from friends of mine in the camera department who roll their eyes at anything having to do with sound. They want to believe it and they spread it and before you know it . . . I've actually heard it taught in college classrooms by people who came up through the art department.

Also keep in mind on a crew of 150 on a film, only three of

them are involved with sound. So you have all these people who know very little about sound and care even less about it and have motivation to favor their own departments. So lets not perpetuate those myths that reduce the value of sound.

KB: Are you finding that you're dealing more with producers and directors and having to educate them on how you can help them?

GT: I think that's fair to say. Almost all directors come from the picture side of things, either writing, or being involved in the camera department, maybe lighting, or editing. I don't know any that came from the sound department and into directing. And I've only met one or two that came from the sound department and got into producing.

If you combine that with schedules that are tougher now, people are expected to do more with less, you have to pack every minute of every day with productive activity. There's just not enough time to think about sound much, they just want it to happen.

KB: It seems like they don't think about it until they get into post, and that's when they realize they should have given sound more time.

GT: And experienced producers and directors do keep that in mind. A lot of times you make a case that something needs to be done and the production manager or the producer on set might say no we can't, we have to keep moving, we'll fix it later. And sometimes they aren't involved in post-production, it's not even a part of their budget. They don't care about what has to go on in post-production. They're concerned about that day on the set.

Sometimes you need to step up and really rock the boat if you feel it's important enough. You have to choose your battles though because you don't want to appear more trouble than you're worth.

KB: Very true. What's your biggest challenge when it comes to location recording?

GT: I think the biggest challenge is to record high-quality dialogue in adverse situations. An example is what we call the "wide and tight".

Normally the best way to record dialogue is with an overhead boom microphone. A high quality condenser mic that is out in front of the actor who's speaking. To do that you have to get the microphone at a certain position, usually relatively close to the actor. In an effort to save time it's pretty common now to use two or more cameras, which isn't necessarily a problem, unless one of those cameras is for the wide master shots. That means you can't get the boom in close enough to have proper perspective for the tight shot. Which means you have to use wireless mics on the actors, a hidden lavaliere, which is always compromising to the sound quality. And it's not a compromise that's small or goes unnoticed. It diminishes the quality of the recording, period. And we see that happen a lot. I'll go to the movies and watch something I've worked on and you never see that wide shot, yet we were forced to mic the actors for the wide shot. It's very frustrating to see those close ups with the compromised sound quality.

So the challenge is to see it coming and go to the director of photography and say can you please just shoot the master by itself and then use multiple cameras for the close ups. Sometimes they just blow it off. Sometimes they understand. Generally if they blow it off I go to the director and make my case. Once they develop a trust in you, they'll usually go along with it.

The challenge is getting the highest quality of dialogue that you can, while working with the things that get in the way. You are working for sound while you are working with people for picture. You try to work with each other without stumbling over each other and getting in each other's way while still managing to get good stuff.

KB: You said that whenever you use a lavaliere mic, it's a compromise. Can you explain that?

GT: Since a lavaliere is a miniature microphone, it can't have quite the fidelity that a full size studio microphone can have. Although, they've gotten quite good. You generally use these microphones under clothing, so it can't be seen. So you have a compromise mic to begin with then you cover it with some fabric. On top of that it's never out in front of the actor it's usually under their chin on their chest. So you have those three factors working against you. And they all serve to diminish the quality of the voice. Now we use them all the time and we get some good stuff with them but it's never as good as it could be with a proper overhead boom mic.

A lot of times a camera operator will say, "We've got lights here, we've got shadows, we've got reflections, you're just going to have to wire them. And they say that really flippantly as if that's a good answer. I wish they were more aware that it's a serious compromise on sound quality when we do that. It might be the best answer we have, but it's never a good answer. The more it's understood that it compromises the quality of the production, the more likely it is that another solution can be found. I've seen both scenarios happen many times.

KB: You spoke earlier about the number one thing is to record the dialogue, can you elaborate on that? Why don't you worry about door closes and some of those other things?

GT: We do worry about them and think about them. I for one don't like to just record the dialogue, I like to record the sound of the room, as well. In other words, if someone is in a room or a set with furniture or wood floors, and maybe high ceilings, I want the ambiance to sound that way I want it to sound like it looks.

We also have to think about how it's going to be cut together. If you have somebody walking down a hallway into a room and they close the door while they're speaking, it might be fine from one particular take, but you need to realize they might cut from one angle to another where that door closes, which is going to cause problems. In that case we will make sure that a door close is muted, maybe somebody catches the door so we don't hear it, so it doesn't get recorded.

Same thing with footsteps, as nice as they might sound naturally, it can cause problems in post when they try and edit it all together so it sounds like one long take. So in most cases we put foam on the shoes, maybe put carpets down on the floor.

KB: Do you approach doing a television show differently than a feature?

GT: Yeah, with TV I like to say, we walk on the set and throw in the towel. You show up and say, "I give up." (Laughter)

It varies a little bit. Many TV shows are shot on a stage so you can control your environment and get some nice stuff. But so much is done on location now, and there you have no control over the ambiance. The sunlight may come from all angles, which will cause shadows, which means you can't use booms as much as you want. Usually we give up and plan to use a lot of wireless microphones. And that's done to save time.

A typical TV show and a feature film aren't all that different now a days. On a typical TV show like the one I just finished, the actor shows up, if they have lines in the script they get wired. It took me a long time to finally give up that battle and go along with it. It's a better way to do that kind of production. For instance if we get in there and start a scene and later realize we can't use the boom because of shadows, there's no time to make adjustments to the light. So we wire everyone in advance and if we can't use the boom, we resort to the wireless. It's definitely a dilemma, because preparing for the worst makes it that much easier for camera and lighting to get away with a scenario that does not consider sound, but that's the way the process has evolved.

KB: Everyone is always talking about how cameras have changed. How much has the audio equipment that you use changed?

GT: The equipment has changed quite a bit, primarily the recorders we use. When I first started Nagra's were in use and they were considered a fairly recent advancement.

KB: I still have mine.

GT: I've got like thirty of them.

KB: I've only got one.

GT: If you want to sell it let me know.

KB: I'm hanging on to it . . .

GT: The recorder went from Nagras to DAT machines, which was not an improvement in quality, it just sped things up in post and it was less expensive to buy. From that they went to non-linear hard disc base recording. And that was about ten, maybe twelve years ago that started and it was a big change. Not only did sound quality improve but also the number of tracks that were recorded improved and we invented ways to use those tracks that are now considered standard operating procedures. It sped things up in post-production and it made things more reliable because duplicates were instant.

Now with HD video, the cameras are non-linear hard drive based or flash card based and the camera people are all acting like, isn't this great, isn't life grand. And I say, listen guys, this is what we were trying to explain to you twelve years ago. Just last week a camera assistant on set was in disbelief that he could receive an email with a file that made his camera work differently than it did before. And I'm thinking we've been doing this for twelve years.

But yeah, the recording technology has changed, it's finally an improvement.

KB: Are you finding you're spending more time learning new equipment now?

GT: I think more time is needed now to learn about equipment. Not only operating the equipment but how it affects the whole flow of pre-production, production, and post-production. Back in the 70s and 80s when we used Nagra's it was complex because we had pull up and pull down to worry about and U.S. TV standards. But there was only one way to do things correctly and understand how it was done. Now there are a host of other variables involved so there are a variety of ways to do something correctly depending on how things are handled in post-production It's almost impossible to know which way is the correct way, but it's necessary to know what questions to ask and depending on what those answers are, know what parameters to use on your recorder. It's a lot more complex but it's kind of cool, it keeps your brain sharp.

KB: Here is something that drives me crazy that I would love to have you address: people come in to pick up gear they really don't know how to use and then I see them take up time on the set trying to figure things out.

GT: That is true. I see it all the time and film schools are known to turn out students with a lot of book sense but when they get on set they trip all over themselves.

KB: Yes they do.

GT: Experience is not only the most important thing, it's almost the only thing. I've seen very bright kids right out of film school trip all over themselves when thrown into the fire on a high-end TV show where there are no second chances. To be fair, I'm sure it's like that with all professions. But also to be fair, I've noticed that students of schools that focus on the technical "hands on" side of film production are more likely hit the ground running on a professional production set.

So it varies, it varies a lot. The more that they can learn about how to use the equipment the better off they are.

KB: Do you think that they should be practicing the night before with their gear, especially if they are going to rent something?

GT: Oh yeah. So many times people come in to rent something for production and they assume it's going to be easy to figure out like a cell phone, and then it's just all screwed up.

KB: And do they usually place the blame on the equipment?

GT: A lot of times yeah, because they don't know it. Here's what I would suggest, I picked this up when I started doing reviews on equipment for trade magazines. Get the gear, get the manual, go through every function of the gear in the manual and if there are menus go through every one of them. Don't just read what they are, go through the menus, make the selections and see what it does. Go from beginning to end on every function of the piece of gear. Too many people just pick up the gear, turn it on and clink around thinking they'll figure it out. It may take a few hours to learn it but its well worth it to go through every function of a piece of gear.

KB: Can you give me any tips on mic placement?

GT: I always say you need a Plan A and Plan B and realize that probably neither one is gonna work because things change and in the last ten seconds you'll have to make adjustments.

As far as using lavaliere microphones, first of all it's always a compromise when you place a microphone under the chin and under the clothes.

Generally you'll want the microphone around the chest. It's better if there is no fabric or clothing between the microphone and the mouth. You want to have a clear line of sight between the mouth and microphone. You can do that a lot of times, while the fabric still covers the microphone from the camera. And the fewer layers of clothing the better. A single layer of certain material may be okay but I would say never more than a single layer.

Then there is the issue of the microphone rubbing against the fabric and you get that rustling sound that everybody deals with. There are several tricks, there are devices made out of foam, or fur and there are sticky things. Most sound carts have a big bag of tricks. I get phone calls from mixers with ten years experience asking how I might deal with a certain wardrobe situation. A lot of students think they can ask the question, how do you solve clothing rustle? Well you work with it every day for fifteen years, then you're closer to having a solution. It just takes a lot of time and a lot of experimentation.

KB: I worked on a period piece set in 1955 and some of the actresses wore this loud taffeta material. The boom mics seemed to work best, but it seemed like no matter where they placed the wireless mics or how they placed them, we got clothing rustle. And it would have been nice to have a conversation with somebody in wardrobe and ask, "Is there any material you could use that looks like what the director wants but is quieter?"

GT: Exactly, a lot also has to do with the crew. On the TV show I just finished I was lucky to be able to fly in one of my favorite boom operators and what he does really well is wire people. He looked at the script and decided he would do the wiring and he handled it. Which allowed me to concentrate on being the mixer. He has a host of tricks and a ton of experience. I would just bring the fader up and there would be the actor nice and crisp, normally clothing rustle free.

Sometimes you'll hear clothing noise and its not because its rustling, it's because the clothing is just making that noise. The fact that the microphone is really close to the clothing they pick it up more. I remember one time the clothing rustle was so bad, we found a way to get the boom in there. When we opened the boom up we heard the same clothing noise. It was just that noisy.

KB: You just mentioned something that I want to follow up on. With all these independent films, I have enough trouble convincing someone to hire a sound recordist that has experience, how important is it to have a good boom operator?

GT: Very important. Most people think anyone can hold a microphone above their head and point it in the general vicinity of someone speaking. It's so much more than that. All the equipment is very light now, so almost any normal healthy person can hold a boom up for long enough, but knowing where to place it for the best sound takes experience. It's also dealing with things like lights, personalities on set, the DP, the operator, the camera assistants, the grips, the gaffers, to get what's needed. It might be turning a mirror just a little to get rid of a reflection, it might be getting the gaffer to put in a little cutter to hide a shadow. It's so many things like that, that if they weren't done the sound would be compromised.

If you hire someone with very little experience your sound will suffer, there's just no way around it. So many times I get a call saying we can hire you but we'll have to get a PA to hold the boom and then they'll go on to say that the sound is extremely important to the show. (Laughs) If you do it this way your sound won't be very good, period. It's like expecting somebody to hop in to a 747 and land it successfully; it's not going to happen. (Laughs)

KB: (Laughs) Right. I'm going to promote you to director right now. If you had to hire a production mixer, what would you look for?

GT: I don't know if the move to director would necessarily be a promotion.

KB: There are a lot more hassles. . .

GT: I would look for someone who could express what is important in their job in the production and see if that idea was in line with the director's vision of the movie.

I would also look for someone that's a problem solver instead of someone who whines about problems. That's a mistake that a lot of sound people make. "Oh well you just don't give me enough time." Or "How can I do my best job, or this, that, and the other. . . " They just complain instead of presenting solutions to the problems.

And once I had that person, a problem solver, I would stay out of their way and if they make a recommendation I would probably take it. Cause when we make recommendations, at least for me, it's always because we feel in consideration of everything else, that suggestion will make the movie better. So if you find someone like that, listen to their recommendations and try not to get annoyed by them.

KB: What are the most important things you think students and filmmakers need to know about sound?

GT: I wish Dynamic Range was discussed more. Some people have zero grasp of dynamic range - the soft parts of dialogue compared to the louder parts of dialogue. Which is one reason why lavaliere mics don't work as well as boom mics, but that's a whole semester discussion right there.

I think that mic placement determines quality of sound, if the mic isn't in the right place then the sound isn't as good as it could be.

Remember even when we are using one microphone we are still mixing. I think the goal of the sound mixer is to make the sound feel like that the person watching the film is actually hearing the person speak. That means a good balance between the voice and the ambiance and the voices of the other actors around them. Sometimes it is just mic placement to balance the ambiance to the voice. Sometimes it involves blending multiple actors on multiple microphones, so it sounds like you're just in a room listening to the actors speak.

Now that gets into a debate between production mixers and post-production mixers because generally if you do that you include a lot of ambiance, and then you take away some control from those in post-production And they seem to prefer building everything themselves from very dry sounding voices and adding the ambiances, but it never, ever is as natural as what was originally there.

KB: What would you tell a student who wanted to get into the sound field?

GT: There are so many different ways that people I know got in to it. A lot of people got into it because they were just really interested in making movies and sound happened to be their way in. And they've turned into really good sound mixers. From my point of view a technical background is very valuable, in understanding equipment and being able to repair equipment and even fabricate certain things. Now just because someone doesn't have that knack, doesn't mean they wouldn't be good sound mixers, that just may not be their forte.

It basically comes down to being able to know what they want sound wise and being able to work with a crew around them - that's probably the most important thing. I say that because there are a lot of talented sound mixers out there who don't get along with the crew, and because of that, they don't get hired. Sometimes the sentiment from the producer is, "I don't care how good you are, we don't want you around," and they will hire someone lesser who is more pleasant.

KB: I think that's true on any level with a crew, anymore. There is so much politicking that you have to get along with other people. Do you still like what you do after all these years?

GT: Yes, I love it. I have been doing it for thirty-five years. Even though this last show was extremely brutal. It was 105 degrees, direct sun light on a black top parking lot for twelve hours then it would storm and we would be in the rain and the mud. But the truth is when I am sitting at the console doing what I do, it's still very enjoyable. Working with a hundred people who are there because they also have a creative bent, the actors, directors, writers, crew, the musicians, we're all in the creative category. To be with those people working really hard to produce something, that's just irreplaceable.

KB: That's cool, that's very cool. Thanks Glen.

CHAPTER 2

It's a Tough Job, Someone Has To Do It.

Post Supervisors

Well, you've survived production but you've still got to get this thing finished. The entire post-production process is a little more complicated than you think.

What do you mean post-production isn't just about editing the film and slapping the sound together?

What if you get a distribution deal? What are the deliverables and who is going to round them up? How many different sound mixes are you going to need to give the distributor? Are you going to make an L-C-R, or do they want a 5.1? Do you still need to do a mono mix? How do you lay out a D-M & E? What's the difference between print masters and intermediates? Who's going to clear that great Bruce Springsteen song you want to use?

And this is just for the sound, what happens if you have special effects? Who is going to schedule everything so all of your elements are finished at the same time?

Did you know in France a film can't be released to theaters or shown on television unless the director signs off on it?

This is where the post supervisors come in. There are so many things that still need to get done and they are the pros. They know what deliverables distributors want and the best way to gather them.

Face it, you don't have the time or the knowledge to do it all.

You need to bring in someone who can keep all of the different elements moving forward and keep an eye on the budget so you can make it to the premiere and hopefully celebrate a completed distribution deal.

Bob Hackl

"You serve the director but work for the producer."

I first met Bob on GOOD WILL HUNTING and it was not pleasant. He and I immediately got off on the wrong foot. He was replacing another Post Production Supervisor who had been fired. I had already done three other films with Gus Van Sant (four if you count EVEN COWGIRLS GET THE BLUES as I had to do that one twice), and he immediately started telling me what to do and how. Naturally I got angry and we spent a lot of time not talking. I didn't realize at the time that he was under tremendous pressure from the Producer to save money and he was getting lots of shit from the higher ups.

We finished the movie before we came to blows and I'd vowed I would never work with him again. So naturally when I got the call to do the re-make of PSYCHO I asked who the Post Supervisor was, and it was Bob.

Bob called me and we had a long conversation. He asked if we could start from scratch. I agreed and it was one of the best experiences I've ever had with a Post Supervisor. Bob was efficient and incredibly funny. He taught me quite a bit about what a GOOD Post Supervisor does.

At the time I was also finishing up my first feature, BIRDDOG. In my off time I was on the phone trying to get deals to save money as all of my funds were exhausted. Bob asked me one day how it was going and I told him, "not well". He asked a few questions, then he got on the phone. He used his connections to get me better deals then what I had already negotiated. He asked for personal favors since he knew most of these people and promised them if they gave me a better deal than the one he usually got from them he wouldn't come back and negotiate the same things for his studio clients.

I was amazed and impressed. A year earlier we wanted to kill each other and now he was helping me. It's a lesson I have never forgotten. What we went through on GWH was not personal, it was business. I found in Bob a hard working caring guy who went to the mat if he was your friend. And he hadn't even seen BIRDDOG!

I am thrilled that Bob agreed to do an interview for this book. Listen to him, he's been through the wars on more films than I will probably ever make.

His credits include: MILK, GOOD WILL HUNTING, ROUNDERS, THE WEDDING SINGER, HAPPY GILMORE, THE COWBOY WAY, THE CROW: CITY OF ANGELS, PSYCHO, MIDDLE MEN, THE GREAT RAID and many others.

If you want to know more about Bob Hackl check out:
http://www.imdb.com/name/nm0352531/

KB: How did you get involved with film? And how did that lead to a position as a Post-Production Supervisor?

BH: I was born in Hollywood and our old black & white Zenith television was quite often the (preferred) babysitter. There were good movies (for free) on television in the 50s and 60s. Hitchcock, Arthur Penn, Raoul Walsh, and many others. In elementary school, we had a movie (16mm) day once or twice each semester, films like POLLYANNA and TARZAN as I recall. It was a nice escape from the drudgery of schoolwork. I thought that old Bell & Howell projector - they let me run it eventually - was marvelous and wondered if a viable career in the movie biz was feasible. I still do.

Most kids in the 50s and 60s were pretty hands-on. Mechanical things were cool back then. I always liked cameras and quickly appropriated my mom's Bell & Howell Double 8 to shoot my own stuff. Film school, student projects and teacher's assistant work followed.

I got a job at Loyola University as a production sound mixer, camera loader and re-recording mixer for student films. They had a pretty nifty "back 'n forth" dub stage, not to mention state-of-the-art TV and film sound stages. The department was well endowed by the Sarnoff family/RCA. Freshman Bob Beemer was one of the kids I trained in sound as a senior T/A. He was the only one to receive a perfect score on his lab final exam which involved demonstrating mastery of an audio patch panel. After college, Bob got a job at Todd A/O as a loader but dreamed of becoming a feature writer. He's since had to settle for a few Oscars as a re-recoding mixer.

KB: Is there a particular film (or films) that were a big influence on you when you started working in film?

BH: I always loved the realism that directors like John Frankenheimer made. GRAND PRIX and THE TRAIN were big faves. Same with Richard Lester, A HARD DAY'S NIGHT and the even fabber HELP. Later, at college, we were tinkering a lot with motion control and opticals in general, so 2001: A SPACE ODYSSEY, THE EXORCIST and, of course, STAR WARS were huge influences. Doug Trumbull was pushing the tech envelope in interesting ways. I remember thinking Coppola was someone who might make it after seeing THE CONVERSATION in Charles Champlin's film criticism class senior year. The Pythons were also starting to make features, starting with MONTY PYTHON AND THE HOLY GRAIL. I wanted to make comedies like that and tried my hand at writing for a while.

KB: What exactly does a Post Supervisor do? Is it different working in Film as compared to TV? (Since you've done both.)

BH: A post super is a combo UPM/line producer (Unit Production Manager) working at half the pay and, until very recently, usually without benefits. In TV, you're typically called an associate producer if you do episodic shows. Usually, a staff post manager handles TV long-form, though I've seen post supers credited as such on cable features. When I started working in the late 70s, many studios and networks employed retired editors as their post managers. In features, "post supervisor" is a solid credit, much better than the more generic "associate producer" which can be someone who fetches the director's laundry.

KB: Do you work closer with the director or the Producer?

BH: All depends on the project. Whoever needs the most attention generally gets it. The straight answer is that you serve the director but work for the producer. Day-to-day I probably spend more time around the editing room or communicating with it.

KB: What makes a good Post Supervisor?

BH: Consummate management/technical skills, patience and a sense of humor, leadership when needed; the ability to check ones ego at the door.

KB: Can you talk about how you manage a project from beginning to end? Who contacts you?

BH: In all cases it's the producer who does the hiring. The bigger the film, the more say the editor or director get in the selection, but normally the producer wants the cold comfort of knowing his person is managing the process.

It usually starts with a budget and a general schedule outline coming from the producer. They want a specialist to review and make sure they're adequately budgeted. From there, we create a detailed schedule as a function of the budget, with the desired delivery date in mind. The schedule is the bible, constantly revised, to be sure, but it's what everyone must work to.

Finally the delivery, which gets bigger and more technically complex every year. It's not for beginners, to be sure. At that point, I want to interface with another professional at the distributor/studio end and have my advisements respected by the producer.

KB: What is your biggest challenge on a film?

BH: Booking actors for ADR and making sure they show up. Hands down. Second to that is making sure the printing intermediates are as spotless as possible. Overly-neurotic directors and/or producer committees run a distant third; beyond a certain point of reason you're no longer on the project, so no worries there.

KB: With budgets changing all the time, and seemingly getting smaller, what is the biggest change you've seen in post-production over the last few years?

BH: There are a lot more independent contractors and a lot less overhead in some areas. Sound, Music and Video FX can be done from home in many cases now thanks to advances in computer technology and affordable specialty software.

As for the picture, the film labs have largely been replaced by the video houses which now endeavor to be the hub of the post universe, though this is not really possible or practical for bigger feature projects.

KB: Do you think good sound is important?

BH: Try watching a movie without it! Back to that old Zenith in my parents' front room. We'd twiddle those damned rabbit ears constantly and sometimes have to settle for a Picasso-esque image that was only watchable because the sound was good. I went to see TROY at the neighborhood 6-plex a few years back. After the trailers, the movie started but without the track. The entire audience walked out, livid, demanding refunds. You rarely see that happen when the projector isn't properly focused (a pet peeve of mine).

KB: How much of the dialogue is usually replaced later in ADR?

BH: It all depends on the production conditions, but seems like less every year, or maybe I'm just working on smaller movies. As a rule, directors would rather live with the original performances on the production track even if it's diseased technically. In their minds it's "the shit" while a loop is something artificial even if the actor manages to exceed his original performance, and it's a perfect sonic match. Go figure. Of course, technology has really come a long way since the notch filter in treating bad dialogue, so you can get away with a lot of sketchy production these days.

KB. Do you believe that sound gets no respect until Post-Production?

BH: I don't see it as a question of respect. Everyone wants to capture the immediacy of the actors' performances on the day. But a day on location for the average studio-class movie costs $120,000. You can loop for $300/hour, and the lead actors have free days for just this contingency. Do the math. Few filmmakers can afford to go an extra day just because of bad sound conditions.

*KB. Do you approach a larger budgeted studio film like
PSYCHO differently than you would a small independent film?*

BH: No, not really. The work is the same, though the smaller
films are usually harder to manage because of budget challenges
and unrealistic appetites (I'd love to be able to set my rate as an
inverse of the post budget).

On the bigger movies, if money is the solution, there's never a
problem. In that arena it's all about personalities, comfort levels
and that nasty ticking clock. Both scenarios can wear you out,
though in different ways.

*KB: If you were the director what would you do differently as
far as post-production and sound?*

BH: First, I'd be so damned grateful to be directing I'd make do
with whatever resources were available and make the best
movie I could. Beyond that, the process has been so refined
over the years that I'd just go with what works.

*KB: What do students need to know about sound from a post-
production standpoint?*

BH: Hire the best production mixer you can afford. Have him
shoot a lot of location environments, crowd reactions, alternate
TV coverage if possible, anything that would have to be replaced
or added later that is unique to the set. A good ADR mixer is a
must, as is the lead re-recording mixer. Today, he must not only
clean up the dialogue but also be great with music.

*KB: What is the most common sound problem that you
encounter? Besides having to work with someone like me?*

BH: Besides having to work with you? Nothing.

The real answer, of course, is noisy production dialogue. Second to that would be a troubled scenario whereby an overabundance of narration is needed to tell the story. In those cases, everyone gets into the act of writing the definitive "silver bullet" lines. During my Miramax stint, Matt Damon seemed to get more than his fair share of that duty.

KB: What's the worst post problem you've ever encountered and how did you fix it?

BH: My first big feature as a post super was NOTHING IN COMMON for Tristar. Lon Bender and Wylie Stateman were the supervising sound editors. We shot an OSTN (Optical Sound Track Negative) at Todd-AO after a four-week final mix with Terry Porter. We had the negative cutter line up the track and got a comp answer print from MGM lab the following day.

One of the reels started just fine, in sync, but then the sync went out, way out. The Tristar VP of post, Jim Potter, asked me if sync was early or late. I couldn't really tell because in some scenes it seemed early and others late. The kicker was that both the two-pop and tail pop were absolutely in sync as confirmed by the negative cutter. Potter the thought I was smoking something. I went to Sound Transfer department, explained the problem and meekly hinted that maybe their optical recorder was to blame. I was roundly lectured on the infallibility of their fabulous sync motors, ridiculed and sent home to contemplate my stupidity. The next day I received a call from the chief engineer in Transfer informing me that another client had a similar complaint, they were now investigating. You can guess the rest.

KB: Anything else?

BH: Many years later, I was working on THE WEDDING SINGER for producer Bob Simmonds at Universal. Adam

Sandler had hired his NYU pals Frank Coraci as director and Tom Lewis as editor. Both were first-timers on a 35mm studio feature. We'd shot the final scene of the movie with Steve Buscemi as the new wedding singer. It involved Buscemi, Gabe Veltri and myself, performing a cover of the 80s hit song "True" on stage at Robbie's (Sandler) own wedding. (I was selected because I'd had a band in the 80s and could show Buscemi the chord fingering and neck moves). We shot, Karaoke-style, to a playback with Steve's mic being hot. It was Friday, the last day of principal photography. We shot lots of coverage because Buscemi was flying home to NY that evening for a long vacation with his family. I drove him to the airport.

On Monday we ran the rushes at Universal and noticed that each take started in sync but then drifted, getting progressively worse. It was a bad camera sync motor getting sicker as the day progressed. The Sandler gang freaked. Frank Coraci wanted me to get bids from a Video FX house to digitally/optically put the picture into sync with the "True" track. This was 1998 and the technology for those kinds of fixes - call it digital interpolating - was both limited and very expensive. I told him as much, and advised them to first cut the sequence using the footage they had and worry about the sync later. The scene was a final button to the movie just before credits, and I knew the individual cuts probably wouldn't be on screen long enough to matter and that the music or dialogue editor could do the rest. He informed me that I was not an expert, insisting I get a bid to fix the dailies. I replied that I was an expert, that the costs would be astronomical but would get a bid. I called Roger Dorney one of the top Hollywood Video FX gurus (ex-Dykstra/Apogee) at Pacific Title. His quote was $1 million, a one-year turnaround, with no guarantee of success. Needless to say, the editor was able to use the existing footage satisfactorily.

You can watch the last scene of the movie here:

http://www.youtube.com/watch?v=HRCcRjf2gsU I'm on
Buscemi's left (right side of frame). It's short, but the best jokes
usually are.

There are other examples as well, mostly involving elaborate
Video FX fixes - remove the Twin Towers in the background in
SERENDIPITY following 911, explore removing a multitude of
Taitinger logos plastered everywhere in the dance competition
finale of SHALL WE DANCE, due to a product placement
dispute.

KB: Have you had any good times or fun being a post supervisor?

BH: Oh yeah. Some moments of real creative triumphs,
including my supervising all post on CONTROL (HBO
Pictures). I had a free hand in supervising the answer print at
Cine Cita, the domestic ADR (Ben Gazzara, Kate Nelligan, and
many non-English speaking international stars) and pre-dubs at
Fona Roma (with dialogue editor Nick Alexander), and the
domestic final dub with Paul Massey in Toronto. I learned an
awful lot on that one and had a ball as you might imagine.
Personally edited the huge Morricone orchestral score for the
domestic version, which was a full hour shorter than the
international feature version (title: THE DAY BEFORE).

Returned to Rome ten years later to loop Iggy Pop who was
touring Europe with his band. I was on THE CROW: CITY OF
ANGELS (Miramax) and Iggy played the antagonist. Then
picked up Ian Dury in London . . . and Roger Moore at
Tickenham around the same time for a different movie, THE
QUEST. I also worked in Munich at FFS, Toronto, Vancouver,
New York with Adam Sandler, Tim Robbins, Jack Warden.
Wonderful adventures, all pre-ISDN, and usually with directors'
blessings.

KB: What's your best advice to filmmakers?

BH: Have fun. Making a movie that gets into distribution is a rare experience that very few get to have. If you can get paid doing it, you're one lucky bastard. If you can sustain a career, you rule.

KB: If you were looking for a Post Production Supervisor what would be the important things you would want to know about them and their work?

BH: Who have they worked with? Can they roll with the sea without appearing too overwhelmed or upset? How personable are they? How responsible? On the most basic level, I think a good parent would have the right stuff as it's all about serving and guiding gently, without being too obvious.

KB: A lot of film students ask me how they can get in to post, what would you tell them?

BH: Just say, "I wanna work in post." That will be followed by a huge, internal sigh of relief by the producer/interviewer who had expected to hear "I wanna direct."

Next Stop: Starbucks runs for the editor.

Seriously, I don't know a lot of people who want to work in post or, once there, make a great living doing it. Many make the mistake of thinking they can use their post job as a stepping stone to "something better." Rarely does that pan out. Your students must realize that producers, like most employers, tend to pigeon-hole people based on their resumes. Think hard about where you really want to be in ten years time and map it out carefully.

KB: Can you think of anything else that would be good for students to know?

BH: Shoot for the stars while you're young, work very hard, move in the right circles, avoid distractions. You have a short window of opportunity, maybe ten years if you're lucky, before life begins to limit your options. The earlier you know what you want to do, the better chance of success you'll have in achieving your goals.

Set a reasonable time line for Plan A and have a viable Plan B. I really admire those individuals who get their bread & butter degrees first, then pursue careers in the arts. Rare breed, to be sure.

Gregor Hutchison

"When shit hits the fan we discuss what the ramifications are both to the budget and to the schedule."

I have never met Gregor Hutchison but he came to me highly recommended. He and I have a mutual friend and when I said I was looking to interview a good Post-Production Supervisor my buddy Richard Mozer said he knew just the one.

Gregor has worked on small films, large films, television, documentaries, you name it and he's probably done it. He worked for Alliance-Atlantic at the studio level and was even involved with twenty-seven episodes of THE CARE BEARS. This is a guy who knows how to get things through post.

His credits include: LUCKY NUMBER SLEVIN, JOHNNY MNEMONIC (who in Canada hasn't worked with Keanu Reeves), a couple of the RESIDENT EVIL films, THE ARISTOCRATS, ASSAULT ON PRECINCT 13, and AMELIA directed by Mira Nair (one of my favorite directors).

If you want know more about Gregor Hutchison check out: http://www.imdb.com/name/nm0404445/

I have worked with quite a few post supervisors and I can tell you that the good ones are worth their weight in gold. They can save you a ton of money and keep you on schedule. Their job is to keep the train running on the right track and make sure that all of the elements are put together for the delivery requirements. The good ones have to know about picture editing, sound, special effects, titles, dealing with the lab, prints and they need to get along with just about everyone. It's a tough job and one I certainly wouldn't want.

Gregor usually works on a couple of films at a time because that's what post supervisors do . . .

KB: Let's jump into this because you probably have half a million things going on today.

GH: Actually not too much but that was the bond company calling me up to ask me questions on some future project.

KB: We're going to talk at some point about having to deal with the Bond Company as compared with the regular production companies and studios. By the time I came on to FAR FROM HEAVEN the Bond Company had taken over and it was not a pleasant experience.

GH: They can be unpleasant. I've actually been able to work very well with the bond companies. I've been on a couple productions that have slid into bond control but they seemed to take my word over the producer.

KB: I don't think they ever took my word for anything.

So. . . anyway you went to Ryerson film school. What were you studying? I mean were you thinking at that point "I want to be a post-supervisor?"

GH: I went to school to be a director. But of course in a class of twenty-two students nineteen of them wanted to be directors and one wanted to be a DP.

Out of film school my first job was in editorial, a second assistant syncing dailies. I worked my way up to editor on that same TV show. By the end of it I thought, "Oh my God, I can't see myself spending twenty-five years sitting in front of, at that point it was a flat-bed, then I saw the transition to 3/4" off line editing and that was just a nightmare."

And the supervising editor was one of these left brain kind of guys, like a surfer dude in terms of his personality and the producer was just so frustrated in talking with him that he turned to me one day and said, "I don't ever want to talk to him, you deal with him." So I became a post coordinator on that show and it was like bells went off "Oh, I get to determine the schedule? I can decide whether I'm going to work late Friday nights or early Monday mornings or whatever?"

KB: You get to decide those things?

GH: In theory I did. In practice? No, not really.

KB: Can you tell me what a post-supervisor does? You said something about having all the responsibilities and none of the power . . .

GH: I basically oversee both the sound and picture editorial crew. At the end of the production when everybody goes home I ensure that the deliverables are created and are "of a technical superior quality." Essentially it's like the production manager for post. I manage the schedule; I'm communicating with the producer. When shit hits the fan we discuss what the ramifications are both to the budget and to the schedule.

In any post-production schedule, or delivery schedule there's going to be a force majeure period which ostensibly is a stop gap for any unseen issues, like strikes or technical issues but more often than not, just getting all of the deliverables ship shape.

KB: I asked you earlier if you work closer with the producer or the director, you said, you report to the producer but you try to take your direction from the director.

GH: Producers don't really know about post-production, about the process. So when the director is in the middle of cutting and he asks for stock shots or stock music or wants to do some visual effects, the producer essentially turns to me and says,

"Can we cover it?" I would move money around from category to category to essentially get the director what he is looking for, always with the proviso that it delivered on time and on budget, (in theory).

KB: How much input do you have with the post-budget at that point?

GH: It depends on the show. I generally take a look at the preliminary budget and flush out the actual details. For instance, in the post-sound category, they'll have a one-line item sound package and put a number beside it and that will include both sound editorial and mixing, and there may or may not be a sound deliverables category as well. I'll make sure the bottom line matches with expectations.

I'll flush out all of the requirements and the specific processes that go into post and try to hit his bottom number. I'm working on a film right now where my numbers came in about $200,0000 over their bottom line number. I pointed out that because it was a digital show, we needed to have in the digital dailies category the kind of money that we used to have for processing, telecine, and dailies dubs which they'd thought they could strip out because it was all digital. I discussed it with the producer saying we need to have this and you need to find the money either from your contingency or in re-allocating some of your production costs.

That's at the preliminary stage. When it gets into post-production, if there's contingency money left we will invade that contingency in order to deal with the unknowns. Oftentimes the unknowns are visual effects where "Oops" they did something onset. For example, where someone is standing in the corner at THE EDGE of the frame.

KB: Why does a film need a post-supervisor? I always thought the producer and the editor could handle all that stuff themselves . . . not true?

GH: Post Supervisors were first brought on to oversee series work where there were multiple shows at various stages. The Producer was watching over the entire series, with shows in prep, production and post. As filmmaking became more technical and complicated, it made sense to have someone overseeing the process who was intimately aware of Post and all it's facets. I find that on a number of low budget productions they haven't allocated money for a post-supervisor. What we're seeing is that the bond companies now are insisting on a post-supervisor because the whole post-production process has become so technically complicated it really is impossible for the producer to be able to manage both the production and the post-process. So you see the bond company stepping in and saying, you need to have this person in for a minimum amount of time. In other cases the producer wants to go on and prep his next project so he needs to have somebody that he can rely upon to oversee the end of the current project.

KB: Once the final mix is done everybody's gone except the post-supervisor and usually the supervising sound editor. We're the ones that have to go through all the different mix versions and the question always comes up during this step why do we even need to record Foley? What is Foley good for?

GH: Foley is good for all sorts of things and I'm talking to the choir here I'm sure you know very well what its for. Foley is primarily used to ensure that we can deliver a good international track, what we call the M & E, or Music and Effects track. When we're doing our primary language mix, in most cases English, there will be dialogue on top of the body movement and the footsteps. Oftentimes you've got footsteps that you can't hear because the dialogue is lower, because the dialogue takes precedence. So we use the Foley footsteps to augment the feet to ensure that there is a full sounding track. We use Foley for specific key moves in terms of props, there are inserts that are shot MOS, there's shots they couldn't cover because with digital technology these days you've got noisy power supplies and fans cooling down the cameras and rigs and that stuff eats up any of the subtleties of the sound that the recordist is trying to record.

I've had several conversations with sound recordists where they get so bloody frustrated over their inability to get the kind of sound that they are expecting to be able to deliver to the editorial crew. So Foley really gives us the stopgap to be make sure at the mix we've got everything we want.

KB: Do most people (like producers and directors) realize all the different versions of the mix that have to be done after the final mix on the deliverables?

GH: Absolutely not. It's so common that the mix is completed and they go, "So you can deliver tomorrow?" or "You're wrapping it at the end of the week?" And I'm going, "Well you've got a TV version, you've got an international version, you've got a domestic version, you've got M & Es, you've got all the video mastering." and 3-D masters that you need to create and it takes a long time. Of course, producers don't want to pay for that kind of stuff and oftentimes they'll say, "Okay, you're on for a three day week for the deliverable period" and I go, "Okay that'll be six weeks of three day weeks or three weeks of full time?"

KB: They try to cut back on your days? Amazing. When we did the Sean Connery film FINDING FORRESTER I think we had to do something like eight or nine separate mixes after the final.

GH: Oh yeah. On big-budget films they have very specific requirements about what needs to be done. With my guys in Toronto they're fully aware right from the get-go what my expectations are. I make it clear before we get into pre-mixing that we need to deliver X, Y, and Z. So they're all cognizant of that and as we pre-mix and mix they're splitting off elements in order to accommodate that. I'm usually able to deliver most of the alternative versions within a week after the print master.

KB: And that's knowing the people you're working with and being able to set those things up ahead of time.

GH: Exactly and it comes with experience. The first time through you scratch your head, "Okay I've got my mix done where do I go from here?"

Back when I was at Alliance a producer had a friend who was an AD and the AD wanted to get into post so this producer made the AD his post-supervisor. I was the post-executive for the studio, and being an AD, he would say, "Okay I've got to take this element right from beginning to end - the critical path." And I'm going, "No, you've got to take them all from beginning to end together." He would get himself all lined up to deliver one element and leave everything else at the starting point. It's really a non-linear process and everything needs to end up ready together. . . You've got to make sure everything joins up together at the end. I ended up having to step in and take over that production.

KB: You said something earlier about being able to think non-linear. Can you elaborate on that?

GH: I've got to think about all the deliverables. I've got to think about the sound work, the budget and the schedule and move them all together slowly as we're moving towards the end. The director may say, "Well, I want the sound designer on from the get-go." On a big budget production I can bring that person in and do a little preliminary sound design during the picture edit. On smaller budgets I've got to back that off and essentially give the assistant editor a sound library of stuff or beg and plead with the sound designer for some of the key effects in order to maintain the budget and still get the director what he wants.

KB: Can you give me a couple of examples of some major challenges?

GH: On LUCKY NUMBER SLEVIN I had a director and DP who did not want to be at Deluxe, (a film processing lab and full post production facility for both picture and sound), they wanted to be at Technicolor L.A. and they fought us every step of the way in terms of doing the color grade at Deluxe. Deluxe in Toronto at the time was fairly new with the digital intermediate process. The DP and the director were saying, "It's too grainy, we don't like the look of it, this is no good."

I had to walk a fine line between what the budget would say and the production would say in order to get it done. Ultimately, the director did win and had his color grade of the picture pulled out of Deluxe and sent down to Los Angeles to do it at Technicolor. It was one of those things that we were never going to get the director to support the film, if we didn't do that. So I ended up having to negotiate with the guys at Deluxe to back out of our deal there. We did the sound deliverables and the sound work at Deluxe but the picture was delivered through Technicolor in Los Angeles. That was one film.

On SILENT HILL the director, Christophe Gans, was very meticulous about what he wanted but couldn't verbalize it. He could critique what he didn't like. With his background as a film critic he knew exactly what wasn't working but he wasn't very demonstrative in telling us what he wanted to do. This was specifically in terms of the visual effects sequences. We were right up against the wall, we were well over budget, and in France you cannot release a feature unless the director approves it. He has to send a letter to the distributor who then includes it to the exhibitor saying "I authorize the release of this film."

The main producer was French as well, so he was literally shackled to the director's wishes and because the director wasn't very good at what he wanted only what he didn't like, it took us a lot longer to get what was going on. It was a massive visual effects film so we had vendors all throughout Canada and France delivering elements. We had one vendor in Montreal that was having trouble achieving the director's vision and we were in the final three days of our mix, because of course everything gets pushed together at the same time, when he basically said, "Its bizarre, this is not my film, I don't like it, I won't have it. Cut it out!"

We ended up going back into picture edit, we cut out half of the sequence that he didn't like. We cut out about three minutes, and what was left was a two and a half minute scene.

So as I say, each film has got its own difficult things.

KB: You need to have great technical knowledge in your job in various capacities to get the different elements together, sound, visual effects, etc, but you also have to be a real politician to get what you need.

GH: Absolutely. Understanding the processes is key, but being able to communicate with all the powers is also key. I'm a fairly personable guy and I try not to get all wrapped up in the details. Every once in a while I have to blow up. On one film I was having a tough time with the editor who was French. He was fighting me tooth and nail in terms of everything and I ended up having to have a big argument with him but a day later he calmed down and came in and apologized and from that point on everything worked.

It's knowing when to lose it. Most of the time I'm able to

navigate the waters, and most of the directors understand what's going on and are able to listen to me when I say we have to make a compromise here. And film production, especially post-production, is a series of compromises.

KB: You also have to think non-linear because you've got multiple balls in the air at any one time.

GH: Exactly. My first question is always, "Which film are we talking about?"

KB: Which has got to install a lot of confidence in the people you're talking to.

GH: Exactly. Just before we went away on our break I got an email from the script supervisor talking about the processes and what slating method to use, etc., and I sent the information to the wrong editors.

I try not to juggle too many projects because I like being directly involved and more at a creative level then some of my compatriots. The way I describe it, I'm there as an adjunct to assist the creative process while still maintaining the producer's requirements of budget and schedule. I sit in at the mix every day of the final, I'm always in and out during the pre-mix period even if the director is not, just to make sure things are getting done.

By sitting in the mix during the final with the director and the sound team, I'm hearing concerns not only about the sound work but also about picture issues and I'm able to address and adjust those to the director's benefit without having a serious impact. The alternative is it gets to the playback where the producer is going, "Well, this isn't working." And the director says, "Yeah, I wanted to make that change two weeks ago but the supervisor wasn't around."

I'm interested in the whole process and because of that I tend to be a little bit more involved. I try to have a little bit of overlap so while we're in the director's cut mode in one film, I'm in delivery mode on another, and maybe in preliminary budget mode on a third. But that doesn't always happen.

KB: Sometimes you have to deal with the Bond Company, what are the circumstances where the Bond Company comes on and how does that change everything?

GH: Well, the Bond Company's involved all along just to ensure that nothing falls off the rails. They've gotten a little smarter over the last twenty years in terms of not waiting till the bitter end to see what's going on. So there's always communication with the Bond Company. I find that because they trust me, there's less communication with me than there is with a lot of the other productions. I have conversations with their post representatives. From my standpoint, I'll alert them if I see things going seriously awry, I'll keep them up to date in both schedules and they get cost reports from the production directly.

On a production that does go into a tail spin or does have a bond claim on it then the bond company will oftentimes talk to me and say, "Okay, we've got no money, we need to get this done as quickly and as cheaply as possible."

There was a film, OUTLANDER which we did a while ago. What happened was the visual effects quote was a low-ball quote. The visual effects company did that in order to get the gig. Unfortunately, the low-ball quote would've meant them closing their doors because the work that was contracted was significantly higher than they could cover in their budget. So they basically said, "we can't deliver, we're going to default unless we can get more money." The producer was maxed out on his ability to fund the production and had to call the bond company. The bond company stepped in and between myself, and a visual effects supervisor, brought in from L.A., we figured out what needed to happen in order to get the film delivered. It ended up being somewhere around a million and a half over budget that the bond company had to eat. But it could have been three million over or it could have been a loss of their twelve million dollar license fee. So from their prospective they bit the bullet and got everything done.

KB: I asked you earlier, do you think good sound is important?

GH: And I answered absolutely not, we can watch silent films!

Silent films were popular for a long time. What's with all the Surround stuff, I mean come on you've got 5.1 and now 7.1. What the hell do you need all those speakers for?

That's literally a question I got from a producer if you can believe it? It was like, "Why do I need to do this, what's going on?"

Sound is hugely important. They say that its 50% of the film. I think its more than 50%. Without good sound no matter how good the picture is you're going to have people walking out. That's why I'm always in communication with the location sound recordist right from the get-go and if he finds that he's getting stonewalled at the production I will make a visit to the set and talk to the producers and the AD's. Basically I'll say I need another $25,000 because you guys are fucking me over and that will usually get the producer's attention. I had one sound recordist who was so bloody frustrated that he just couldn't get any kind of sound and it ended up costing us $68,000 in ADR in order to get the sound we needed to deliver the film.

KB: Why is it so many people think it's cheaper to do ADR?

GH: On studio pictures they tend to be a lot more particular about the sound, the quality of the voices. Often times they will have ADR shot for a lot of the film but when it gets into the final mix I find that the director is constantly losing the ADR and going back to the original sync because that's where the performance is, that's where the film lives.

It's crucial that we have good sound right from the get-go. SILENT HILL was the film that we ended up spending all that money on for ADR primarily because the lead actress was in Australia. We had to do a session there. We flew one person to Australia for one ADR session for three days but we didn't get enough. So then we ended up tying in two studios and the director and the supervisor and the ADR editor and literally it took us five days of major ISDM. I think it cost something like $21.00 a minute.

KB: Why do you think sound is looked at as the easiest or the cheapest thing to fix later on in post?

GH: Well, I think that it is the cheapest and easiest thing to repair because with digital technologies you can repair and change picture but with astronomical consequences cost-wise.

Some of the environments people are shooting in are so bloody boomy but they want to have that look and they bite the bullet for it. Really there is no alternative. It is not that sound recording is cheap its just that it is cheaper than recreating the picture. Look at AVATAR, they created all their stuff, what was the budget on that? Four hundred million?

Sound design is a completely different thing and we're seeing huge creative leaps in terms of the use of what I call "not normal elements" to create soundscapes.

On SILENT HILL we had a sound supervisor from France to work with the Tattersall crew. He arrived with a 5-0 mic rig so he would have three microphones in the front and two that he would position in the back and he would record all his sound effects and sound design elements that way (both Atmospheres and specifics). Even when we shot ADR we would go in and set the mics in each of the corners of the room (as well as in front of the Talent) so that we could spread out the sound across all five speakers (the sub being a derived signal). For the loop work and crowd ADR he wanted to have that ability to translate it directly without having to manipulate it in the mix. From my standpoint SILENT HILL was one of the most interesting sounding films that I've worked on, specifically because of the attention to detail in that environment.

KB: That sounds pretty awesome actually. You made the comment that features are the director's medium and television is the producer's medium. Could you elaborate more on that?

GH: If we start talking about television you're often talking about a television series, or a M-O-W (Movie Of The Week). A M-O-W is like a mini-movie so it kind of slips into the feature world. On a series you've got an arc of say twenty-six episodes a season and you've got a story line that the writers (and oftentimes the writers are the executive producers) are building from episode to episode. They've got continuity in the season. They hire a director to shoot a few episodes but they need to prep one episode while they're shooting another. I call it the "Machine". The Machine starts rolling and it keeps on rolling. Because they are tied to air dates they can't say, "Oh we're going to take an extra five weeks on this one episode because we're waiting for our director to shoot his third episode." It doesn't happen that way.

The producer steps in and ensures A.) He can meet his broadcast schedule, and B.) He can keep things going with the writers and executive producers making sure that the story arc goes all the way through. So as a matter of course the director is brought in for one or two episodes and can't have that big vision.

A feature is a director's medium because the whole concept of the auteur is very prevalent in Hollywood (and indeed throughout the industry). You're seeing that a director who is successful on one feature will get bigger and bigger budgets and have more and more control. Oftentimes the first time director will get a "Director's Cut" but won't have final say over the picture.

On a picture by David Cronenberg for instance, he will have Final Cut. He will have say over and above the producers and even the studios, "This is my film this is the way it goes out." And as I mentioned before, in France every feature film has to have the approval of the director before it can be released or shown on-air. From that standpoint the director is definitely in the control position. As you well know, a director who doesn't have control has the ability to take his name off the project and then a pseudo-name is put in. I can't remember right now what the pseudo-name is but its something like. . .

KB: Alan Smithee.

GH: That's right. You often see that for films where the director has lost control and has basically stormed off the picture. That is the worst-case scenario. I worked on a couple of pictures for Miramax and the Weinstein's are known for their control over a feature film. The story on SHAKESPEARE IN LOVE is they shot over 25% of the film after the director had delivered his cut including re-doing the ending because they didn't feel that it was a film that was going to maximize their investment.

I worked on one film with a director where the first preview tested fairly low. The Miramax guys had their own sort of shadow editorial going, to do notes and showing them to the Weinstein's directly. Then the Weinstein's would give very specific notes back to the director based on what their own shadow editorial group had shown them. It became quite funny because our editor was cognizant of the fact that with their specific notes, talking about takes and portions of takes to be used (including time code references), that they were in fact cutting the picture themselves. But the Weinstein's made sure that the director had his say and any kind of discussion or disagreement between them was negotiated to keep his name on the picture which he did do.

KB: He is known as "Harvey Scissor-hands" for a reason?

GH: Oh absolutely. At the end of the day they have to release a film that they think will make money.

KB: So if you're supervising a television series, how many episodes are you dealing with at one particular time as a post-super?

GH: That's a good question. On the first episode you're only dealing with one production, right? It shoots say for two weeks, director's cut for two weeks, producer's cut for a week, and then it goes into sound editorial for a week, and mixing for a week, and then it's delivered. That's about six weeks from the end of principle to delivery.

So that first episode keeps moving forward but the next two weeks while we're in the director's cut we're shooting the second episode so it leap frogs. By the end of it all you're dealing with five or six episodes all in various stages of post. And of course the problem is when the producers look at an episode and say, "We need a re-shoot. Put that on the shelf, let's move this episode up ahead or what have you.

Not so much now because they're so tied to the story arc but in previous times where each episode stood on its own, especially when they were looking at syndication. They would rush one episode and hold back another episode so you'd end up having a couple of weeks where you're only dealing with three episodes and then the next weeks we were dealing with six.

But the good thing about a television series, I always say, is you've got a hard out. You've got a broadcast date and you need to deliver on time. The last thing you want to do is to miss a broadcast date.

When I was at Alliance I was overseeing post on a number of series. A series that you might be familiar with called DUE SOUTH, basically got behind on a number of episodes and needed to get an episode delivered very quickly. I believe it was eight days from end of principle photography to delivery to the studio to the broadcaster. Literally they had three days after the wrap of the picture to fine cut the picture, three days to cut the tracks and mix it, and two days to deliver. And this series had visual effects shots. The worst part of it all was that it won a Canadian award, a Gemini award, for best episode.

KB: *"We did this one in eight days, so let's do that again . . . "*

GH: Exactly, I had to explain that it was an exception with considerable overtime - it only took eight days, but still cost what the regular three week edit would have because we had people working around the clock. I still get "What do you need six weeks for?" even after the cost report comes out.

KB: *What's the thing that young filmmakers need to remember about all this stuff?*

GH: In my mind the process is a collaborative process. You need to listen to the people who have experience. The sooner you can find your sound supervisor or your sound designer even if he's not on payroll, begin a discussion so that while you're still in production you are thinking about how things will play. You can use off-camera sound to set things up and to segue from one sequence to another, as long as you're cognizant of that, you're going to end up with a superior project.

It's the people who don't listen to others that end up at the end of the day saying, "Why isn't this any good? And you're saying, "Because you shot everybody on your team down and they just phoned it in." And I've seen that happen where the sound crew feels so frustrated because no one is taking them seriously that I've stepped in and said, "Listen guys we need to make this good. It's your reputation, and your next job is going to be based on what you do today. Let's not worry too much about what he wants and put everything on the table so that at least when we get into the mixing theater we can preview stuff for the director and hopefully wake him up."

KB: With so many sound recordists now using eight and sixteen track recorders, what is the most common sound problem that you're seeing?

GH: You've got these little radio mics, the RF mics that you can pin on to the actor's bodies, but the costumes are rustling, making some of the recordings virtually unusable. You go to all the trouble to get a nice close mic sound for an actor that you can manipulate in post but because of the costume design or the placement of the microphone its all unusable and the recordist is pulling his hair out going, "I have no control over the costumes!"

I love the concept of polyphonic recording with digital technology now you can have eight, twelve, I've even had twenty-four tracks done on location. In fact, Robert Altman used to use the old two-inch tape recorders and have twenty-four tracks of audio on the set. Those old two-inch audiotapes that we would master for music because he was so concerned about sound. The bloody thing is the size of a large dishwasher.

KB: A lot of my friends worked for Altman back in the day, so I got a lot of lessons on how that all worked. He did drive them all crazy but his sound was superior.

GH: It was phenomenal. The level and the complexity of what he got in the tracks when you really start to analyze it, here's a guy who really listened to sound and it's great.

KB: And speaking of Altman, I asked you about films that were a big influence on you. Can you give me a few films that you think young filmmakers should see?

GH: You've got some great old westerns, STAGE COACH and RED RIVER that are great stories. APOCALYPSE NOW is one of my favorites in terms of the whole use of sound and picture, it's a classic. THE CONVERSATION has stuck in my mind for years, just the use of sound and the lack of sound as we piece together the pieces of this conversation throughout the story. Just phenomenal.

Francis Coppola was a very big guy in terms of sound. ONE FROM THE HEART, a film that he did almost video-style, directing from the inside of his truck - I went and saw the re-mastered version when it was playing at the Toronto Film Festival and Coppola did a Q & A afterward. I found it inspiring, he was so cognizant of what he was getting in terms of both picture and sound.

And there are the big films that we all love and enjoy, films like, TRANSFORMERS, a brilliant use of the Surround Sounds. It may not be a great film but in my mind it was one of the films that started to use the rear speakers as more of a storytelling thing rather than just sticking atmospheres in the back. Most films don't take advantage of the Surround Sound environment they just throw the music in and spread it out a little wider and throw the air in the back and the occasional zip that will come from the back to the front. But that was a film that I thought really did have good sound work.

KB: If you were looking for a post-supervisor what would be the important things you'd want to know about them?

GH: Is he or she a people person and do they have enough confidence in himself/herself that they can stand up to the director and the sound guys and the picture guys and keep things on track because its so easy to get steamrolled by these guys. Certainly the director is a very driven guy who wants what he wants. I worked on a couple of films with Paul Anderson of RESIDENT EVIL fame and he's a director who knows exactly what he wants. My job was to make what he wants happen. And by doing that successfully the producer was happy because there weren't any issues in getting the film done. So a post-supervisor needs to be cognizant that the director is creating his baby and hopefully give him as much support as he can and still stay on time and on budget.

KB: Film students are always asking how they can get into post-production and your first comment was "run away." A lot of people I talk to say the same thing "Get out! Don't get in the business!" Do you like what you do?

GH: I do. I actually enjoy what I do. There are an awful lot of rewarding things I love when a film comes together. As I mentioned earlier I love being on the mixing stage. I also love being in the color correction suite, being able to see the vision of the director come alive is so huge.

KB: Did you really make people call you three times before you'd take their call?

GH: I did. I wanted to see how persistent they would be. They would call and leave a message, occasionally I would pick up and they'd get lucky. If they called and left a message that was one thing if they sent in a resume that was another thing and then if they followed up again I would usually talk to them. Rule of Threes (for post).

Basically I'd say it's a cruel business and I don't have anything for you now but keep bugging me every six weeks or so and something will come up. And the people that I hired were the persistent people because there is so much of a demand to get into the film industry even in post, that you really have to be driven, you have to be hungry to do it. It took me a while to get in the door, I was lucky to get my first job, two weeks of syncing dailies when some guy went on holiday. I went in and interviewed, they looked down their nose at that fact that I had just graduated from film school. They said, "You're starting at the bottom just like the rest of us." And literally the first day I'm thinking, "What I learned in film school has absolutely nothing to do with reality here."

KB: I feel the same way. I learned some basic stuff in film school but they did not prepare me for what a ride this business is.

GH: It's so true. I think that the practical side is you come out of film school having a really good grasp of all the various roles in film. The downside is you have a really good grasp of all the roles in film and you think you know it.

KB: Well put.

GH: You get to your first job and you go "Okay, I know how to set up a light and the Gaffer's looking at you with that "You touch that and you're fired." Or "Help me with the dolly tracks" and the grips are going, "You're not in my union get the fuck out of here."

Once I understood the realities of the real world and how different it was from school things started to get into motion. From my prospective it was like doing a good job each and every time because you're only as good as the recommendation from the last job you had. It doesn't matter whether the film or picture was any good they wanted to know was he a nice guy, did he work hard, was he late, all that kind of stuff.

It's whom you know not what you know.

Again I stress that film production is a collaborative industry. You're always collaborating with people. Directors, if they're any good, will listen to suggestions. They may not follow them but. . .

I just finished a low-budget film, it was the second feature that this director had done and I got brought in at the very end when all the money was spent. I was doing a favor for another post-super friend of mine. I came in and basically took over. I'm a fairly hands on guy and as Richard may have told you I'm fairly strong willed, I make my presence known. And right off the bat we had a few sparks, but as she said to me at the end, "You know your suggestions may not be good but you care and I'll hire you again in a minute." And that I think is the important thing. You've got to care about what you do, you've got to care about the project that you're doing.

KB: Absolutely.

CHAPTER 3:

Cutting Film with Sound in Mind

Picture Editors

A picture editor's job is to cut the film together using the best performances from each take and hopefully this cut will make a good movie. Remember that most scenes are shot over many hours and often the sound of a location will change during the day. This change can affect the backgrounds on the dialogue.

What kind of a movie are you making? Is it a comedy? A horror film? An action film? Or is it just a straight drama that is heavily dialogue dependent? All four of these films have different sound needs and their sound will depend on how the film is cut.

An action film is usually fast paced and often has lots of special effects like explosions, so much of the dialogue probably will have to be ADR'd. But in a horror film the pace can be slower and the tension comes from longer, slower shots and atmospheric sounds where every tiny effect on the audio track is intended to get a reaction out of the audience.

A comedy not only relies on sight gags and fast cutting, but a lot of the comedy in a film can also come from a well-placed sound effect. In a dialogue driven drama your dialogue has to be front and center and usually the pacing is slower to allow the drama to play out.

Think about different films that you've loved. Now think about how they were put together. Were they cut fast, or were scenes allowed to play out slowly?

Some of the best picture editors I know have a keen understanding of how sound can pace a film. What types of sound can build tension or make us laugh out loud.

Having an editor that understands sound will give your film a better feel.

Harry B. Miller III

*"I basically hated being on a film set. I found it very stressful. In
an editing room I felt like I was in control of my environment."*

Harry Miller is the best editor I know. We met at USC, he was
the editor on my film CLOWNS. He is always thinking in terms
of story and what's best for the film. He really studied how
films were put together and he put in the time, first as a sound
editor then when he had the opportunity as a picture editor. For
years he went back and forth between sound and picture but
now works on picture exclusively.

If I were making a film Harry is the guy that I would want on
my team. When I made my first doc (CRIMINAL JUSTICE)
Harry came up to Portland between jobs and fine cut the movie.
When I made BIRDDOG I was stuck. The editing worked great
on paper, when we shot it. It felt right, but when I put it together
it fell flat. Harry came up for two weeks and figured out the
problem with the scene as he did the fine cut. We have an
interesting way of working together. I was not allowed in the
editing room for the first week while he was editing. When I was
finally allowed in it was for a screening and I couldn't say
anything until I watched the entire movie. Sure enough when we
got to the problem scene I started to jump out of my chair when
I saw the beginning of the scene. Harry grabbed my leg and kept
me in place. I watched the scene and was blown away. He had
figured out the problems with the scene and fixed them. I have
never told Harry that I believe he saved my film because of what
he did with the ending. (I didn't want it to go to his head.)

In the 80s and early 90s, I used to crash on Harry's couch when
I had a gig in LA. He has always been one of the greatest and
most generous supporters of my films. I have learned a lot from
Harry over the years and I hope you will too.

Harry's credits include, TALES FROM THE DARKSIDE (the movie), A MURDER OF CROWS (a very under rated film), DUNE and CHILDREN OF DUNE (mini-series), episodes of BONES, COLD CASE, WOMEN'S MURDER CLUB, CAPRICA, WAREHOUSE 13 and HAWAII FIVE-O (the new one) among others.

If you want to know more about Harry B. Miller III check out: http://www.imdb.com/name/nm0587823/

KB: Is it a good time to be a student and want to get in to the film business?

HBM3: Not Really. There are more things happening in reality based, unscripted television than there is in feature films, and even in series television. The feature world is way down and extremely competitive. The television world is down, but still very competitive. It's a very difficult time. There are more opportunities to make things that are unscripted. Getting in to scripted isn't a very good idea right now.

KB: How did you get in to editing both picture and sound?

HBM3: I was at the University of Kentucky, planning on going to Law School. I was going to follow my family's footsteps and get in to the legal business. I took a class in film appreciation, and it seemed like it was a lot easier to watch movies then it was to become an English major or something that may be useful. When I was approaching my senior year I applied to law school and to two film schools, UCLA and USC. I was accepted at Kentucky Law School and I was accepted at USC Film School. I made the decision that it would be more interesting and more fun to go to USC, which I did.

USC was a great background as they force you to do all aspects of production and post at some point in your schooling. I did one of the upper level films as a picture editor. I liked it quite a bit because I basically hated being on a film set. I found it very stressful. In an editing room I felt like I was in control of my environment.

When I got out of film school it took a while. I took a couple of assistant editing jobs and it wasn't long after that some other people from USC hired me. First to assist, then they moved me up to editor. A good friend of mine who had done an upper level project at USC got to direct a feature and he was able to hire me as his feature editor.

The problem with the picture editing side is that you have to know someone who is going to hire you as a picture editor. And it's usually the director. Getting out of film school you don't know a lot of people. On the first picture-editing job I did, I hired the sound editing crew. They were friends of mine from USC. Soon after that they got to do the sound work on a feature film called NADIA. They asked me if I wanted to work on their film as a sound editor. So that's how I started editing sound.

For the next several years I bounced back and forth between working in sound and working in picture. I've always tried to do picture work but it has tended to be more sporadic than sound work.

Because it's about who you know, picture work is harder to get. The second aspect to this is that a movie will only have one picture editor but will tend to have seven or eight sound editors so there's more opportunity as a sound editor. I would get lots more offers for sound.

It's only taken me twenty years to establish myself as a picture editor and to work pretty consistently as a picture editor.

KB: Do you have a preference?

HBM3: Absolutely! The great thing about picture editing is you get to make lots of choices and lots of decisions and you are essentially creating a story.

In sound there is creativity, but you are pretty much stuck with the picture that you're given. I enjoy picture editing more because I am able to create and tell a story where sound editing is a lot more fixing someone else's problems.

I did a lot of ADR supervising. ADR is Automatic Dialogue Replacement where you're fixing either badly performed dialogue or badly recorded dialogue. It's fixing a problem rather than creating something unique and interesting. Although there are people who do very good sound design and sound creation to help tell a story, that's pretty rare. A lot more of sound is mechanical and repairing a problem.

KB: Do you think your background as a sound editor helps you as a picture editor when you are working on something?

HBM3: It helps me tremendously. First of all having gone to a film school I think I have a broader perspective of the whole process than people who just started in one department. I was able to see the whole process in film school. Saw how things were produced and directed. How things were done. How sound was done and what's going to happen to the sound. Knowing about sound editing and having done a lot of it I am able to make better creative choices as to how I add sound to my picture cut. I have a very substantial library from the post-production companies that I have worked with. I have a lot of resources for good and interesting sound effects. I think I understand it better.

I also grew up as a guitarist and played in bands for many years.

I know a lot about music and how to edit music better than a lot of my contemporaries. So I think I'm pretty good at taking dailies and cutting a pretty effective scene and then helping to tell the story with effective sound effects and music.

KB: Do you think good sound is important?

HBM3: Good sound is really important. One of the things we're always dealing with in television and features is clarity. And if you're dialogue isn't clear and well mixed, it's hard for people to follow important story points. Having it recorded and mixed well so it's audible and intelligible is not an easy thing to do. And it's critical.

In terms of sound effects, it depends on the movie whether sound effects are important or not. Some movies are very much dialogue and character based. Sound effects aren't that critical. It's nice to have stuff that doesn't stand out. When you are adding effects you want to add stuff that is appropriate and mixed at a level that isn't annoying.

But then there are other pictures where sound is absolutely crucial and tells more of the story than the dialogue does. There's a movie I like where there is very little dialogue, but the sound was so impactful. It was a movie that William Friedkin directed called SORCERER. It's set in South America and all of the characters speak different languages. Spanish, Arabic, there's a French guy and a German guy, very multilingual. It's hard to follow the dialogue. But the sound work is tremendous, it really adds to the storytelling, the tension, and the excitement of the movie.

In the 40s and 50s the movies all seemed like they were done with one piece of music. I mean the music would feel almost continuous throughout the film and the sound effects weren't very important. These days there are some films that have almost no, or minimal music and depend much more on sound effects. MAD MAX is a movie where there is music but the sound effects are so much more important to the storytelling than the music is.

KB: Is it true that a lot of the production dialogue gets replaced?

HBM3: It's not true at all. I'd be surprised if on average in television 3% of the dialogue is replaced. Sometimes it's 5% or 8% but it's not very much. There are big action features where there may be 70% or 80% of the dialogue replaced, but most features I would say maybe 10%. That's not including where we add stuff with Group ADR and Walla and additional dialogue that we do to add to crowds and that sort of thing.

KB: How come sound gets no respect until Post-Production?

HBM3: Boy that's an interesting question. The structure of the business is about the writers, actors, producers and the directors. And the people that are responsible, the cinematographers, the editors, the sound people don't really rate. For example, a lot of the technical craft awards at the annual Emmy awards are done at a separate session from the main Emmy ceremony which is all about the actors, directors, producer and the writers. In the general public's view they really don't know what a sound editor does, or what a picture editor does. It's easier for them to know what a cinematographer does. But most people don't understand what we do.

I'm working on a TV series called CAPRICA and we're getting dailies every day, between five and seven hours of media, photographed media, and we have to wade through that and edit a scene that's probably ten minutes long. So it's a huge amount of work that we do to wade through a massive amount of material to construct a story. Most people don't understand that, because they don't see it. It's hidden so they just think a cameraman shoots it and then it's put on the air and that's great! And a lot of people truly don't understand that the sound you see on television isn't necessarily what it sounded like when they photographed it. A lot of work gets done to fix the sound that's there. To add to it. To mix it. So they don't see it and they don't understand.

KB: Do you think that most people when they see a movie think that the sound occurred while they were shooting the movie?

HBM3: I think in television they believe that. I think in features it depends on the feature. In a James Bond movie, for example, I bet that most people don't understand that every sound effect is added. They presume that the guns sound that way and they presume that the cars sound that way. Something like TRANSFORMERS, that's a different thing. Many people are more sophisticated and they know that those are special effects. Those transformers don't actually exist, they're computer generated so the sound has to be added in. But I really think that on a James Bond movie for example a lot of people wouldn't really think that the sound was added later.

SAVING PRIVATE RYAN is an awesome sound job. I'll bet a lot of people don't really think about someone going through and cutting every gun shot, every body fall, every ricochet, the air backgrounds and the water sounds.

A lot of people don't realize what a fabulous job the sound was on FORREST GUMP.

If you said the name Gary Rydstrom most people wouldn't know who you were talking about and yet he is one of the most honored sound people in town. His work is amazing. People don't think about it, you know. They don't think about sound.

KB: You've worked on a lot of television shows, documentaries, features even IMAX films. Is there a difference to your approach as far as one or the other?

HBM3: Everything is different. I got to work on a show called WAREHOUSE 13 this past year. It was not the biggest budgeted show, it was not the best-written show ever, but it is charming, Very enjoyable. And the great thing about television generally is they shoot it, you cut it, it airs, and it goes away. It's a very quick process.

I was on one feature for thirteen months. I could have cut five television shows in that time. In features you spend a lifetime going over the same issues and re-editing the same thing. But there's no thrill like going to a theater and having your feature premiere. It's a pretty great feeling.

IMAX is a very special type of project, a very special skill. I actually got to go to Berlin for the premiere of a 3D IMAX movie, the CIRCQUE DE SOLIEL JOURNEY OF MAN. And to see that on the big screen with a lot of people was fun. There was another large format movie that I worked on MUMMIES: SECRETS OF THE PHARAOHS. I happened to be in London last year when it premiered for a charity event, and I got to go to that. It's pretty awesome to go in to a big theater and get applause, it's a lot of fun.

A huge part of the business is political and that is true as a sound editor and as a picture editor. There's a lot of politics that go on. You have a lot of people who depend on you to do a good job but also depend on you to present a good product, present yourself well, and be politically astute to help out the process. There are a lot of people involved in making a film and there are a lot of people you have to work with to make everybody happy, to make the best product. Each project has it's own political issues and problems.

KB: Do you approach each genre differently as a picture editor or a sound editor?

HBM3: I do. I cut film differently for a television show, or for a feature. A television show generally is much more cutty than a feature. A large format film is way less cutty. A large format film is so much more about the image, the size of the image and letting people absorb the image. Television is all about having the dialogue tell the story with some visual support.

I did a horror film last summer, that was much more about the atmosphere and anticipation of something happening. So the editing style was much slower paced in a lot and depended much more on the audio to tell the audience what was going on.

And then I go on to a television show and it's all about the dialogue, about making things happen pretty quick and fixing the dialogue so some producer can understand it.

KB: Do you find a big difference in the way things are shot digitally now then the old film days?

HBM3: I love digital. A lot of people don't. A lot of people don't think it looks as good as film. It doesn't have the quality that film has. I disagree. I think it's a great change in our business. It's the cleanest image. Film has the problem of being analog; it has a lot of imperfections. A lot of what we had to do in the past is to get around those imperfections. For example in film you can't necessarily use the same shot twice. You wouldn't want to, but if you had to use the same shot twice or the same frame twice you'd have to print it again, make an optical and you would lose quality. In digital there is no issue there. You can use a shot as many times as you want. A lot of times in television I have to be so clear, I have to repeat things. Like in a recap. I have to have that flexibility. If I were cutting film it would be much more difficult.

Having said that, having had the experience of working in film has been invaluable to me. I understand how things are the way they are and how we work the way we work. I am smart enough to adapt to the way the business is constantly changing because of technology. I feel like I am better than most at adapting to the changes in the business and the changes in technology.

KB: Are people changing not what they're shooting on, but the style of what they're shooting?

HBM3: In television with the transition to digital technology the result has been that they shoot a lot more than they ever shot with film. That's why I am getting five to seven hours of dailies every day on a series like CAPRICA. They have three cameras and two of the cameras don't get all that much that is usable. In one sense, it is making television directors lazy. It's easier for them to turn on cameras and shoot everything than to actually be selective and only shoot specifically what is needed. So that's a negative. I don't like that at all. But having a lot of choices is not the worst thing in the world.

The feature film I did last summer was shot digitally and it was a single camera shoot. It helped being digital, as they needed much less light. So they were able to be conservative on how they lit the show and it really helped quite a bit in producing the film.

Large format films, it's unlikely they will make the transition to digital because the resolution of the cameras isn't good enough yet.

KB: With budgets changing all the time, what is the biggest change you have seen in post-production (sound) over the last few years?

HBM3: One trend was that producers wanted to get cheaper and cheaper equipment and software to work with in post. There had been a push in the last several years away from the Avid Media Composer to systems such as FCP (Final Cut Pro). That has actually reversed a little. There are a couple of things that have happened, first of all the Avid Media Composer started around $100,000. Now you can buy the software package for $2000 or if you're a student you can buy it for $300. It has become much more price competitive with FCP. And I think producers are finally listening to editors and post producers that FCP doesn't have nearly the tool set that the Avid Media Composer has. A lot of things they want to do can't be done well, because of those limitations. So there has been a little bit of a reversal where producers are more willing to say you don't have to use FCP. Avid is making a resurgence in that area.

Another area where we've been pressured a lot is visual effects. Because we have been working in the digital arena, and with the advent of very powerful personal computers and really sophisticated visual effect software, producers are coming to think that anything can be a visual effect. And anything that was done wrong in production can be fixed with a visual effect. And they're not wrong, but . . . how much you spend does determine how good the final product is. And one of the downsides of this show WAREHOUSE 13 is that they made a deal with this company in Canada. A lot of visual effects get shipped to Canada because they'll do it cheaper. And this company isn't the best at visual effects work. They're cheap. It's always true that you get what you pay for.

With CAPRICA there is a bigger budget for visual effects and they look pretty good.

KB: What do you think the biggest challenges are when it comes to doing post sound now?

HBM3: It's all related to budgeting. The last show I worked on was not a huge sound budget. It was certainly adequate. My friends tell me there are less people employed to do the same work.

On the other hand the software we are working with enables you to be much more productive then what we able to be before. It used to be, we'd have to print sound takes to magnetic film, we'd have to cut multiple tracks, we'd have to take multiple tracks to the stage to mix it. Now, one editor can work in Pro Tools and cut hundreds of tracks of sound effects. The software has really been able to make people more productive and more creative.

But as a result of this there are less jobs and fewer people are being employed. And the budgets are getting smaller. It's also true that mid level and low budget features are disappearing. There is less of a market for those films in terms of sales and there are fewer and fewer being made. So there are fewer jobs and less opportunities to get work.

Television, I'm not sure, I haven't done any television sound cutting in quite a while. I know that the schedules have always been short. But you can only make the schedules so short to actually make it and deliver something.

KB: I know it sounds crazy, but a lot of students ask me how they can get in to sound, what would you tell them?

HBM3: You have to be very passionate about sound to get in to it. That's a pretty rare person, who gets in to it, really understands it, and loves to work with it. If you don't, it's not a very good area to try and make a career out of. The problem with careers in movies and television is there isn't much security in these industries. You finish a job, then you're out of work, then you have to find another job. If you're good you might get more work and be steadily employed, but there are always times when there is no work. It comes and goes.

As far as sound, you have to be passionate about the whole product. Recording it, editing it, and mixing it. And if you can do all that, you're really going to be valuable to people. It's helpful to have a broad understanding of the whole process and be passionate about it.

KB: What's the most common sound problem that you encounter?

HBM3: Poorly recorded dialogue. Part of the problem we are having today is that increasingly sound recordists are using multi-track recorders. They are using digital recorders that can record eight channels of audio. One of the problems with that has been that people haven't figured out how to integrate that appropriately in a production sense and then move that in to post production. Some people do a good job of recording it and sending it to post production, some people don't.

When I worked on a show called WOMEN'S MURDER CLUB, they had individual lavaliers on most of the actors and would record each one on to a separate channel. And they would record a boom mic as well. And what the recordist did, which was really helpful to us in post-production, was he made a live mix of all of those elements. The editors got a single track of audio and it was generally pretty well balanced between all of the available microphones. So we generally got a clear track without much noise.

On this current show, I am not sure how they're doing it but we're getting two tracks of audio and they tend to be extremely noisy, lots of ambient sound. At times I can't figure out what they're recording because one character will be in a wind tunnel and the other character next to them sounds perfectly fine. And they tend to give us more than one track and I don't know if they're making very good decisions about which track they're giving us.

There's a lot of indecision and that's part of the problem. Fifteen years ago everybody did the same thing. Everybody shot, everybody recorded and edited in the same way. You shot on a film camera, you recorded on a mono Nagra recorder with a boom mic and occasionally you used a lavalier, but that was rare. And everybody cut with film either on a flatbed or a Moviola. Today there are multiple editing platforms. There are multiple ways of recording sound. There are multiple ways of shooting it and every change in technology creates a new learning curve. It creates new problems. It also gives you new opportunities.

We could potentially have the best sound in the world because everybody is on their own microphone, if they could figure out how to give it to us in the editing process so it doesn't sound like crap.

KB: What do students need to know about sound? Both location and post production.

HBM3: They need to know that even though the picture is extremely important, the sound is also important. If you can't understand what people are saying, if it's not clearly recorded then your film is not going to be effective.

In large format films, I have a director that I have worked with several times, Keith Melton. We've come to a common approach to the way we work. When he shoots large format films the cameras are very noisy and it tends to be that you can't get very good audio. And if you're shooting in 3-D then you have two 65 mm cameras and it sounds like rain on a quonset hut.

What Keith and I have done is a "work around". It's hard to move cameras so you don't do many set-ups in a day. So when he does a set up and he gets a take he really likes, then he gets a safety take. So he gets several takes of every set up. After he gets done with a set up to where he really likes it then they will do a take of the same scene without the cameras rolling. So they will record the audio with the same people, in the same environment, with the same emotion, with the same micing, performing the scene and we will use that audio. Even though it's not truly sync audio, we will use that to replace the recorded audio because the sync audio will have camera noise.

We did a movie in India, called MYSTIC INDIA and all the characters spoke Hindi and I was able to replace, all the spoken dialogue with wild tracks of audio that was recorded after they turned the camera off.

It made an enormous difference in the post production process because they didn't have to re-record those actors as loops. They didn't have to bring them in to ADR and a lot of people aren't very good at ADR. Some people are fabulous, but non-professionals aren't. So we had really good audio and we had the ability to mix it clearly and cleanly. It was very effective.

The other thing I always love to have and I make sure that a director is cognizant of it, is every location has it's own ambiance Whether you're at a park, or in a basement, or in an apartment, every room has a sound signature because of the nature around it. I always like directors that will slate a take and wait for a second. Pause. Then call action. What that does is it allows for a little bit of ambiance for every take that can be used to fill in problems.

I don't particularly like when sound recordists record ambiance tracks. Ambiance tracks don't specifically help unless it is a specific noise that's in that location. Like a water background or pipes. But just for room backgrounds you always want to draw the ambiance from the specific take that you're fixing. It's great when directors aren't so anxious that they call action as soon as the cameras are slated. If they give a little bit of air before they call action that gives me a little bit of sound to use to fix problems easier.

KB: What are the advantages between doing wild tracks and ADR.

HBM3: Production people, line producers, directors, get the idea that the only thing that is important is the camera department. As soon as the camera gets a good take that's all they worry about. A lot of times what can happen is that the good camera take can have a lot of extraneous noise. There is a car passing by, an airplane. There's a bump on the microphone. There's a dog barking, whatever . . . Producers don't want to wait for sound. So they move on and you end up having to loop that take or you have to loop that scene.

If they had simply turned the cameras off and waited until there was a quiet moment and recorded a wild track with the actors doing that same scene it would save a lot of time and money. What happens is the mics are the same as in the production. The actors are in that same emotional performance state, their voices are as tired or as fresh as they were when they performed it a few seconds ago. The audio signature of the location or the room is exactly the same as in production. You don't always have to replace all the audio. You might have to replace one line, one phrase, or even one word. And if you have it as a wild track that is cleanly recorded it will match in every aspect better than it would match if you went to a studio later and tried to record it.

Now there could be a case when the persons voice is no good, you want to replace it or it's just a bad performance and you want to change it. That's what ADR is good at or is useful for. To change what you couldn't do on the set.

The best actor that I ever worked with was Anthony Hopkins. I was the ADR Supervisor on a picture called THE EDGE. Anthony Hopkins was the only actor I have ever worked with that wanted to watch more of the scenes in the movie because he would watch a scene and say, "I can do that better." He was concerned about the performance. And that he could do a better performance later than what he had done on the set.

I had only marked certain things on ADR for Anthony Hopkins because of noise problems on the set. But he had a lot of instances where he wanted to do something a little differently. It didn't mean the director had to use those takes. But he had the opportunity to use something cleaner and better if he wanted to.

We had a scene in an airplane and it was very noisy. They actually shot it in an airplane while it was flying. Anthony Hopkins could match his tone, his sync, in every take. It was just perfect. He would also do impersonations of other actors doing his ADR which was hilarious. "This is how Sean Connery would do it!" He was brilliant.

There was an actress in that movie and I had to do some ADR with her. I'm sorry, she's a beautiful woman but she didn't even understand what ADR was. I told her there are three beeps, and you start talking on the fourth imaginary beep. And it would go beep, beep, beep . . . I would say "you gotta talk now. On the fourth imaginary beep you gotta talk." She didn't get it. She was totally clueless. Her session was kind of a disaster.

The other person who was pretty terrible at ADR was Quentin Tarantino. I did a movie called FROM DUSK TIL DAWN and Quentin was enthusiastic, but not very good.

The more you can get recorded on the set, the better it's going to sound and the easier it is going to be to match. And you'll be happier.

KB: If you were looking for a sound designer what would be the important things you would want to know about them and/or their work?

HBM3: People are evaluated in this industry by their previous work, and their previous associations. The way I find a sound designer or sound supervisor is I look at somebody who has done a similar kind of project and I listen to what they've done. There are some people I have worked with that would be good for an action movie. Some people would be good for special effects movies.

I also look for someone I can work with. It's very difficult to work with someone who is moody or lazy or doesn't do what you want. We are going to be spending lots of time together and getting a long is really important.

And then I talk to people they've worked with to find out what their experience was working with this person. I'll ask, was this person good? Where they easy to get along with?

The two aspects you have to deal with in post-production are, you have to find someone who is talented and can actually do the job. And you have to find someone who you can work with on a co-operation level.

I worked on a museum film a few years ago and the producer came up to me and said this person called me and wants to do the sound supervision. And I said let me look at his credits and I'll check him out. I saw that he had worked on a movie that I knew the editor on. So I called the editor and the editor said, I wouldn't hire this guy. He didn't do a very good job. So we didn't hire him. There are a lot of politics involved in this business and you have to be nice enough and good enough to have people recommend you. That's how you get jobs.

KB: What is it that you've learned that they never taught us in school?

HBM3: There are an infinite amount of things they didn't teach us in school (Laughs). What I would advise in terms of learning and personal growth is that you have to work with other people and see how they do things. One way I learned a lot is by opening up another editor's sequence. See what techniques they have. See how they organize things. See how they cut sound, see how they organize their tracks, organize their bins.

We are really in a world where you have to keep learning. What we learned in film school was fine, it was great, and I really enjoyed it. But it's a constant learning process. You have to stay ahead of technology and to stay ahead of people you are competing against. So treat this business as a learning experience.

The other thing that I got a little of in film school but not enough is that it is a political world. You have to be cognizant that you are getting along with other people. That's really important.

Lee Haxall

"Sound is not the enemy!"

I rarely see Lee anymore but I always hear about her through mutual friends. She was a sound teaching assistant when we were in school and she was one of those people you could call after hours if you needed something out of the sound room. She had keys.

After school she worked doing location audio for quite a few people and then transitioned that in to a career as a sound editor. She has worked on some impressive films and was quite sought after as a sound editor before she made the transition in to picture editing.

I hadn't talked to Lee in years when I tracked her down to do an interview for the book. We spent an hour catching up, a couple hours talking about post-production, and three hours laughing. She has some very specific ideas on audio and as a picture editor brings a lot of sound experience to the table.

Her credits as a sound editor include: GHOST, AFTER DARK MY SWEET, NIGHT OF THE DEMONS, and OPPORTUNITY KNOCKS. Her credits as a picture editor include: CRAZY STUPID LOVE, THE SHIELD, ARRESTED DEVELOPMENT, MEET THE FOCKERS, and NCIS: LOS ANGELES.

If you want to know more about Lee Haxall check out:
http://www.imdb.com/name/nm0370448/

KB: How did you get into sound and then sound editing?

LH: In all honesty, it was at USC. Dan Wiegand (a USC Sound Professor) gave me a Sound TA-ship. I really knew nothing about sound, but it was the only way I was gonna get through USC. When I got into USC I had no idea how to use the sound room. I was that bad. Ultimately, sound was very, very good to me. I did eventually figure it out though.

I lied my way into, (I was way over my head), doing the sound on Tom Neff's movie, I supervised it. He hired a bunch of us to do his feature right out of film school. I was the sound mixer and supervising sound editor and one thing led to another and next thing you know I was actually doing sound.

KB: Was there a particular film or films that had a big influence on you when you started?

LH: PASSAGE TO INDIA was the film that made me understand sound and how important it is. I remember I had a very creepy feeling while I was watching the film and after I finished watching it, I thought, "Why did that movie creep me out?" I didn't like that movie and I should have. It's the kind of movie I would love. And I couldn't figure it out. After I started studying sound I realized I didn't like it because 100% of that movie, I believe, was ADR'd and the backgrounds were all replaced. It was shot in modern day India and it was set in the 1800s. Apparently there were so many cars and airplanes and modern things running over it, they had to replace all the natural sound. They did a beautiful job I'm sure, but something felt wrong to me and it creeped me out. And that's when I realized that replacing all of the sound affected how I liked that film. It was psychological.

The quality of the sound was all good, the recordings were beautiful, the backgrounds were nice, but something was wrong in my brain. I did not process that film correctly and did not like the film because the sound felt so weird to me. That's when I realized the naturalness of sound, if it's not there it can be absolutely detrimental, as much as if it is there. It's why I don't think we necessarily have to ADR things. Obviously with a period piece you can't have airplanes going over dialogue, but in most modern day films I'll work extra hard to keep the original dialogue in. I like natural sound.

KB: You are one of the few people I know who has been both a sound editor and a picture editor. Do you think that your sound editing background helps you as a picture editor?

LH: Oh my God yes! Sound is so critical. I was a sound editor for years. Even though I was a sound editor before Pro Tools and digital editing, I'm very fast with sound and I understand the importance of it. With picture, one of the main things you're cutting is dialogue. Picture edits don't work for me if the dialogue edit isn't working.

If the cut bumps, I usually straighten my dialogue tracks out, almost as fully as a dialogue editor, because I can't even look at the picture subjectively without having the dialogue nicely cut. It helps me tremendously because by the time the director steps in to look at the edit, the cuts aren't gonna bump because of sound. If a cut isn't working, if a performance isn't working, it's gonna be because those elements aren't working. We can try to change things without having to figure out, well gee, maybe that cut only bumps because presence dropped off right there like five decibels and everyone went "what was that?

I think being a sound editor has been tremendously helpful. Now, you're expected to have a very thought out cut by the time you're showing it to people. You would never deliver a cut without color, sound effects, and music, right? I'm pretty fast and pretty good with it because I had all that experience cutting sound, I know when a sound effect is going to work with the image I'm seeing and when it's not.

KB: Do you prefer picture editing to sound editing?

LH: I love sound editing, don't get me wrong, but for me personally, picture editing has been more fulfilling. I enjoy editing actors performances, sound helps the performance, but you don't get to make the performance selection in sound as you do when you're cutting picture. And that for me is very exciting and fun. I do enjoy cutting picture more, but if I spent the rest of my career cutting sound I would still have been very creatively satisfied.

In many respects I think sound can be more creatively satisfying, especially if you're in the horror genre or animation. With sound you can create an entire universe that doesn't exist in reality. I enjoy picture editing because of actor's performances and storytelling.

KB: I've always said that sound gets absolutely no respect until you're in post-production. Do you believe that?

LH: It depends on the director. It's certainly true often, but not always. It depends on how it's gone for some directors in their career, whether they end up hating ADR or not.

A lot of directors will happily wait for the location sound person to get set up because they detest ADR and they don't want to have to do it. And if they give the location person five more minutes, they might get a track that's usable. Other times sound doesn't get the respect because there's this prevailing attitude that's been around since the thirties that, sadly, you can fix it later. And you can. But back to PASSAGE TO INDIA, often times it doesn't feel right. Maybe the synch isn't perfect, or it doesn't feel like it was really recorded there or whatever. That's why people don't like ADR.

The great actors have no problem doing ADR and they can be right in synch and everything. With very well-trained actors it's not a problem. But often the spark of the location isn't there. I've cut a lot of TV and what I've discovered is, often in TV you just gotta get it done. You try so hard, but sound is gonna get a little bit pooped on. There's no way around it. They've gotta get it today. They shoot eight pages in a day, they've gotta get it done.

In features, with a smaller daily page count, there's a little more time for the sound guys to see a rehearsal and formulate and plant some microphones. They have more time to try to get good sound on the set. But the more I'm in the business, the more I'm realizing a lot of these directors are catching on to the fact that if you give the sound person some respect right from the start, on the location, it can save you a lot of time and money in post. ADR is not cheap. You gotta get the actor back, you gotta book a stage, a mixer, it's not cheap to replace the dialogue.

Now sometimes you can't help it. I mean, if you're shooting under LAX, fine, you're probably gonna be replacing dialogue. And there's no way a great sound mixer can deal with certain problems. You're stuck. But other times if the sound person just gets five minutes to plant a mic, he might get really good sound. It's great if the director will give it to him. And the ADs, too. It's the ADs as well as the directors.

KB: One of the statements that comes up all the time is that 80 - 90% of the location dialogue in movies is replaced. Is that true from your experience?

LH: In my experience, absolutely, totally not true. I would say anywhere between 10% - 30% is replaced, more often it's closer to 10%, if that. Most people will always go back to the production tracks.

I edited a movie with a lot of car material in it and, well the most polite way I can put it is, it was disastrous! It was a disastrous series of recordings, and that director had the mixer sitting there on the re-recording stage and work with that material for like a day trying desperately to avoid putting in the ADR. He didn't like the ADR. We ended up with production because the director was willing to sacrifice a little bit of comprehensibility for the performance. What I'm seeing is a lot less dialogue is replaced now than perhaps might have been a few years ago. Usually if you can use the production at all, they will sit there on the re-recording stage and work and work and work with it before they'll go to ADR.

I think even on a messy episode of television, where you're down at the beach, that you're only going to maybe have 30% ADR at the tops. Plus in TV the actors get annoyed because they don't like having to go ADR. It's like, they're down there shooting all day and then they have to come up to a studio and ADR. They really don't like that. It's grueling in television just to get the shooting done. In all honesty, if they're having to ADR a whole lot, the location mixer may not keep his job. If the stars of a show start complaining that they're having to ADR too much, the location mixer's job is in danger. The location mixer has to try and figure out how to get great sound all the time. It's really a hard job.

KB: And sometimes it's not their fault.

LH: Absolutely. And obviously everyone understands that. Like I said, if you're by the airport or by the ocean or places like that. I can usually fix the production. Even recording by the ocean. If the sound recordist gives me some wild tracks and if the director waits ten seconds before he says action, and you have the mics in the same position you've recorded the actors on, you can save a lot of dialogue that way. If you can fix the ocean you can fix almost anything!

KB: Tell me how you really feel about ADR. I hate it.

LH: ADR is necessary sometimes. But in a lot of the acting classes here in Los Angeles and probably the rest of the country, everyone's into the mentality of acting. How do you get into the character and study the character and become the character, the method and all that stuff. It seems like they never teach the craft of acting. And acting for film is not acting for theater There's a whole craft involved. Every once in a while, I would just love to take every acting student in Los Angeles, sit 'em down and tell them about the things that we in post-production need to edit them. Matching is number one. If you do it in the master you have to do it that way in the coverage or I can't necessarily cut to you. That's number one, matching action.

Number two - ADR. Learn how to do it so that by the time you step into that ADR stage and you hear those first three beats you're comfortable with the process. You've rehearsed it, you know what you're doing and you know that your performance won't be destroyed if you have to do ADR, which you will have to do in your career.

There's going to be a scene in a car, by the airport, by the ocean. Something's gonna happen where you're gonna be ADR'd. And many of these young actors come in and say, "I don't wanna do ADR. It's gonna ruin my performance." That's no way to approach it. You should approach it as a professional. That would be like me as an editor saying, "I don't wanna make a jump cut." Well, that's what you're gonna have to do here. The director asked for it and we need it. This is your job. Learn how to do it.

To me ADR is part of the craft of film acting, and I wish people would teach actors, acting craft. Obviously I think they should be taught how to act, all the wonderful things of getting into character, but once every few months let's have a craft class.

Let's see who can stand up and sit down on the same line every time, you know? Or throw their arms open so I can cut. That's a real pet peeve of mine.

KB: I believe sound can truly improve the story. Have you had an experience where you feel that something that you did in sound really improved the story you were telling?

LH: Number one - if you can't hear the dialogue the audience isn't going to understand the story. And that means the location sound and the re-recording. Dialogue rules in movies. Obviously all the other stuff is fun and creative, but there's nothing worse than going to a movie and turning to the person next to you and saying, "What did they say?" That's awful.

Number two - in my career, millions of times, we have actually saved scenes, performances, and whole storylines with wild lines. Lines that weren't scripted or shot, but something's happened where the movie comes in too long and you have to take some time out. You can cut a scene in half, but suddenly an important piece of the story that was in the second half of the scene is gonna be lost. You gotta figure out how to get it in the first half of the scene that you're keeping, 'cause the second half is hitting the cutting room floor. Well, the way we do that is to put in a wild line or two. You'll be on the back of somebody's head and have 'em say a line that the actor didn't originally say there. And I'm saying this for students, the wild lines can actually end up helping you tell the story where it never was meant to be told there, especially if you need to take time out.

Also, wild lines can help when a story is kind of fuzzy. I've edited a lot of television and often times, the studio will watch it and they'll send it back and say "we're kind of confused. How did this character end up here? How did he know to go there?" Things like that. And suddenly you go "Oh my God, that's right!" You know, either we cut that out or, gosh, they forgot to write in a line that explains that. And then the producer will say "well let's put that line in here," and we'll do a wild line. So wild lines can aid immeasurably in telling stories. That's the dialogue end of helping with stories.

In the fun end, the sound effects end, I find sound effects can help the story and the filmmaking process. Sound effects can add comedy. You can actually be laughing because the sound of that lady pulling the chair out is so funny that you're starting to laugh before she even says the line. So I think sound effects are immeasurably helpful in story and comedy.

They're also helpful if you've got an actor reacting to something like a phone ring. What kind of phone? Is it an old traditional phone or is it a cell phone. The selection of the sound effect is helping tell the story. It's telling the audience about the character, you know, that was an old dial phone. That must mean that this guy's a Luddite, you know.

Watching the TV series THE PACIFIC, all the bombs that were going off in the background, they're just constantly going off all the time. These guys couldn't escape from all these bombs, you know. And it color's their mental state, where these actors are in their heads. It's storytelling with sound effects.

And of course the ultimate is sci-fi and horror films. You're not only telling the story, you're creating a whole world. I love that kinda stuff. I love horror movies for that. You have to create a whole universe that doesn't really exist. I think that's awesome for sound. That's the ultimate storytelling.

KB: Have you ever worked on any science fiction or horror stuff?

LH: I was the supervising sound editor on a bunch of horror films. Do you remember a guy named Kevin Tenney? He did horror films. I was the location mixer and then the supervising sound editor and I had so much fun! There were people, you know, eating people and it was hilarious, great fun and I was able to be so creative. I remember just looking at the backgrounds and stuff that we created for this movie. And I sat there thinking, "This is some of the coolest stuff I've ever heard". It was in the 80s and the movie was like $50,000 or something. I kept on saying "God, it's so sad that none of the horror film people can ever get nominated for an Oscar, ('cause it's all low budget) but boy, they do some of the most creative work. And the sci-fi guys, sci-fi guys are getting recognized because some of those are very big films now. I think that's some of the funnest sound editing in terms of just creative, let-loose kind of things.

KB: If you were looking for a sound designer what are the things you'd want to know about someone and their work?

LH: The most important thing for me is getting along with the people, 'cause at this point I'm working with some pretty big people, so the resumes are all gonna be pretty impressive. With the quality of people we're interviewing, you're not going to have somebody that's going to be a flake. So a lot is the personality, 'cause you really go into the trenches together. I need to have a person that is completely willing to help me out no matter how peculiar the request is. You also wanna be respected and there are some people who aren't particularly respectful of picture and you know we're in this together. I've done both, I like to have a team. I want us all to be on the same page and work together because I think sound is absolutely as important as the picture.

KB: When you started cutting sound you did it on magnetic film. For our students what was that like?

LH: Totally different. It was tactile, and everything had to be done by hand with physical tools (splicers and razor blades).

There were no computers or programs. We cut SFX on Moviolas and dialogue on Synchronizers. I didn't cut dialogue on a synchronizer because what I learned was on film the way you spun the synchronizer with your thumb, remember that big synchronizer wheel with a circle on the front and the way I would spin it, I would slow it down or speed it up to make the backgrounds match. Subconsciously, right before the cuts were happening I would do this, and the cuts would work and then when I put the track on the Moviola at speed, the cuts didn't work. I got so fascinated with that, I started making the sound supervisors rent me a three headed Moviola and I put my three lead dialogue tracks up on the three headed Moviola with picture and really listen to it under headphones and make sure it worked.

I got vindicated on GHOST (this was the last movie Lee cut sound on), when Walter Murch said, "your tracks are great just great", and I cut the scene with the damn frickin' pottery wheel. That pottery wheel in GHOST was about the end of my life! Every single take the damn thing was live. It was on all the dialogue and it was in a different pitch on every take. You know how fast it goes. It goes "weeoooo," and it wasn't rhythmic. It was, like, how fast she pressed that freaking little pedal! And I had to trail all these things out and make 'em match, and join it all together to make all these various different tones match. That fucking thing almost killed me!

KB: You realize that if I had a hat on I would be taking it off right now, because the fact that you were able to do that in mag . . . I'm impressed. Really fucking impressed. I mean, 'cause that's hard..

LH: Awww. It was, yeah. And I didn't use chemicals. The other cool thing was my friend, Duncan Burns taught me how to do fades and everything with a razorblade instead of the chemicals. Remember that old chemical wipe stuff that would turn your skin white?

KB: I learned with razor blades. I always used razor blades.

LH: Thank God for the razor blades! 'Cause I could do a big old wipe, I could lay out four feet of mag on the table and with the razor blade do a four-foot wipe and never bring out the chemicals. I learned on the chemicals and I noticed it was turning my skin white, and I knew it couldn't be too good for you. It's film cleaner and an acetone.

KB: I remember learning to cut shapes and diamonds into the mag to get rid of stuff, pops, clicks, and juicy mouth stuff.

LH: Yeah! That's a gone art.

KB: When you're sitting in the mix how much say do you have? How much control do you get over the things that you've done?

LH: Well that's really interesting, because that plays directly on an earlier question. Picking the re-recording mixer for me is really, really important, because having come from sound I want to be listened to. And every picture editor is going to be different. Some just sit there quietly and let the sound folks do their thing. I will do that for a long time until we're getting close to the end and then I usually have very strong opinions about sound, especially in the comedies. Something will strike me as particularly funny and with the director's permission I'll make the guys work on it a long time until it sounds funny. Just the right funny.

Sometimes I have sounds in the temp tracks that the sound people didn't record, which is a big pride thing with sound people. Most of the stuff they record themselves and there's a lot of pride in the work and I usually love it, but once in a while I'll have some cheesy-ass SFX in there that makes me laugh harder then the professional sound, and I'll want to use that in the end. I like working with a person that has the same sense of humor

120

and will say "that's funnier, let's go with it. Yes, it's from Hollywood Edge (a sound library we all use. . .), but we're gonna go with it." That says to me that we all want the best for the movie. At the same time they know that I'm saying "please, please, please Mr. Director or Ms. Director, please let's get the Foley up." They know I'm gonna stick up for them. I love sound. I love Foley.

In TV sometimes where they're so married to the dialogue, it's like you have a scene in a restaurant and they don't even want walla, let alone music. Walla, and tinkling dishes and stuff, and you have to say, "Guys, come on!" People expect these sounds there and then you have these restaurant scenes that are just dead quiet dialogue and that disgusts me. Honestly I will be the picture editor out there fighting and clawing for the sound people. I've had a lot of sound guys come up to me and thank me for trying to get their work heard 'cause I'm so into the sound stuff.

I love Foley. I think Foley rules. If it's mixed really well. It's like, "My God, you've added life to a movie," and all these specific sound effects and things that are really funny are helping tell a good story.

Back to your story thing, when do you use the footsteps? When do you not use them? That's good storytelling with sound effects, cloth movement has saved me on hundreds of occasions. The cloth movement track! Sooner or later in every movie mix I'll be like, "We're putting in cloth movement." Something will be bothering me like a buzz or presence or something and cloth movement will fix that. Everyone just laughs, but cloth movement also rules!

KB: Speaking of sound problems, what's the most common sound problem you encounter?

LH: Lately it's been technical. What's happening now in production sound is we're going back to the old Robert Altman style where there was a guy mixing like eight, ten, twelve tracks at once. When we were young it was just a person with a microphone and you'd have some radio mics going. You'd have radio mics on track one and the boom on track two, and most of the time you transfer the boom only, unless you had a problem and then you could go to the radio mics.

Now just about every character has a radio mic, and then there's the boom. And what I'm discovering is some of the location mixers aren't learning how to boom, and that should be the primary track. So a lot of location work isn't as good as it could be. A couple of years ago I remember working on a wide screen movie and I remember hearing a radio mic on the actor, and I was like, "Why is this guy not boomed?" On a close-up of the actor, why am I having to suffer through cloth noise on a radio mic?" And radios never sound as good as booms. It turned out there was a miscommunication in the transfer process and the wrong tracks were coming to me. I visited the set like four times before we figured it out and I said to the sound guy, "You gotta get up here. You gotta hear what I'm getting, 'cause I don't think it's what you're getting." That was an enormous technical glitch that went on for weeks while we were trying to figure this out. So early communication with the location mixer and the editor is a very important thing that's almost never done.

There should always be a meeting with the transfer people, or the facility to discuss how the tracks are going to get to the editor and what the editor wants, because now they're recording like ten tracks on a take. And they'll have a bunch of radio mics and a boom, maybe some plant mics, and things like that. On the Avid I only want one track. I want a mixed down track. And then I want the post-sound people, the dialogue editor to unspool where necessary (separate the tracks). But I need a mixed down track. I can't have ten tracks of dialogue going when I'm cutting a movie. I can't carry all that. I can only carry one track. It's not that the Avid won't, it's that I don't have time to cut ten tracks of dialogue.

Sometimes it's a problem for the location mixers because the mix down isn't necessarily sounding as good as it will in the end, so they're terrified that they're going to get fired, but that needs to be communicated. We all have to figure out a way to make this new way of doing sound work for us.

It's getting more complicated actually.

The other thing that happened a couple projects ago was the location mixer had everyone on radios and he would point the boom to the room, not to an actor. He'd just stick the boom in a room and get presence. And, I swear to God, Kelley, a lot of guys are mixing like that now! I'm getting these eight phasing radio mics with cloth movement and it's a mess! And I say, "Get me the boom, get me the boom, there's plenty of headroom here, we should have the boom." And we'll get the boom and everyone's off mic and you realize it was just the guy pointing it at a wall to get background. And this guy lost his job because it was making us all crazy and the actors were losing it 'cause they had to ADR a lot and it was not going over well. Location mixers need to be steered away from that style of mixing. If that's how somebody's teaching you to mix, learn from somebody else. You need to call the Angry Filmmaker and learn how to do some good location mixing.

KB: Harry Miller was telling me the same thing, with all these multiple tracks and they're not recorded well. So it's not just you.

LH: They're all using radio mics, and the quality of radio mics is a lot better than it was in my era of location mixing, but nonetheless, you can't tape a mic to the back of an actor's shirt and think you're not going to get cloth movement. I don't know what's up with that, but I'm hoping that we swing away from that pretty darn promptly. And I'm glad that Harry said it, 'cause I thought "Oh my God. . . is it just me? Am I being too picky with this stuff?" But I'm like "no, if I'm on a medium tight shot on a couple guys and there's plenty of head room I expect a boom. I'm sorry."

Obviously if there's an A camera that's super wide, fine. You're in on the radios. And everything now is two camera, but if you're in a medium shot or a medium close up, why in God's name would you not have a boom on the actor? I can look at a shot and say there's no reason they should have these actors on radio mics here. Those should be the desperation, not the norm. And now it's turning into radios are the norm. Not the go-to desperation mic. It's just bizarre.

And getting a good mixed track can be very difficult, too. 'Cause if you mix eight microphones down you often have phasing issues and reverb and stuff, so you've got issues with the mixed track. I know it's hard on the location mixer 'cause they're trying to get a good mix on everything they do. I think they're expected to have an isolation mic on everybody now. They're all isolation mics, which are the radio mics. And they phase. If two guys are standing next to each other you're going to have two isolation mics phasing with cloth movement. The wrong kind of cloth movement. Not the kind that rescues us, the kind that we're all going "oh no, what's that?"

Another problem I encounter in post is, generally speaking there's the spotting session, and you say something in the spotting session, you ask for something very specific and then it doesn't show up. I just wish sometimes the sound people would take better notes, or pipe up if they don't understand what the editor or director is asking for, rather than getting onto the stage and having nothing there. I say, "I asked for this." "Well, I didn't know what you were talking about." Call me up and say, "I don't know what you're talking about. You're not making sense." And I probably don't make sense half the time.

KB: Some people don't listen or they have their own agendas. I've run into this before, too.

LH: The thing that's kind of fascinating is youngsters now, and this is generational, it sounds like I'm an old puke, but kids now aren't taking notes and they don't write. They don't actually use writing utensils, everything's done on their cell phones. Literally, I had one student taking notes on his iPhone. I was just blown away. My brother and I were joking about it 'cause he just got an MBA and they were all teasing him for using a pencil. People don't use them anymore.

KB: I've got the greatest pen collection from different motels I have stayed in across the country. But when I go lecture at universities I see so many kids just sitting there and not taking notes and it's like "how do you expect to retain any of this? You're not all brilliant. Trust me."

LH: Like I said to my assistants a couple times, "When you come in here it would be great if I see you with a little pad of paper." That will make me feel better. I might just be old, but when you come in and I've got eight things for you to do you can't possibly remember all eight. And that's not saying anything bad about you. You're a great person but no one can remember eight things at once.

KB: What was the worst thing that happened to you when you were cutting sound?

LH: The nightmare story that I have is so film specific. My assistant walked in to the room when I was cutting reel one dialogue, and this was on mag film, and dumped a Coke into the trim bin with the entire track in it! It was the entire cut of reel one's dialogue! We grabbed all the tracks and went into every bathroom in the building and rinsed them all off. We ran all the tracks into the sinks in the bathrooms and we were washing it all off. The Coca Cola did not have time to eat the mag because we washed it all so fast and we hung it to dry and darned if the thing didn't dry out!

KB: What about the worst sound problem you've ever had?

LH: The worst problem I had as a picture editor was I had a director with super, super acute hearing who was hearing something that I couldn't hear. It was making him crazy and for me that was terrifying because I wasn't hearing it. I just didn't understand what was going on. And the supervising sound editor came to my rescue. He said, "You're hearing something that's going to be rolled off in the academy roll-off." It's like a vibration he was hearing. That to me was terrifying because I didn't understand what he was talking about. I just didn't hear what the problem was. And whether that's because I've lost hearing from being a dialogue editor I don't know.

KB: What are some of the biggest change you've seen in post-production over the last few years?

LH: The shortening of the schedules. It's so hard on the sound people and I know they hate us, but the schedules are shortened so much that we don't have picture finished by the time they're starting to work on it. And we're changing picture sometimes right through final dub. I just want all the sound people out there to know, we don't like this. We would never be changing picture on them, not late in the game, but the schedules are so short because of the new technology. It's not easy on sound at all. Technology or not, they've got hundreds of tracks to conform, no matter how you slice it. So if you're doing a picture change late in the game, they've got a massive conform and it

126

takes them a day just to do the conform.

It's part of the game now and we all know it. We apologize in advance. And the sound people all know that it's happening. And the mixes are shortened, too. By the time a film comes onto the big stage to do the final mix, everything's been built, the sound editors do the pre-dub before it even gets to the stage. That's a whole new thing too, the sound guys pre-dubbing from their own Pro Tools before they ever get to the stage.

KB: Do you think that's a good thing or a bad thing?

LH: If the sound designer or supervising sound editor is the one that's doing it and it's his or her design, that's fine. But sometimes if you get the pre-dubs in and you can't pull things apart it can be a little frustrating.

Everything's shortened, all the way through the process, so we're all together in the trenches doing the best we can. I don't know how these poor guys on this TV show I was just on do it. These guys had five days to do all of the sound for the whole show and half the time picture came in so late they only had like one day before the mix. It was nutty.

KB: What are the most important things students need to know about sound, both location and post production?

LH: Sound is not the enemy! In my era as a location mixer, it was just torture. Hopefully it's not as bad for these younger guys, but I think it probably is. If the location recordist needs a few minutes on the set, just give it to him. It almost always works better than ADR. You give the camera crew the time, can't you give the sound crew a little time? And people say, "Well they should have been ready while we're setting up lights." Setting up lights is not like having an actor change something. It's like, yeah that plant mic's there and the actor changed the performance and suddenly that plant mic's not useful anymore. So give the location recordist time to plant another mic or something.

Students also need to know about creativity in location mixing. If you can't get a boom in and you have to use radio mics, everyone's relying on them so heavily now, remember there's a lot of ugly sound that comes married onto the dialogue on a radio mic, get creative with plant mics! Try and plant the microphone on the steering wheel of the car, try and plant it on the gearshift if the guy's leaning over to his buddy to talk. Have plant mics all over and mix them in there. Get creative. You can be just as creative in location mixing as picking the right bomb explosion in post. It's like sound editing. It's a very creative job. Don't be afraid to get creative with location mixing. Do anything you can to keep the mics from rubbing against clothing and costumes and being muffled under a necktie or a lapel.

For sound design, I'd like to make a pitch for using the original sound as the basis for your design. The original sound always has a feel to it, right back to PASSAGE TO INDIA. There's a psychological naturalness to the original sound, that's how that place should sound. Don't be afraid to add sound in, but use the original as much as possible.

If you're gonna go into television don't fall into that trap of thinking that your written word is so holy that you should have no other sound on it. Listen to a restaurant next time you're in one. Listen to all that stuff going on and know that you can add all that in to a mix. Keep it low, but still give it the feel and your dialogue will still shine through happily.

The other thing is get creative and go too far. The director will reel you in. But have fun and experiment with things, and never be scared to try something. Even in a reality-based movie. Just yesterday, I had my assistant trolling around because I saw an actress pull her chair back and there was a really funny chair sound effect as she pulled it back, and I thought, "That's a funny sound." I think the director probably thought I was crazy, "What's so funny about that?" It was the way the leg rubbed against it. Even in reality there are some very funny sounds and even in a movie that you think is just a walk and talk, it's not. There's tons of room for creativity. Here is the neighborhood of one family and it's gonna need a totally different sound than the neighborhood of this other family.

And last but not least, these two departments have a traditional history of warfare and it shouldn't be. Music is not the enemy. Often, half the sound work gets blown away by music and the sound guys feel frustrated. Once again, it's not the enemy. In a beautifully mixed film your re-recording mixers will find the balance, if they're given the time. Everything shines through.

Sometimes, sadly, one department or the other is going to get the balance, is going to be favored and it's not always going to be you and it's not always going to be music. A lot of supervising sound editors have come up to me afterward and said, "Thanks so much for sticking up for sound here and there." But I wouldn't have if I didn't honestly feel that I wanted to hear the sound effects there more than music. I would've said, "Bury 'em" if the movie would've been better with music instead of sound effects. It's all for the good of the film. Shut your ego down and say, "What's the best mix here for this scene?"

It's not about how much work you put into it or how much work that guy put into writing the score. It's what's best for the movie and, once again, your director's the ultimate decider, but there are no enemies here.

And one last thing, louder is not necessarily more powerful. Sometimes you get into this quagmire. They raise the sound effects and they have to raise the music and then everyone's got orange earplugs in their ears while they're making the movie. If you've got orange earplugs in, what's the audience gonna do? I would say find the balance.

KB: Can you think of any films that you think young filmmakers should see?

LH: I'm classically oriented, but the three movies just popped into my head were NORTH BY NORTHWEST, NOTORIOUS (the two Hitchcock movies that I like the best), and BEING THERE. BEING THERE, oh God, I love that movie! If they like international films, THE DISCRETE CHARM OF THE BOURGEOISIE, history of film kind of stuff.

It might have been 1900, I just remember the shot where the crane starts on this leaf blowing across the driveway and sweeps up and it was Bertolucci so it's gotta be 1900. Beautiful. Anything shot by Vitorio Storaro. There's a movie called I AM CUBA that was shot in 1961, prior to steadicam shots. The first shot of the movie, I don't know how they shot it. They ended up in a swimming pool, and there's a second shot where my friend and I turned to each other and said, "How did they shoot that?" We don't see any track. And it was before the era of wire removal. It was a documentary propaganda movie. I don't know if you've seen it, but there's a shot in there going through the streets of Havana and the camera's above the city looking down and there's no track, there's no wire, there's nothing, and we were just like, "How did they do that?"

For sound . . . gosh, I remember being blown away by OUT OF AFRICA. The version I saw of OUT OF AFRICA was six-track magnetic sound. Remember that old style six-track mag? Today you never see a six-track magnetic Dolby print. We saw a few of those in our era and I think some of those are some of the greatest sounding films of all time. If they can ever see a print that is 70 mm, six-track mag of anything they should see it. There are tons and tons of great movies for sound. I'm terrible at thinking things up off the top of my head. You even gave me that question, and I didn't have anything written down.

Oh! MY OWN PRIVATE IDAHO! Tell them to watch that!

KB: Well, thank you. That was a long time ago. I think I had dark hair back then.

LH: Yeah, that's awesome. That was an awesome movie.

CHAPTER 4:

It's the Dialogue Stupid!

Dialogue and ADR Editors

Years ago, when I was first starting out I had the opportunity to work with a bunch of veteran sound editors. Back in the day we cut all the sound on upright Moviola's and 35 mm magnetic film. The editors I learned from had amazing skills. They could take a razor blade and cut fades and shapes on to the mag. I was taught you could minimize (and sometimes remove) microphone bumps by scraping off some of the mag on a piece of dialogue. I watched as one of these guys scrapped a two second fade out in just a couple strokes on an ambiance track. These sound editors did amazing things with primitive tools by our standards.

Although the tools have changed, Dialogue and ADR editing hasn't.

The goal is still to make the dialogue sound as clean and understandable as possible and when you can't fix something you ADR it. Dialogue editing may be looked at as a craft but it's also an art form. A good dialogue editor can save an awful lot of an actor's performance.

When they encounter problems like microphone hits or clothing rustle or RF (Radio Frequency) noise a good editor will find single words or phrases from other takes and place them seamlessly in to the desired take. They can take syllables and add them on to words to change meaning and they can make an off-screen line sound more believable.

A good ADR editor doesn't just re-sync new takes; they handle all of the Group ADR and that can add meaning and believability to background action. They work closely with the picture editor to add lines that were never recorded on location to explain away plot holes or speed up the film. Many films have been made better by clever use of off-screen lines.

Doing ADR is hard work and a lot of actors can't do it well. There is a reason why many directors don't like to replace dialogue in ADR, it's a crap shoot as to whether the performance will be as good as what they got on the set. As a filmmaker you don't want to put your actors through a really grueling scene where their emotions are laid bare because you didn't give your location recordist enough time to mic it properly. Good dialogue editors can often save those scenes and salvage the best performance.

Remember, audiences don't care that it took twelve hours to shoot that scene and the backgrounds on all of the characters mics changed throughout the day. The audience wants to believe that the entire scene took place in the three minutes that it lasted on the screen. You need to make your dialogue seamless.

David A. Cohen

"Your job is to make it so nobody has to worry about the dialogue, so they can worry about the music and the sound effects and the ADR."

I first worked with David on EVEN COWGIRLS GET THE BLUES. He was the first person I met who was editing sound on a computer workstation. It was called the DAWN and, it seemed like he was light years ahead of everyone. The rest of the crew were still on upright Moviola's and we had one flatbed.

Since then David and I have worked on a lot of films together and I've always respected his attention to detail, because cutting dialogue is all about the details. Dialogue editing is one of the most challenging and can also be one of the most tedious aspects of post-production. And you better get it right if you want the dialogue to sound good.

When I first got out of school I had the opportunity to work with a lot of old time editors who made magic on those old upright Moviola's. They could cut shapes and scrape mag film with razor blades and eliminate microphone hits to really clean up a track. I have seen David do the same thing with a computer. He can take words from different takes and put them together to make a nice sounding line of dialogue that we thought we would have to ADR. I have seen him save performances by fixing the production. There are a lot of actors who should thank him for making them sound better.

His list of credits is long and includes: CORALINE, ALL THE KING'S MEN, INLAND EMPIRE, THE LAST SAMURAI, LOST IN TRANSLATION, SEABISCUIT, WIND TALKERS, GLADIATOR, THE SIXTH SENSE, GOOD WILL HUNTING, FAR FROM HEAVEN, and of course my favorite, BIRDDOG.

David is one of those editors when he does his job right, no one notices.

If you want to know more about David A. Cohen check out:
http://www.imdb.com/name/nm0169314/

KB: How did you get involved in sound and specifically dialogue in particularly.

DC: It was kind of an accident. I lived in the Northwest back in the 70s and I decided to stop working for Seattle City Lights as a saw operator on their logging crew and move to LA. I got my ears tested because OSHA required it and my hearing tested better than anybody the guy had ever tested in his career.

He actually told me you have to stop running a chainsaw, you have the best hearing I've ever encountered and you're going to destroy it.

So I moved to LA and enrolled in Santa Monica College. I was taking a few classes just to see what I wanted to do when I grew up. I took a radio production course. And the guy that ran the program there told me I had a pretty good voice and I ought to consider this as a career.

Eventually I got a job at KUSC as a full-time staff engineer. It didn't really occur to me that there might be a career in something where I could actually work on feature films probably until the late 1980s. It was around that time I started getting exposed to people that were working as mixers and sound editors on films. They started telling me why don't you work on this stuff, you could make more money and it's a nicer gig. I got to know a guy who was a picture editor and he was working for this company called Ediflex, you remember Ediflex?

KB: I remember Ediflex.

DC: Yeah, I knew you would. This picture editor was working for Ediflex and they needed somebody to take the AudiFlex out and show it to sound editors around LA. They were trying to get a foothold in the then developing digital sound editing field. AudiFlex was geared toward dialogue editing. I got the job and showed this system to sound editors all over LA. A couple of places started using it, so I got to know all these dialogue editors.

I would discuss dialogue editing with them, their approach, and how they did things. I spent eight or nine months getting this tutorial from just about every dialogue editor in LA. Modern Sound had looked at Audiflex, but decided to stay with an analog system that was a tape-to-tape format, very popular in a few editorial houses in LA in those days. They asked me if I wanted to edit dialogue and ADR for them because the guy that was supervising MACGYVER thought I might do a good job. I said sure so that's how I got hired in 1989 to cut dialogue on MACGYVER.

KB: A roundabout way to get in to sound, from chainsaws to sound editing. Tell me exactly what a dialogue editor does? What are you responsible for?

DC: Specifically the job is to make sure the sound recorded on location, is laid out and ready for the mixer to mix it during the pre-dub phase of the mix . What I mean by that is your job is to make sure that the mixer can put his faders literally at zero if that's what he's after and all he has to do is hit play. Then he can go through and start EQ-ing all the different lines within each scene to try to make them sound like they're all part of the same continuous take.

Nowadays I'm working in a digital format but it worked the same on the Moviola. Let's say the editor in scene 25, liked scene 25-H take three. You try to put everything from that take on one track so that theoretically the background is similar no matter which person is talking. In a live-action film, maybe 25-H-2 and 25-H-3 have slightly different background sounds, different time of day, the way the people were talking, the way the wind was blowing, whatever. So you're splitting everything out on to different tracks from different takes.

If you've got a scene where they use twenty-five different specific takes, well you don't have twenty-five tracks obviously because the mixer only has so many faders he can deal with. You've got to give the mixer time between different takes if he needs to go in and come out on a track and be able to hit record.

I don't like working in time code, I go back to the days when we were measuring film in feet and frames. I set my Pro Tools even on a time code movie to a footage counter so that I can see footage.

If I can't set it up to where the mixer is going to have at least fifteen feet between different pieces of audio, then I'll just add a new track rather than put him in a position where he's not going to have the time to do what he needs to do. If it's like Scene 25-H take three, I don't care if there's two feet between each piece of sound if it's the same take. But if we're going to put 25-H take one on that same track I try to give the mixer at least fifteen feet between the different takes.

So all he has to do is concentrate on the EQ work. The mixer is trying to match the EQ on each take so he can mix a few things down on to fewer tracks and he won't be stuck in the final mix having to undo what he has already pre-dubbed.

KB: I think you're simplifying it to a point, because you're also responsible for cleaning up the dialogue.

DC: Well yeah, that's my second job. First job is to make it so the mixer likes me. Pure and simple.

KB: You want to be like Sally Field, "You like me, you really like me."

DC: Yes, but it's not just a matter of being "Little Davey Sunshine." This is a job where you're only as good as your last gig.

If you want the mixer to be happy when he sees you, you need to lay your tracks out so he can do his job efficiently because you're helping him look good too. And the supervisor looks good if the mixer says you're good so everybody's happy. I once had a Supervising Sound Editor ask me, "What do you think your primary job here is?" I started to say something about "massaging the tracks", creating a pristine production track, etc, and he cut me off after a few seconds. His quote was, "You're here to help make the mix go faster." I thought about it and realized he was right. A dubbing stage cost around $450 - $650 per hour in those days (Now it's more like $550 - $1000 per hour). I was, and still am getting quite a bit less than that to prep the dialogue. If I do my job right we'll save a good deal of time on the dubbing stage struggling with the dialogue. Time is money in other words.

So your number one job is to lay the shit out so everybody can do their jobs efficiently and smoothly and make the dialogue intelligible. In my mind, dialogue is king, if you can't understand what they're saying then the movie is a waste of time.

If the mixer starts hearing a bunch of crackle, snap, and pop in the tracks, there's not much he can do with EQ knobs to fix that. He's going to want to know, and so is the director, why you didn't fix those things. This job is like holding a wire toothbrush, and having a pier full of barnacles and being told this should take you a month, do it in a week.

Fixing the snap, crackle and pop, that's where the editing art comes in for a guy like me. I have to be good at knowing what tool I need to go about fixing this stuff. There's not a lot I can do about noisy backgrounds, that's where we get into do we ADR it or can we fix it in the mix? My job if there's shitty background is to make sure that there's plenty of that crappy background that they can use and blend in and out to make a pure crappy background sound.

KB: How do you do that?

DC: I always want to have access to all the dailies that were recorded on the set and hopefully they recorded a few takes of everything. Sometimes they don't because they're in a hurry or the budget's low. I go in and listen to other readings of the same line and maybe I can take a little piece of a word and feather it in so that you get a seamless feel. I've gotten rid of an impurity in the sound that will distract people from actually knowing what is being said.

Something else I do a lot is when somebody walks off camera, I'll go find some footsteps in that scene of somebody walking off somewhere. Maybe there's somewhere where we caught some footsteps and I'll make a little bit extra and put them on our production effects track so as the actor walks off the mixer can feather them off without having to go to the Foley which will now sound more natural.

And I'll make a little piece of air for each take, we call them handles and depending on how loud and noisy everything is I'll ramp these handles in and out of everything I do. I try to make fairly long ones if I can so they very subtly blend together so you never get the sense that you're hearing a different take each time.

KB: Let's talk about ADR because, film students for some reason think that just about everything they see in the movies and on TV. . . all the dialogue's been replaced, its all ADR.

DC: I don't know where they get this idea. I've had that happen too. As a matter of fact, I would say that if you polled ten directors, eleven of them are going to tell you they hate ADR.

KB: Right.

DC: It's weird because I do more ADR than dialogue nowadays. I'm getting stuff where they want to change what the person says or there was some technical problem with the dialogue. Sometimes they want to add new lines. But I'm finding that a lot of the time even the stuff that needs replacing because of technical difficulties in the recording they'll try to save almost to the point of fanaticism before they actually go with the ADR. And you know some editors only do ADR, they'll always fight for their ADR but since I do both, when I'm the ADR supervisor a lot of the times I'll say let's use the production first. There are times where I think the production's not working so I'll go with the ADR. But if the powers that be really want to go with production we go with it.

KB: I'd be surprised if we ever replaced more than 5% of a movie. We might have recorded 5% of ADR for a film but I can remember only a few lines here and there in an entire film that were ADR, everything else was the original.

DC: I've even gone into movies that the production was so poorly recorded that we recorded seven hundred lines of ADR. Seven hundred lines! Some of it was added lines but a lot of it was replacement lines. In the final release of the film out of those seven hundred lines I'd say we probably put two hundred and fifty of them in.

KB: Wow. And two fifty is still a huge amount of lines.

DC: That is a huge amount. A lot of it was added stuff, we probably took a little less than a quarter of what we recorded and put it in. It's the same with group, the ADR supervisor a lot of times makes group ADR a bigger deal for you than the actual production lines because you've got to get the right stuff in there for the background people.

Yeah, ADR in Hollywood films is pretty rare, a lot gets recorded, a shit load gets recorded for protection purposes, but it is only used if we can't make the production work.

KB: What is your biggest challenge when it comes to cutting dialogue anymore?

DC: Time and budget more than ever. I just don't have the time to do as much as I used to do. It used to be if there was going to be seven or eight weeks you had two or three people working just on the dialogue.

Now even if you're on a studio film you've got a dialogue editor, an ADR supervisor, a show supervisor who is also usually a sound designer, and he usually has one sound effects person helping him, then you have a Foley person and one assistant for the whole crew.

And you're stuck doing everything in a really short amount to time. It's really compressed. You get on a studio film and they'll do two or three temp dubs while you're doing the final mix. If it's not a high-powered production, to the director your time is compressed down to nothing with a really small crew. So, my biggest challenge nowadays is just doing the job that my standards dictate that I turn over.

KB: Right. Where do you think post-sound stands as far as importance on a film crew?

DC: We're the janitors.

I talk to quite a few people about this over the years and the general consensus seems to be that they spend so much of the budget in production, and during the picture editorial process that when they get to the end which is when we come on, all of a sudden they realize they have no money left and so we're the ones that end up having to do miracles with nothing.

KB: No shit.

DC: And over the years what's happened is there's been a lot more emphasis on the commercial viability of any project. In the early 2000s a lot of studios went to what they called their independent wings. They began to see the independent feature films in terms of what they were worth, how much could they make off them, what their commercial potential was. I think that a lot of them started to feel it doesn't matter what the movie sounds like because the people that are on top of the food chain believe that the "Indie" crowd who pay to see these films aren't interested in how it sounds. In fact, there might be a belief that a super pristine sound job may put those folks off a little.

I just think that there are a lot of people making decisions that may not have the most sophisticated taste when it comes to the final product that they're putting out too.

In their mind they're looking at widgets and they're looking at dollars and cents. I understand that it's a business we all like making money but as far as they're concerned, if we spend that money and we do this or that, how is that going to make me more money when we release this. Can you guarantee me that I'll make X amount of dollars if I spend more, but if I don't spend that amount of dollars I am pretty certain that I'm going to make the same amount during the release.

KB: As a dialogue editor, how do you manage a project from the beginning to end.

DC: That depends on the project, who's doing it, how many people are on it and the budget. If I'm doing dialogue on a picture and we're going to have an average amount of time for pre-dubs then I'll try to keep my tracks down to right around sixteen to twenty.

If I know we're not going to have any time for pre-dubs I'll keep it down to eight or twelve tracks. If I know we're going to have shit loads of time for pre-dubs, we have a big schedule and everything, I've gone as far as thirty-two tracks just on a dialogue but that's pretty rare.

I'll do a track lay out and every reel is going to be the same. I'm going to have this many dialogue tracks, this many PFX (production effects) tracks.

If it's a movie that we're going to be doing some futzing for telephone conversations or TV or whatever, I'll look at the film first and then decide I'm going to need three or four PFX tracks. In the old days, when I had the time, I would actually make room "fill" tracks, I would run a separate track of matching room fill. I would make it out of production in every scene, which would be better for the M & E. Occasionally they would use it in the regular mix too, but that's something I tossed away when I didn't have the time anymore.

So then you've got your X-tracks where you're going to prep the lines labeled as ADR, but like we talked about since a lot of stuff that you're X-ing over is going to get ADR-ed, you put fill on your dialogue tracks so they can have matching background on it.

You still want to cut the dialogue so you got your X-tracks with your cut dialogue in it and you want to make sure the mixer pre-dubs because they're probably going to wind up using it. Then you've got your X tracks that have the crap on it that you know nobody wants but just in case you mistakenly identify something as crap that somebody really doesn't think is crap.

So those are the different kinds of tracks that you're going to lay out. You count how many you're going to need of each type of track and then you just make it consistent on every reel, the same amount of tracks.

Then I'll go through and start splitting everything based on scene and take number without even listening to it. Once I've done that I'll go back and make a real time pass through it listening to everything and seeing if the EQ didn't change within the same scene which it occasionally does, which will cause me to split out everything even more.

Once I've got everything split out on the tracks then I go through another pass much slower. Now I'm making the fixes on the impurities and putting those handles we talked about on, splitting the production effects off to a separate PFX track, filling in when its appropriate in the dialogue track, matching background tones so it all plays smoothly and seamlessly.

After I'm done with that which usually takes a few days per reel, then I go back and do a playback on the reel and listen to everything. That's when I make my final adjustments as I'm listening to the playback. You know, much like the way we do a mix.

KB: Right. When you're doing your last pass in Pro Tools are you EQ-ing things yourself, are you using any plug ins to make the pre-dubs go quicker?

DC: No. The only time I ever did that was on a really low-budget film. They wanted me to pre-dub the dialogue too. But that was a special circumstance.

KB: So most of the time when you're editing you don't get into EQ-ing or any of that other stuff?

DC: Well . . . there are some pretty good plug-ins out there, if there's some really bad rumble on the track what I'll do is put the un-rumbled stuff on an X track and then I'll de-rumble it with something like Sound Soap Pro. I also have De-Crackle and that's about all I'll ever do. Maybe I'll roll off everything below 50 hertz just to get some really bad rumble out. Sometimes I do a tiny bit of de-popping, but mostly I cut the pops out myself and hand smooth them over you know.

One of the things I want to emphasize is that when I cut production, when I cut dialogue, I always cut on headphones.

KB: Why?

DC: I feel that when you're using speakers when you're cutting production it is almost impossible in my mind to really know how things are going to match unless you're on a dubbing stage. If they're going to let you cut on a dubbing stage . . . fuck use the speakers. But if you're not on a dubbing stage, if you're in some little cutting room on a lot somewhere you're just not going to be able to play it loud enough and you're not going to be in an acoustically correct room that will give you the correct prospective.

When you're on good headphones you're getting every fucking sound that's on that track really tight to your ears and there's no distractions from the outside world. You're really getting an idea of how everything is going to match together. You can be reasonably assured when it gets put up on that dubbing stage nobody's going to get any surprises. There's not going to be a hum or a tone or a crack or a snap that you didn't know about.

I will use speakers for ADR because that has nothing to do with background and everything to do with performance and sync.

KB: You've done dramatic films, you've done animated films, and you do the occasional documentary. Does your approach vary from film to film or is it always pretty much the same?

DC: Its all based on budget, and how much time I have to do it. So depending on how much money they have to give me that will dictate how much time I have. I do have certain things that are essential and I know they're essential and it doesn't matter if your film has a $5,000,000 budget or if its got a $500 budget for sound. If all you have is $500 for sound, if I agree to do it there are certain basics that you're going to get out of me. Beyond that, I know what is absolutely essential and time dictates how much else you're going to get.

If you've got a thousand bucks you're going to get a thousand dollar job, if you've got a hundred thousand dollars you're going to get a hundred thousand dollar job.

Now the thing that I hate to admit, but everybody that works on such a wide range of budgets like I do will tell you, that unfortunately your professional pride won't allow you to do a thousand dollar job. If they've only got a thousand bucks they're probably going to get the $5,000 job.

KB: Right. And it puts us into a tough bind because if somebody says I don't have much money and you agree to do it and you give them whatever you think the minimal is and then they say, "God, you know we paid that guy all that money and this sounds like shit." Which is such a ridiculous thing.

DC: Yeah. I try to avoid those gigs anymore. I've been pretty successful the last ten years or so not putting myself in that position, but you're right in the past I have been in that situation.

KB: How much control do you have over what you do? Do the directors leave you alone or . . . ?

DC: When I'm doing dialogue everybody leaves me alone. Once in awhile the picture editor will come in hang out for a little while. Cutting dialogue, is like watching paint dry to most people. So when you're doing dialogue you get a lot of leeway.

It is an interesting gig because anybody that's interested in being involved in the sound crews, very few people say I want to be a dialogue editor once they see what it entails. It's a weird job because when you're doing your job right, you're invisible. When you don't do your job right, then you're noticed.

Your job is to make it so nobody has to worry about the dialogue, so they can worry about the music and the sound effects and the ADR. And the Foley to a smaller extent, but Foley is kind of in the same boat.

KB: Right. Do we really need all of these footsteps?

DC: Yeah. Foley's really there to supplement and that's it. I once told an editor who was complaining a lot of his stuff didn't make it in to the movie, "You want your stuff to be heard? Start cutting dialogue. They've got to play it."

It's a nice gig if you like being left to your own devices and like to be creative on your own because there's a lot of design work in dialogue in its own way.

KB: Sure.

DC: Now ADR is different. A lot of the time you're collaborating closely with the editor and for me that's a cool thing. There's a lot more interaction, plus when the stars are there you're sitting there circling takes and maybe the director will ask you a few questions here and there, "Should we get something else?" You're working with everybody a lot more closely on a daily basis.

I love going in to a group ADR session and directing the group. I really enjoy it when I get a good group and we get good stuff.

KB: When I was directing loop group stuff I always wrote tons of lines. I gave them stuff to say because there's nothing worse than leaving actors up to their own devices.

We've talked about the loop (ADR) groups a couple of times but we really haven't explained what they are and how we use them. Could you tell me what a loop group is?

DC: Group becomes really important where there are crowds and you can't have this hubbub all the time of just a bunch of voices overshadowing the dialogue. The dialogue has to be the most important thing people are hearing, but if you've got a crowd reacting something's got to be there. Usually when they record on the set, especially if the actors are talking then people in the background can't be talking because we need to hear what the actors are saying. So the background people are just flapping their gums, not saying anything. Something's got to be put in there so if there's a break in the dialogue maybe a word will come through here and there so you get the feel that there really is somebody back there.

Your job is to assemble a group of actors and I have to cue everything that I think might need to be filled out with voices. I'll record multiple takes, individual stuff and larger group stuff. What we call walla. Walla is a general hubbub in the background. I'll go through every scene in the movie and I'll fill it out every which way from Sunday with a loop group. On some shows we may take two to three days to record everything with the group. Now after I record all this, maybe 5% is going to get into the movie.

There are group wranglers that I like to work with, one in particular in LA, she's really good. I'll spot the show with her and we'll talk about what we're going to need here and she'll know which actors to bring in based on how many we're going to be able to hire and how much money the production's willing to spend.

I'm not somebody who will sit down and write specific lines. When I go through my ADR program and cue all the stuff, I'll have a general idea of what these people need to be saying. Then I'll look at it with the actors and the group leader. The group leader and I have already discussed what they should be saying so we'll tell the actors we want this kind of a conversation.

I find it's better to let the actors try to make something up because then they feel like they're participating. The thing that most of them don't get real well and it is hard because you don't want to destroy their creative juices but look, you're not a character in the movie, you're a word or two. You just need that word or two to sync with that person in the corner there.

Some people like to get a big group of people in front of a microphone and have them all start just mumbling and talking. I don't like doing that because it creates a situation where you're stuck with everything in the center. What I do, even in a scene where we might have a huge crowd, is make five or six passes of anywhere from three to five people each and have them all talk. You still have them talk about things pertinent to the scene that's happening and let them ad lib. There are always one or two people in a group that talk louder than everybody else. They want to get their voice in the movie. What they don't get is their voice is being cut out first because you want it all to blend.

Here is a good example of Group ADR. I cut the dialogue and the group ADR on GLADIATOR. Chris Jargo was the ADR supervisor. We had a good budget and he spent a lot of days shooting group. In this one scene, there's a couple of Roman senators in a marketplace and they're discussing what to do about crazy Joaquin Phoenix Caesar. In the background you hear all the people hawking their wares in the marketplace and that's all group.

What Chris did is he shot all these people walking by the microphone and he would tell them, "Okay, you're selling olives, you're selling cloaks," or whatever and they would be acting like they were selling stuff. Then I got it all from him and he said, "I want to set this up so we can play this through the surrounds so it sounds like people are walking by them and around them and its like this marketplace is three hundred and sixty degrees around them." It was a fucking great idea.

I cut it together into a coherent sequence, everything overlaps by just a sentence or two on the tracks. I would use five tracks and I would go one- two- three- four- five, one-two- three- four- five all the way through the scene. When I gave it to Chris and he pre-dubbed it he said, "Great! You got it man." He and I became instant friends on that movie because he realized that I understood what he was trying to do.

If somebody gets GLADIATOR and watches that scene in the marketplace, if you listen to the background people hawking their wares, every voice in that background is loop group.

KB: What's the most common sound problem that you encounter?

DC: When a film is in production the location recordists get stuck dealing with the sounds of the generators and the lights. They sometimes struggle with where the boom is set up, and where the lavalier mics are being set on the actors. They don't always have a lot of control over these things on the set. Those are problems that are avoidable in my opinion. If the location recordists aren't allowed the time to get the sound right, how am I going to overcome the impurities that are now being created that can't be fixed?

KB: What's your best advice to give to filmmakers?

DC: Don't go into it for the money or the glamor or any of that bullshit because it's a trap. You're probably not Steven Spielberg, you're probably not even Seymour Spielberg. You've got to go into it because you really want to work on films.

Seriously man, you can't do this because you think there's a payoff because there probably isn't a payoff. I thought one day I might become an actor. When I realized that I wasn't a very good actor I saw that there was a way to make a nice living and still get to work on stuff that I enjoyed. So that would be my piece of advice. And get off your fucking high horse, you're not a filmmaker until somebody else says you're a filmmaker. I don't sound bitter do I?

KB: Actually you don't.

DC: Good. Do it for the love of doing it. Its not very financially rewarding unless you're one of a select few, but it's a great way to earn a living. And you get to meet some really good fucking people. I think there's a large concentration of really intelligent people working at least on the sound end of films, then you would find in most other jobs you're going to do.

KB: You work from home, what's your set-up? What equipment do you use?

DC: I have a Mac Pro Desktop, quad-core. I've got two 21- inch 1080P ltd screens, and I've got some self amplified speakers for reference, and Pro Tools I've got a sound editorial room and I've got two sets of headphones. I use Beyer DT990s when I'm cutting at home, I also have a set of Sennheiser H2-280 Pros when I'm on the stage. The Beyers are more of an "open ended" set of cans. Great mid-range response, so they're perfect for dialogue editing. On a dubbing stage I need a more isolated pair, so the Sennheiser's work for that. When I do animated films like CORALINE, I use my speakers for that because I'm not listening to backgrounds.

Cutting sound for animation is totally different than cutting production.

KB: How is cutting animation different?

DC: Animation is all about sync and it's about characters. When you're doing animation the amount of characters you have in a reel dictates the amount of tracks you have. Track one might be this character, track two will be that character, you're splitting out by character so if a character has only one or two lines in a reel there might be a track that has only one or two things on it. You have to do it by character because that's the way the mixer wants to have it set up for his EQ settings. Theoretically the EQ for each character doesn't change much because it's all done in the same studio most of the time.

You may have a different amount of tracks per reel depending on how many characters are in each reel. If one character is track one in reel one that character is track one in every other reel in the movie.

The other thing with animation is sync. They usually record the characters to the storyboard and then they'll animate to the voice track. Once they start animating maybe they'll change out the takes a little bit or they'll stretch them or compress them a little bit or whatever. The animators can't always get the sync exact. They're not spending a lot time worrying about animating for the dialogue they're looking more at the animation.

When I'm cutting production dialogue mainly I'm watching to make sure nobody screwed up when they sunk the dailies but if they did then I have to bring it to somebody's attention and we have to get to the bottom of it.

With animation it's like, "Oh, shit," I spent weeks maybe months going through that movie line by line as they finished the animation and then going back and looking at it again. Adjusting it little bits and pieces at a time to make it so the character's animation fit the line that they were going to use in the movie.

I've always felt that not enough time was spent worrying about whether the dialogue and the animation are really sunk properly. I'll tell you what man, I find it's easier to get the sync you like doing ADR in a live-action film than it is in animation. I could do an animated line ten times and then a week later look at it and just start working on it again, you know?

KB: I know that one. I spent a lot of years in the clay factory, remember?

DC: That's right, you know what it's like.

KB: Can you think of anything else that we haven't talked about that students or other filmmakers should know about audio?

DC: It's more important than you think. And a lot of the times it is not going to be fixable in post so it might be worth taking a little extra time to make sure you've got somebody who knows what they're doing recording the sound for you. Not your cousins, uncles, hairdresser or some guy from Craig's List. It'll really pay off down the road if you hire somebody good. It's always better to have a pro if you can, and if you can't then it is better to have somebody that really wants to learn location recording. Remember, what you record out on that set is really going to dictate how your final product is going to be perceived.

I talk to filmmakers that don't have a lot of money and not a lot of experience. If they spend a lot of time and effort and maybe a little extra money getting a really good sound job, especially getting it recorded well on the set, it may not mean the difference between you getting that big deal or getting in to Sundance. But if you're looking to impress and you give them something that sounds amateurish, most of them are going to know and their perception of you will change.

If you give them the best edited, best looking, best sounding product you can, it is going to help your chances somewhere down the road. Maybe they'll actually give you the money to make something or take your work and put it in a good festival. You may not get any immediate payoff out of spending a little extra time, effort, or money on making sure it sounds good, but it will help the perception that people have of you as a professional filmmaker.

KB: Do you still love what you do?

DC: I really like what I do. I love getting gigs and I love the fact that I'm not on the same gig all the time and I still bring just as much enthusiasm to the job as I ever did.

I've been working as a sound editor for twenty-two years and I still really like it. I'm hoping I can keep doing it for another ten years or so.

Milly Iatrou

"A good dialogue editor can figure out a way to make nearly every line of dialogue usable."

I first met Milly on a film where she served a (very) short stint as the Post Production Supervisor (uncredited). She came on during a re-edit. She was amazingly organized (which was a real change after a few of the other post supervisors I had worked with) which I came to find out was because she had been an editor as well. Her background allowed her to come in and help us get organized and be as efficient as possible and she was always able to get me what I needed.

We had a few conversations in those days about film and how we got involved in the business. She was a big fan of foreign, experimental and art house films which lead to many interesting discussions. She always seems to be busy but I was able to speak with her just before she started on a new film.

Milly has been a Supervising Sound Editor, an ADR Supervisor/Editor and a Dialogue Editor her credits include: X-MEN ORIGINS: WOLVERINE, X-MEN, THE LAST STAND, THE X FILES: I WANT TO BELIEVE, HAIR SPRAY, WALK THE LINE, CATCH ME IF YOU CAN, and L.A. CONFIDENTIAL.

If you want to know more about Milly Iatrou, check out: http://www.imdb.com/name/nm0406375/

KB: How did you get involved with film?

MI: I was fortunate enough to take a filmmaking class in high school and fell in love with the art form. I decided I wanted to be a filmmaker. I made 16mm films in film school and found that my favorite part of the process was editorial. After film school I tried to get a job in post-production in New York and found it very difficult. A few years later I moved to San Francisco and was able to get a job as a sound apprentice at Francis Coppla's, American Zoetrope.

KB: Is there a particular film (or films) that were a big influence on you when you started working?

MI: It was the experimental films of Maya Deren, Buñuel and other Surrealists that made me want to be a filmmaker. I was also influenced by Coppola and Scorsese who were heroes because they were some of the first film school graduates who were able to work in the studio system.

KB: You have worked a lot as a dialogue editor and an ADR editor. What exactly does a dialogue editor do?

MI: A dialogue editor takes the picture editor's audio tracks and smooths them out by cleaning out pops and clicks, replacing words or syllables that have unwanted noise with alternate takes, and cleaning up the production sound fill.

The picture editor often works with a mix channel from the production sound rolls. The dialogue editor has to check the other channels in cases where the mix channel is off-mic or noisy to see if the other channels are clearer and the dialogue more present. (For example, sometimes the body mics are a better choice.) These dialogue tracks are prepped for the sound mix by splitting them by set-up, adding handles, and providing alternates for hard to understand lines.

KB: Then what does an ADR editor do?

MI: An ADR editor goes through the picture editor's audio tracks and programs lines which should be replaced by ADR because of loud background noise, bad recording, low level of recording - basically anything that's hard to understand. One also has to program added lines requested by the director, picture editor and studio. These are often story points that need to be reinforced.

I also spot for areas that will need additional Group ADR.

KB: How much of the dialogue in the "average feature" is usually replaced later in ADR?

MI: I would agree with you that we usually replace less than 5% with ADR. Most filmmakers agree that production sound will always sound more real and true than ADR and will use it over ADR whenever possible.

I believe that getting a good production sound recording is one of the most important elements of making a good movie. It will save the filmmaker money and stress further down the line. The reason filmmakers don't ignore production sound and replace everything with ADR (except for in Italy, but I'm not even sure if that's still the case today) is that it's extremely time consuming and expensive and sounds very strange.

KB: What makes a good Dialogue Editor and a good ADR Editor?

MI: A good dialogue editor can figure out a way to make nearly every line of dialogue usable, and prep the production sound so that it's as clear and present as possible, and easy to mix.

A good ADR editor knows which dialogue lines need to be replaced by ADR, which lines can be improved in the mix without ADR, also when to fight to record an ADR line even if the actor doesn't want to.

KB: Can you talk about how you manage a project from beginning to end?

MI: I start by spotting the movie and giving a line count to the director, editor and post supervisor. The director and picture editor usually have a list of lines they want to replace before I even start so I take that list and incorporate it into my line count.

The post supervisor uses my line count to schedule the ADR sessions. I supervise the recording sessions. The director or picture editor are usually there to direct the actor. If not, I direct.

We are usually replacing lines for technical reasons in which case the actor should try to repeat the same performance. Sometimes the director wants a change of performance. Sometimes, it's a line change. If the director is present my primary role is to call sync or point out if there's a technical problem. I keep a log of all the lines and circle takes.

Afterward, I cut the ADR lines and prep them for the final mix.

I also have to spot all the areas where Group ADR is needed, supervise and direct the Group ADR recording sessions, then cut and prep the Group for the mix.

If the budget permits, I have an editor cutting behind me to help prepare all the ADR and Group for the mix.

KB: If you were looking for an ADR Editor what would be the important things you would want to know about them and/or their work?

MI: I usually go by recommendation and ask if they're good with sync.

KB: What is your biggest challenge on a film?

MI: Dealing with the demands of creative and powerful people.

KB: You've also been a Supervising Sound Editor, can you tell me what that role entails?

MI: A Supervising Sound Editor prepares the sound editorial budget based on the post production schedule, hires the crew, supervises the crew, usually also performs the task of ADR supervisor or SFX supervisor, edits sound, supervises the final mix and temp mixes, oversees the delivery process, and checks sound on the release prints.

KB: With budgets changing all the time, (and seemingly getting smaller), what is the biggest change you have seen in post-production sound over the last few years?

MI: Crews are getting smaller. When I started in 1986 there were around twenty people on a sound crew. The last movie I supervised we had five core people with a couple of people helping out during crunch time. We have to work really hard now. Not so much time for schmoozing like in the old days.

KB: Do you believe that sound gets no respect until Post-Production?

MI: Sometimes sound doesn't even get respect during Post-Production. Often, so much of the budget gets spent before post that you really have to fight for what you need to make a good sound track.

KB: You have worked on a lot of different types of films with all kinds of budgets. Do you approach a larger budgeted studio film like X-MEN or THE X-FILES differently than you would a small independent film?

MI: Yes, because of different crew sizes and different

expectations. On a big Effects film you have more to play with. You can be more imaginative. On a smaller movie our mandate is usually to make it sound like the picture's editor's track as much as possible - very little ADR, they usually like the SFX they've been using, etc.

KB: What is the most common sound problem that you encounter?

MI: Badly recorded production sound - usually an over reliance on body mics, not enough boom mics used, or they didn't get close enough or record it at a proper level.

KB: What's the worst post problem you've ever encountered and how did you fix it?

MI: A conversation in a car - the windows were open and every line of dialogue had a loud "car by" which obscured the dialogue. Some lines were inaudible. We looped the whole scene.

KB: If you were the director what would you do differently as far as sound?

MI: I would give the production sound mixer ample time to get a good recording - ask him to hang boom mics whenever possible. Also, if it's a scene where there's a special sound situation, i.e. a crowd reaction, I would give the mixer time to record wild tracks.

KB: What is your best advice to filmmakers?

MI: Get good production sound recordings! It's the best thing you can do to save yourself millions of headaches later on.

KB: A lot of film students ask me how they can get in to post, what would you tell them?

MI: Get good at post while at school - learn Pro Tools, learn professional editing room protocols if possible, get good at sound editing, learn about mixing, and then find someone to intern with.

KB: Can you think of anything else that would be good for students to know?

MI: If you can figure out what you want to do (besides direct) and aim for that you'll move ahead much faster. For example, if a student came up to me and said they wanted to be a dialogue editor (instead of "I want to work in film"), I would have a much clearer idea of how I could help them.

Dianna Stirpe

"If a film is well recorded, production sound is priceless."

I met Dianna through mutual friends and almost immediately we had a great conversation about writing, art, Iowa, Portland, Oregon and San Francisco. I don't think we talked about film until much later. I knew she was a friend of Jim LeBrecht's who had just re-located to Portland and that was good enough for me. The sound business is like a very small high school and if a friend says you should meet someone, then you do. It was later that I found out that she had been a dialogue and ADR editor in the Bay Area for quite awhile before she moved to Iowa to attend the Iowa Writers Workshop.

Dianna is quite unassuming, until you start looking at her credits. She has worked on "little films" like FORREST GUMP, THE ENGLISH PATIENT, THE RAINMAKER, THE TALENTED MR. RIPLEY, and lots of others, and she cut quite a few episodes of THE ADVENTURES OF YOUNG INDIANA JONES. She has been a dialogue editor as well as an ADR editor and I'm sure she's cut quite a few effects in her day.

We've become good friends and her input has been invaluable on this book.

If you want to know more about Dianna Stirpe check out: http://www.imdb.com/name/nm0830572/

KB: How did you get involved with film in the first place, and then sound editing?

DS: Hmm, a convoluted story. My awareness of sound probably

began in high school, though I'm not certain I realized it at the time. I spent a lot of hours under headphones, like many of us, listening to music. And I stayed out very late at concerts and clubs, or slouched in the corner of mix studios during overnight recording sessions. I worked backstage at concerts too, when I was about fifteen or sixteen (I don't think they knew how old I was), so I watched how they set up each gig, what the challenges were. I sometimes dreamed of being the one behind the mixing board, but the music business was enormously unwelcome to any woman who wasn't either a sexy lead singer or a sexy girlfriend on the arm of her musician boyfriend. I was certainly neither. And I didn't have a thick enough skin to fight for more. It seemed too tough a road for me to take then.

Just about all the time I wasn't either in school or doing that, I spent in independent movie theaters, soaking up runs of European or experimental art films. Anything by Wim Wenders or Francois Truffaut or John Cassavetes, I was there. When I headed into art school later, I learned something of the fine arts but mostly I took classes in both film and sound. I remember one class assignment entailed compiling an audio-only short that contained no dialogue, but told a story. It was my first time playing with sound and I had great fun. A never-ending ringing telephone played a huge part in my plot - truly thrilling stuff. I think I envisioned myself eventually living a deeply creative life, poring over experimental or political-activist films that I would make in obscurity.

But, like the best and worst of us, I needed a job. I did music retail and distribution right out of high school, before art school, but a few years later I was able to nab an office/production assistant job in a small company that produced music videos, commercials, that sort of thing, right about the time that MTV was exploding. And, soon after, the first Macintosh computers came onto the scene. I helped with this company's productions, and I learned a ton about everything from brainstorming concepts to budgeting to final online and mix sessions. They produced a small independent feature too, back when "independent" truly meant independent. And I learned how to work on Macs there, which helped me a lot later on. I felt lucky, to learn so much about the whole process with them, both technically and creatively, and in a relatively short span of time.

Sound kept rearing its head, though. And I kept craving more feature or documentary work. I heard more and more about the reputation of the Bay Area sound editors - at Skywalker, Saul Zaentz, and the like - and I decided to aim for that, partly for my interest in sound but also just to get more steady work on bigger projects. The storytelling nature of features was a big lure. I hammered away at that door into features for a long while and, eventually, thanks to the big heart and supportive nature of Vivien Hillgrove [picture editor and, then, sometimes sound supervisor], I got my first apprenticeship on THE UNBEARABLE LIGHTNESS OF BEING. That started me into almost exclusively going for sound jobs and, even though I wandered back into production and other realms since then, sound became the most predominant, most specialized skill in my film career.

KB: Is there a particular film (or films) that were a big influence on you when you started?

DS: When I started, it felt like everything affected me, since the film medium is so absorbing. But I don't think I quite understood what I was hearing or seeing in any film. Not enough to explain any of it back then, anyway. Scenes from several films have stuck with me - in some obscure French feature from the mid-70s, a woman in a bulky red sweater sitting on the floor just below an open window, hugging her knees and sobbing, the sunlight falling on her hair and the very subtle melding of the sound of the wind lightly buffeting the house with the sound of her crying, it was like a living landscape in a painting to me. I couldn't tell you the title of that film or what else happened in it or why that specific moment stayed in my head, but that might have been one of my first conscious recognitions of the visual and aural together in equal measure. Subtleties like that can be just as moving as the big stuff.

I think, when you view a film, if you have any susceptibility to the medium at all, you are affected by much of it unconsciously. All interesting or evocative art does that. So it's difficult to identify which film or films in particular influenced me. On some level, probably they all influenced me. Even though those early art-house films still stick with me, I did not at the time stand up and scream "this is an incredible use of sound" or "this is great filmmaking." I simply felt something somewhere other than my head and it resonated. And I loved that. Still do.

KB: You have worked as a dialogue editor and an ADR editor. What exactly does a dialogue editor do?

DS: Dialogue editing is about cleaning up and smoothing out what is there in the original production sound recordings, and doing what's needed to enable the dialogue mixer to move through the material and easily incorporate ADR options wherever necessary. Sometimes an original sync take is a beloved performance, but it has a flaw in its recording - a mic bump or a jet overhead or a dolly creak, some unwanted glitch. Since that flaw usually distracts, a dialogue editor needs to either clean up or cut (if possible) alternate takes of that area that could be seamlessly cheated in so the original, beloved performance isn't entirely lost. Mostly, it's all about making the production sound as clear to understand and as seamlessly presented as can be, before a mixer hones it further.

KB: What does an ADR editor do?

DS: Production takes that cannot be saved with other production cheats, or any takes that the director wishes could be different for whatever reason, all need to be re-recorded and replaced. ADR editors work with those re-recordings, shoving them into a sync that can work. They also flesh out scenes with recordings of other vocals, like extra lines that weren't originally scripted, loop group background voices, beds of crowds and such.

One function of ADR that can be a little more complicated is working in new lines that change or further develop areas of a script. On a few of Anthony Minghella's films, like THE ENGLISH PATIENT and THE TALENTED MR. RIPLEY, he ran into areas of his final cut where, if one off-screen character could just say one perfectly crafted new line, it would turn the focus of the scene on its head, or even mildly better explain something the original script didn't quite explain as well as it could have. Anthony worked with his picture editor Walter Murch to create the opportunities for such placements, and with his ADR editor Mark Levinson, who also loved to write, to come up with additional lines that could enhance or refine a scene. When it worked, it was masterful.

Ultimately, just like with almost all other facets of filmmaking, an ADR editor's work is all about believability. Is this re-recorded performance, which was done in a recording studio months after the shooting has stopped and all the other actors have gone home, which I as an editor have pitched and squeezed and folded up and tweaked, is it going to mask itself beautifully enough that no one will ever notice that it's not the original performance? It's a con artist's game. Good ADR editors know how to manipulate something into complete, or at least unremarkable, believability. Film, of course, is all about taking apart what's real, duplicating each component of someone's notion of that reality in a mostly manufactured or semi-controlled setting, and putting it all back together in a more elaborate and almost more persuasive version of itself. It's quite a task. This is the reason for that endless scroll of credits at the end of many films.

Each director, each budget, each production is different. No one should compare a big-budget feature containing complex action sequences or layers of added lines and loop group, with a simple, low-budget four-person narrative recorded in only one or two locations well enough to allow for use of almost all of the original production performances. There is just no formula to it.

If a film is well recorded (or even mostly well recorded), production sound is priceless. Performances done by an actor in the moment are often threaded with an energy and accuracy that can be very difficult to replicate in a recording studio later. Some actors are experts at ADR and can add something extra to their own performances, and it's a joy to watch them in action, but I find that often ADR performances shift just enough that they don't feel even half as strong as the original. It can be too hard for an actor - especially for beginning actors - to match that spark they had on set, let alone get anywhere close to workable sync. As a dialogue editor, if a line is slated to be replaced purely for technical reasons, I always try to find alternate production takes of it to include in my tracks, just in case an ADR version of it doesn't quite wow the director.

Another note on production performances, you might run into instances where the production take is truly impossible to replicate, no matter how good the actor is at ADR. I had one scene in FORREST GUMP - when Robin Wright is throwing rocks at her old house and basically letting loose on all that had happened to her in her childhood. As she threw those stones, she kept bumping her radio mic, so there were bad mic bumps and rustles throughout the entire chosen take. But her performance was too good. No one, least of all the director, wanted to go into a recording studio and try to get Robin Wright to cry and breathe and fight herself through that scene again. It would undoubtedly never match the magnitude of her original performance. So the sound supervisor had me cut out all of the mic bumps and rustles. Now, it may sound somewhat simple with today's electronic editing, but this was back in the film-and-tape days. I had to cut all this in mag, with all the splices and tiny bits of filler I had to fit in to keep the whole thing in sync. This very short section must have ended up with twenty or thirty splices in it - I can't remember. Managing to keep all those splices from creating audible bumps as they traveled over the sound heads was a challenge. But it worked, in the end. The director made the right choice to keep production. It never would have been better than what Robin had done that day on location.

Getting back to your original question . . . beyond whatever you choose to add in for vocal fillers like loop group, et cetera, how many lines you ADR is all about whether something you hear - as a director or as a viewer - distracts or takes you out of the moment or makes you too conscious of a mistake. If something does, and you have the budget to do so, you can try to replace it with ADR and see if that works better. But if the ADR distracts just as much, it may be better to keep with production or try a production alternate. Again, it's all about believability.

KB: What's the difference between working on an action film like K-19: THE WIDOWMAKER or one of the YOUNG INDY TV shows as compared with something like THE TALENTED MR. RIPLEY or THE RAINMAKER? (Action films vs. smaller dialogue driven films)

DS: Actually, I'm not certain I would call K-19 a true action film. It's certainly suspenseful and there are moments of intensity and dramatic intrigue, but a lot of the dialogue moments carried the plot. And the YOUNG INDY TV series had a lot less action in it than the original Indiana Jones movies. But I've worked on a few bigger horror/sci-fi films [MIMIC,

SPECIES, THE HUNTED] with lots of monster mayhem and large swaths of reels devoted to special effects or stylized vocalizations. On these films, the dialogue editor has to make any usable production dialogue as clean as they can and, everywhere else, just get out of the way. Production sound effects are almost always dropped from big action sequences, so usually I don't spend much or any time on them. And it's a given that many production dialogue lines, even if they seem clear and perfectly usable when listened to on their own under headphones, will end up being replaced by ADR just because they have to compete too hard with all the other sounds that will end up in an action scene. A mixer has to push up the dialogue so far to match how loud and layered the sound effects and music get in the final mix, that they often have to go with the closer-recorded ADR versions regardless. But unless you're told specifically not to, dialogue editors prepare all production so the choice of whether or not to use something can be made later by the director.

Diverging for a bit here . . . I worked on one film that progressively escalated in intensity from beginning to end, and the mixers discovered maybe nine-tenths of the way into the final mix, that they had escalated everything so much with each new reel that they had literally nowhere else to go. Few of the sound editors wanted to sit in that mix room while the mixers worked, it had become so unbearably loud. But mixers' ears can sometimes grow numb after sitting with everything that loud day after day. They ended up having to go back to reel one and temper the entire progression all the way through to save both everyone's hearing and the studio's equipment.

In contrast, something like a dialogue-centric film concentrates mostly on the original performances and the storyline. Each delivery of dialogue contributes to the story, so you want each line to hold itself above any other distracting tone or effect, be the point of the scene and not something a viewer has to reach for. And you want it all to reflect the best of what every scene is about. Editors should get rid of any problems as best they can, and simply aim to give the directors and mixers all the options they might need later.

KB: What makes a good Dialogue Editor and a good ADR Editor?

DS: Attention to detail. And a good eye-to-ear sense - knowing if the sound fits what you're seeing. And that's about more than just knowing sync when you see it.

But attention to detail is foremost. I might say that's true of almost all other areas of filmmaking, though. Dialogue and ADR are not only about the details, but it helps if you have a personality that is naturally driven to dig into the smallest anomalies and finesse them into whatever will make each element, each line, each scene its best.

I think that can make filmmaking a real challenge for some people. I've met a lot of folks who desperately want to make films or work in film, perhaps because they have an idea of how creative or exciting or prestigious the work could be, but I think many of the most successful filmmakers tend to possess the type of diverse personality that can both focus in on and decipher some of the most intricate details while also being easily able to keep in mind the larger perspective and their own vision of an entire project. It's a singular yet comprehensive perspective. Filmmaking requires both at once, a great range of view and a great deal of versatility, along with pure gut instinct. Plus, the ability to communicate those things to others, since other people have to help you make those ideas happen.

KB: Talk about how you manage a project from beginning to end? Do you spot the film for ADR or is it done for you, setting up the sessions, directing the sessions - what are you looking for - performance or sync?

DS: It depends a bit on the expectations of a supervisor or filmmaker, and upon the budget. If I'm editing, I'm usually given my allotted reels that I spot with the supervisor (whether I'm editing dialogue, ADR, or both), and eventually all the ADR lists to help me know which lines to split, what's important to work on. I just plow through each reel as I get them. Adapting my cut tracks for changes made later by the picture department can sometimes be a challenge but it's usually all in a day's work, so to speak. Frankly, it's just methodical, detailed work.

If I'm supervising, of course I spot all the reels with the director, to see what that person's goals are, what sticks out for them as needing specific work, relate what sticks out for me, and in doing that I usually glean what that director already understands about the capabilities of sound and how adventurous they want to or can afford to be. And I get a sense of how involved they wish to be in the details of the whole process.

Setting up ADR recording sessions has always been done for me, but once I get to the recording studio I try to create a relaxed, respectful dynamic with any actors involved. If the director is hands-on during the session, I tend to my line lists and notes and let my attention be more on whether each re-recorded delivery is close enough to what we need or whether there are technical problems during the recording. It helps if a director is able to be there to guide an actor's performance, because that director knows better than anyone what he or she wants. I usually only interject my ideas as to performance if I feel the approach is too far from what we'll have to match in the rest of the scene.

If I'm left to direct an ADR session myself, I balance between guiding the actor for the performance I feel we need, being articulate in my instructions from an actor's perspective (because they don't hear what I hear and they don't approach these sessions with the same priorities I do), following whatever instructions the director has given me beforehand, and - most importantly - paying attention to whether I'm burning out an actor with needless re-takes. Even if sometimes you are not quite certain you have everything you need, sometimes you must simply move on and make do with the components you have. To be any good at directing ADR sessions, I think you have to have developed an ear for those performance and technical issues, understand how to articulate what you are looking for, and understand when to stop fussing. That kind of acuity only comes with experience.

KB: Do you have any tricks with ADR to make it match better?

DS: I'm one of those people who always hears the flaws in ADR. I'm impatient with it. I can't help it. I forever notice its imperfections. If I get stuck hearing everything wrong about a take, I'll have someone else listen to it for me, and it's usually better than I am imagining. Only once in a very blue moon will something reach out and bonk me between the ears and I'll know it's dead-on. And then you feel ridiculously proud of yourself.

One piece of advice: don't be scared to take a line apart into syllables and play with each element slightly differently. Editing technologies today allow for all kinds of play, and if you know how to use that technology well, and don't get carried away with it, you can surprise yourself at how much better you can make both the sync and the pitch. But if you do a lot of this, leave those versions alone for a while and go back to listen to them with fresh ears, because you just can't tell how contorted or utterly weird you've made something until you can hear it anew.

KB: How often is the director around when you are pre-mixing the dialogue or the ADR?

DS: Usually, unless there are picture or visual-effects problems that demand their attention, or the director is already busy on their next film, I've found that most of them like to at least drop in during the premixing. If there are two premixes in action at once, the director might bounce between two stages. It's good to have a director there at least intermittently, especially if there are a lot of ADR choices to be made. If the director can't be there for a premix, we usually carry along the best ADR takes along with any production alternates for the director to decide on later, but delaying those choices until the final mix, when there are usually complex music and sound effects issues to face as well, can make the final mix one step more complicated than it needs to be. But it all gets done in the end, no matter what.

My experience with ADR recording is that the directors more often than not have been in the session or direct the session from a remote location over the wires. It's the smaller name actors or the loop group sessions that I've usually been left to corral on my own.

KB: When you work with someone like Walter Murch who is both an editor and many times the re-recording mixer do you take a different approach to your work, is he looking for different things?

DS: Every single one of us hears and sees things differently. Walter has distinctive ways of viewing just about everything. I'm not certain I take a different approach to my own work as an editor when working with him, but I suppose I try to anticipate what will be more important to him. I aim to just give him all the options I think he might desire, so he can do what he hopes to do, without having to ask repeatedly for more from me. I'll say also that, when you've worked with someone several times, you begin to notice what they notice. Not always, but it's interesting when you do. I enjoy that part. We all get to rub off on each other a little. For good or ill!

I think Walter's evolved in his approach to sound over time too. Not that I would dare to try to quantify how, but a while back I began to notice slight changes in the way he treats some things that he might have treated somewhat differently years before. Perhaps that is what all of us should always hope for, a continuing evolution in our own approach.

KB: Can you explain what Group ADR (or Loop Group) is? How does that help a film?

DS: Oh, we've all heard those ridiculous background voices slopped into ancient foreign films that sound too loud and too closely present to be real - those hordes of fighting Romans or spaghetti-western cowboys in cheesy action films of the 60s and 70s. That's really awful loop group.

When a film crew sets up, say, to shoot a scene in an outdoor café where the leading actor and actress are supposed to have a fight, in public, over breakfast - banal example, I know, but here we go. All the secondary actors and extras in the background are told to keep quiet in order to make sure the production sound recordist can get the best possible recording of the main actors' dialogue. Extras walk by in the background pretending to be in avid discussion with one another, or other diners sitting nearby mouth the words to imagined conversations to appear as if they're all talking in truth - lip flap. Some lower budget filmmakers go ahead and let a few background actors mutter away, but more often it's easier for the dialogue mixer if it's all kept quiet on the set, except for the main ensemble.

So, when we sound mavens get down to premixing that sort of scene, after the dialogue mixer has finessed the couple's production dialogue to perfection, and possibly replaced a line or two (or maybe none!) of an actor's dialogue with an ADR version, we then need to add in a few layers of cut loop-group tracks. All kinds of loop groupers have been previously gathered into couples or large groups, or whatever suits the scene, and recorded in a studio (or sometimes the great outdoors, as needed). They chatter up wonderfully innocuous café-style conversations amongst themselves. The ADR editor usually knows how dense the mix should be, based on the scene - how many people are truly sitting in the background in that café, and how many, realistically, are all talking at once. You might do a number of two-person interchanges, then one larger group pass of four or more people talking at once, if the background contains a lot more people, then maybe a run of a few waiters or waitresses talking about what they would normally talk about, and then a few walk-by conversations from the people that might have walked by on the sidewalk in the background . . . if those people appear to be talking when they're on camera. You record whatever you think the scene is lacking, and all this is what you spot for in detail when you do your initial spotting of the film for ADR. You just have to match the density of what each scene contains. Of course, a scene shot in a stadium, with a crowd of thousands, requires a whole other approach.

If it's a true low-budget film, though, the production sound recordist on that café set may be wise enough and be given the chance to record the café crowd in a separate non-sync wild take, with the lead actors either gone or just sitting there silently. The entire cast can run through the same scene, but just not deliver any dialogue lines. This way the production ends up with some quick-and-easy loop group for the scene, along with a bit of possibly helpful ambient sounds, without having to book a studio or loop groupers later on to record it.

In their cut tracks, ADR editors layer in all of these original or re-recorded café conversations however densely until everything feels realistic and the dialogue mixer then can play with them during the premix. Keeping loop group voices separate like this allows the mixer to manipulate each element separately, which is probably the single most important help you can give a mixer.

KB: Do you believe that sound gets no respect until Post-Production?

DS: Frankly, even in post-production, sound can be considered an annoyance for some people. Not often, but some people just don't feel it's as crucial as everything else in a film's construction. Our brains are wired to respond more strongly to visual over aural, every time, so I can't blame anyone, but once a person begins to hear and understand how much sound influences their film, once a director who has never before really known how to use sound and then discovers what a post sound crew can do, there's no turning back. I've never seen a director, once they go through that experience, then decide to back away from it.

A reluctance to use sound to its best advantage can also depend on other factors. If the film is behind schedule or running way over budget, post sound can sometimes be where the producers suddenly hope to make up the difference. I've also seen directors who are just tired of living with the same material for so long and eager to move on to the next project, or even just a well-needed vacation, so they end up not caring or noticing much about the sound. That's a rarity, because just about every director wants to make the best film they can make, but it happens.

I do think things are changing fast. More and more filmmakers are recognizing just how much sound contributes, even though a great many of those same filmmakers still primarily consider sound only in terms of showy sound effects or music. Often, when I say I work in sound, or even more specifically say I cut dialogue, people outside the industry automatically think that means I cut music for film scores. Or I cut all the flashy sound effects they keep hearing so much about - sound design. They have no concept of anything else. There is a whole lot more to it that few truly get.

Of course, as someone who enjoys language immensely and is perfectly happy with my dialogue tracks, I feel the quality of a dialogue-driven soundtrack is just as valuable to a film's success creatively as all the explosions and metal scrapes and blood spatters and crescendos of music. Hey, take out all the dialogue from a film and what do you have? There is no story there, or at best only an imagined fragment of one. I think what we all crave, at our core, is a great story. It's probably another thing our brains are wired for. Who knows why, but I can't think of anyone who doesn't enjoy a good story. Sure, we also love the pure sensational and emotional exhilaration of all the rest, but the best films are really all about the story. Aren't they? Be honest with yourself. And yeah, I can have fun at a testosterone party just as much as the next gal, but sometimes it's just plain tiresome. I want to sit down somewhere quiet and have someone whisper something delightful into my ear.

KB: If you were looking for an ADR Editor what would be the important things you would want to know about them and/or their work?

DS: You need to know techniques of the editing software, certainly, and you must have an ear for making things sync, which usually takes a whole lot of practice. Some people have that talent more inherently than others. But I think it's also very important to have the ability to work comfortably with actors and directors, which not all editors have a good handle on. There are certain personalities who do well in those settings and others who do better in more technically driven environments. As with anything in life, you're better off knowing your own strengths and playing to them.

KB: You have worked on a lot of different types of films with all kinds of budgets. Do you approach a larger budgeted studio film differently than you would a small independent film?

DS: Absolutely. I learned that lesson early on, embarrassingly so, when I wasted money on buying items for a low-budget documentary that I didn't really need, just because I had grown too used to the bigger-budget projects. I kicked myself a long time for that one. Especially since the producer was working on such a good cause and did not deserve to have her funding squandered.

Everything is different - on a lower budget project the money sometimes comes in fits and starts, because funding can be staggered. The time you have to do the work can be fragmented or shortened, or come in fits and starts that reflect the money. The experience levels of the crew vary and, therefore, sometimes the quality of the sound recordings or the mixing isn't as good as you wish it could be, or maybe as consistent. The experience of the director and producers can be varied too, as to what it is they are hearing, or whether they can even articulate what it is they are looking for. Just everything. If you work in both realms, you learn what's important to each and try hard not to impose one working style over another. It's all too obvious once you get in there.

KB: What is the most common sound problem that you encounter?

DS: On some of the lower budget projects and documentaries, I would say it's often mic placement and background noise. On the higher budget features, a lot of the problems can be fixed because they often have the money to do so, but I suppose one - and this is certainly not a frequent problem - is the inability sometimes of a director to hear the subtleties in or even recall the importance of their own production tracks. They've been listening to the picture cut's sync tracks for month after month, so they begin to take for granted what they've been hearing. Sometimes this means they don't recognize why or how it could be better, or even think anything should change from how they've been hearing it for so long. It can be hard for any of us to see the same ol' face in the mirror every single day and try suddenly to see ourselves with new eyes . . . or ears. I guess I've had some trouble with digital production recordings a time or two as well - technical issues that came up because the equipment and its limitations or its quirks weren't well known to the sound recordist at the time of the recording. But those issues are usually ironed out with a little work.

KB: If you were the director what would you do differently as far as sound?

DS: Ah, tough question! It's so much easier to critique someone else's work than it is to produce your own, isn't it?

I suppose I might try to lighten up the load. I mean, I think a lot of soundtracks are overcrowded these days. And not just with the very best combination of sounds, but with everything, as if it's all become one big expensive soup of whatever anyone wishes to throw in there. Just because they can. And everyone does love to throw something in there.

Sound long ago became a grand manipulator, too, and even though that's somewhat inevitable, I dislike that trend. As viewers, many of us now expect to have either all of our heartstrings yanked or every ounce of our adrenalin pumping throughout every film-going experience. I tend to prefer more intricate ideas. They are always more effective for me. It's all a matter of personal taste, of course, and at times thick layers of rampant sound are just what a particular film requires.

Also, I'll say that it's dangerous to just do what an industry has been doing only because everyone has become used to hearing things always done that way. Being alert and inventive enough with each new project, to approach each one as its own beast, is what I'd like to think, as a director, I'd be able to do. I'd also hope that I could have the fortitude to listen to many different ideas from the people at work on the sound, because I do think there are a lot of good ideas out there and, regrettably, not all of them can be mine!

KB: What is your best advice to filmmakers?

DS: It seems absurdly boring to say it, but just listen. Pure and simple. Unless you're a prodigy of one kind or another, most of us don't grow up naturally learning how to pay attention to what we hear as much as we pay attention to what we see. But hearing is an enormously influential, powerful sense. Listen to the soundtracks of all your favorite films and figure out what in particular about the sound contributes to why you like that film so much. Maybe you won't find anything and maybe, then, that tells you how ignorant to sound you are. Sometimes it takes a concerted effort to really hear what's there, or even identify why it's effective. We can all easily pinpoint mistakes, the glaring things that can't help but show us that something doesn't fit. But can we also recognize what's working, what's superbly helping that scene become richer and, in essence, better?

You know how, in film school - in some film schools, anyway - they give you that exercise to turn down the soundtrack of a film and just watch the images go by. It's often to show you how the picture cuts work or don't work, how the editor paced a piece. Clumsy picture editing can become more apparent when you do this. But I also think this exercise shows how essential sound is to telling any story. If you did the reverse - closed your eyes and only listened to a film's soundtrack - you can almost always follow the nugget of a story with just the sound. You lose important facial expressions, body language, and maybe the texture of a landscape. But how much can you hear? Sure, this includes the ambient sounds and the effects, the rain falling, or the car-bys and the door slams. But it's also the elaborate ways in which we each speak to each other. Language can say so much about who we are, if we only pay attention. Just like body language, we each have inflections and rhythms that say so much more than we often realize.

Also, as you listen, there is so much your head and heart - and maybe even your skin - reacts to with sound. It's much more subliminal. And, sometimes the best sound is remarkably simple. Today, we are all so filled with experiential expectation, so in love with being distracted, or amused, or entertained by every single thing we encounter at every moment of our day. Sitting still and hearing how the tone and rhythm of someone's voice reflects or how quiet sounds can determine an entire mood just as much as the more elaborate, overly present ones - that can all be just as important to understanding anything.

KB: Can you think of anything else that would be good for students to know?

DS: Not a damn thing. Most, if not all, of the best things we learn, we learn by experience. So I'd say just get going. Find all the ways you can discover more of these things yourself, or develop your own ideas. There may be methods developed over much time and experience that work extremely well and should be learned, if you wish to be successful in filmmaking, but there is also always room for innovation in any craft or art. And learn too by collaboration, I would add, because even if you're the sort of person who prefers to work alone, sometimes a tiny little bit of perspective can give a world of help to an idea.

CHAPTER 5:

Turn It Up!

Music Editor

We all know the effect that music can have in a film. We have memories of favorite scenes where the music worked perfectly. Think about the running scenes in CHARIOTS OF FIRE, the dance scenes in DIRTY DANCING or any scene in AMADEUS. There are some movies where we remember the music better than the film itself. And certain songs are timeless because of their use in a film.

It is usually the music editor that has to walk that fine line between the wishes of the composer and giving the director what they want.

I worked on a film where we moved the music around to different scenes than what the composer had intended them. The composer didn't have a problem with this, she realized by moving some of her music it gave those scenes a greater emotional impact.

On another film I was on, the music editor fought so hard for the music and to keep turning it up louder (after awhile we had to strain to hear the dialogue), that they eventually fought themselves out of a job.

I wonder if filmmakers are using music in the right ways these days? There seems to be an over-reliance on music to tell the audience how to respond emotionally to a scene instead of letting the actors convey that emotion through their performance.

I think many filmmakers are taking the easy way out with music. As filmmakers we manipulate the audience through sound, but when you rely on music to do that you are telling the audience exactly what to think instead of letting them come to their own conclusions. If your character is supposed to be lonely, instead of using a song that tells us they are lonely, why not surround your characters with quiet? Or maybe a distant train whistle, or a lonely wind? Show us isolation and a stark, empty audio track. Don't tell us what people are feeling with music, find new and different ways to show us.

I believe that the more music you use in a film the less impact it has.

Well-placed music can evoke mood, tip the audience off that something is about to happen, or it can make you laugh. The music must feel integral to the film and in that way it can live on in our memories.

Ken Karman

"I would rather see no music than music used improperly."

I have been lucky enough to work with Ken on a couple of films, GOOD WILL HUNTING and FINDING FORRESTER. He is easily my favorite music editor because of what he brings to the table. He has an amazing knowledge of not just music but sound in general and he's easily one of the mellowest people I've ever worked with. I have never seen him pull rank on an assistant and if you're having a problem with your own system he'll do what he can to help you out.

On FINDING FORRESTER, Ken got to work without a composer and the editing of the music is brilliant. The way he worked with the tracks by Miles Davis and Bill Frisell really brought the music and the film to life. I still listen to the sound of that film all the time. Ken is one of those guys when you find out he's on a film with you he makes everything more pleasant.

His credits include: WHO FRAMED ROGER RABBIT, THIS IS SPINAL TAP, FORREST GUMP, GOOD WILL HUNTING, PIRATES OF THE CARIBBEAN: CURSE OF THE BLACK PEARL, MEMOIRS OF A GEISHA, BACK TO THE FUTURE 1, 2, & 3, MILK, and so many more. His career has spanned more than thirty years and yet he is one of the youngest guys I know when it comes to attitude.

If you want to know more about Ken Karman check out:
http://www.imdb.com/name/nm0439741/

KB: Shall we talk a little bit about sound? How did you get in to the business?

KK: Well, I dropped out of high school in my senior year and needed a job. I was vaguely interested in film, but didn't really understand anything about the process. Elsa Blanksted, a friend of my family happened to be a prominent music editor and was kind enough to introduce me to some of her associates in post-production. This led to my first job as a driver for a sound effects house called Edit International. It was 1970, I was nineteen and thrilled to be able to afford gas money and my own apartment. I was also enchanted with the world of editing. Even as a driver, I was exposed to all the secrets of bringing a film to life. The Foley stage, in particular, blew my mind! Of course, this was before digital editing. The union was more powerful back then and mandated a rather burdensome series of steps one had to take before being able to even touch film, much less edit it. When the job at E.I. ended I was hired by a non-union production company that produced product films and for Chrysler Corporation. The post arm of this company was run by two music editors, Jim Henrikson and Dan Carlin Sr. They were true mentors and it wasn't long before I was editing film, sound, and music for them. I learned an awful lot in a short period of time in that place.

Eventually, Dan opened La Da Productions, the first post house devoted solely to music editing. He invited me to join him and I eventually did. The truth is that back then, nobody really knew what music editors did, which was convenient because I didn't either. It was a wild and wooly time in the early days of La Da. There was so much work, and so few music editors, that you could be promoted from driver to apprentice to full-fledged editor in the space of a couple of weeks! One day you were cleaning splicers, the next day you were on the dubbing stage with a major motion picture! A lot of music editors started their careers with Dan - Bob Badami, Curt Sobel, and Jeff Carson to name a few.

KB: Did you ever want to go back to picture editing, or was music editing the thing you enjoyed the most?

KK: I harbored that notion for a while, but I liked the fact that, as a music editor, you could have somewhat more of a life than a film editor, which requires total immersion for up to a year and more. And, not only did I love the job, but the phones have never really stopped ringing. I don't think I've looked for a job in thirty-five years so that's a good reason to keep going too.

KB: When you first started is there a particular film that was a big influence on you?

KK: The 70s was a golden age of cinema - THE CONVERSATION, KLUTE, MARATHON MAN, CHINATOWN, and ALL THAT JAZZ. These films all inspired me, but not necessarily in terms of my profession. I was young, my salary was a hundred dollars a week and my rent was eighty-five dollars a month. I was a happy guy. I was rich! I don't think I ever said, "I want to be a music editor." I just suddenly was.

KB: Have you ever watched a film and wished you had worked on it?

KK: Absolutely. Dammit! BOOGIE NIGHTS stands out. The use of music in that film is just so intelligent, exhilarating . . . really fantastic. It informs the action and captures the era perfectly. Martin Scorsese puts music together in an anachronistic way that just blows me away. Michael Mann and Quentin Tarantino are also fearless in their use of music. There's a film from the early 70s called O' LUCKY MAN. It's a Lindsay Anderson film that incorporates original songs into the storytelling in a way that I've never seen equaled. I really love that film.

KB: That is an amazing film, I have the soundtrack for it.

KK: Yeah, it's great! The songs all stand on their own. Alan Price, the keyboard player for the Animals was the composer. In the middle of the movie, he and his band become swept up in the story. The concert finale of O' LUCKY MAN is fantastic.

KB: I think anyone interested in filmmaking needs to see O' LUCKY MAN.

Do you think good sound is important?

KK: I think it's absolutely essential. Basically, my first look at every film is with little or no sound. After all this time, it's still tough to get used to. As much as you try to overlook the missing elements, you can only suspend your sense of disbelief so far. Even music tends to flatten out without the support of good sound effects and sound design. I just saw a work-in-progress film that my daughter and a group of fellow actors self-produced called THE FALL OF 1980. It was a very good film but really suffered from the lack of a complete sound job. The missing backgrounds, specifically, marked the production as incomplete.

Good sound can focus your attention on what's being said and why. It can help establish time and place as well as underscore every emotional element that the filmmakers are trying to express. It is, in my opinion, equally important to every other aspect of film post-production. Obviously music can be extremely powerful, but can also be subject to misuse and overuse. I think a restrained use of underscore is important. I would rather see no music than music used improperly.

KB: As a Music Editor at what stage do you usually come on to a film?

KK: Generally, a music editor will come on board near the completion of the director's cut when there tends to be a lot of focus on getting the film ready to screen for the studio. Sometimes I will inherit a fairly complete temp track that the director and film editor have assembled in the Avid. They will usually have a wish list of cues that they want me to improve upon or cues that need a little editorial love.

In the case of the film I am working on now, I was handed a blank canvas . . . my favorite. The director and editor both felt that putting in music during the initial editing phase interfered with their ability to make judgments about structure and pace, so I had a real opportunity to build a consistent temp score from the ground up.

KB: On FINDING FORRESTER you were there early on because the music source was Miles Davis.

KK: Yeah . . . Gus rang me from New York and asked if I could come out for a couple of months to create a sound track based on the entire Miles Davis catalog. I thought I was dreaming! Gus, Miles, New York . . . also the fact that the work I did was going to stand as the final soundtrack. That was a rare opportunity.

KB: What was it like working with all those Miles Davis tracks?

KK: Amazing. We listened to all of it, everything we could find, and we didn't stop with Miles. We listened to a lot of great jazz, especially from the 50s and 60s. Ultimately, I relied mostly on a mix of Miles Davis and Bill Frisell, sometimes in combination. That was fun. For example, in the scene where Jamal breaks into Forrester's apartment, we created a "mash up" using a very ambient Frisell track underneath edited phrases from Sketches Of Spain. Gus let me try anything and most of it stuck. That was just a fantastic experience.

KB: Is it easier for you to work with a composer or with existing music?

KK: I like both. Working with existing music requires communication with the director. It's a lot of fun to experiment with different ways of telling a story with music and very gratifying when you can create an approach that informs the final score.

Serving a composer is a different process. Every composer has a different methodology and my job is to figure out how I can best facilitate that. Sometimes it's a technical job, sometimes a communication job, usually both. Most of my career has been spent working with Allen Silvestri and it's been a gratifying experience every time. I started with him on BACK TO THE FUTURE and I hope we'll continue together until he retires to his vineyard. Over the years, I've also worked with Thomas Newman, Danny Elfman, Cliff Eidelman, John Williams, and Hans Zimmer. But to answer your question . . . since films generally continue to change even after the score has been recorded, it's all existing music. Still, there's nothing quite as exciting as watching a ninety piece orchestra kick into gear with the movie playing behind them on a forty foot screen!

KB: The Music Department seems like an entity all its own. Sound designers have to deal with dialogue and sound effects. How do you integrate with the other members of the sound crew?

KK: Post-production sound has changed a lot over the last several years. Sound effects crews have gotten much smaller and, I have to say, those that survived the retraction are all very good. Also, the mood on the dubbing stage is much less territorial then it used to be back in the day. The music and sound departments really do work together to create an effective mix. This isn't to say that we've achieved a true integrated collaboration. Until we get to the dubbing stage, we tend to work on parallel tracks and trust that things will sort themselves out in the mix. On occasion, there will be something rhythmic in the sound design that demands that the music give way, or sync with it. That sort of thing should be worked out in advance. But generally speaking it all shakes out on the dubbing stage in a generally cooperative environment.

KB: (Said with dripping sarcasm.) You mean it wasn't always that way?

KK: Ha, it used to be like three separate encampments lobbing mortars from one end of the desk to the other. It was a major transgression for a music editor to make any comments about the sound effects and vice versa. I'm sure it had something to do with the cumbersome nature of making changes on film. One misplaced comment could open up a real can of worms. You couldn't simply hit a key on your Pro Tools and re-sync a cue . . . you had to take down the reel, set up on an editing bench . . . splicers, tape, grease pencils and sync machines. Now, of course, you can accommodate a suggestion with the push of a button and undo just as easily.

KB: My memories when mixing was that everybody would go home at night except for the music editors who always seem like they were getting tracks for the next day, that night. Do you still feel like you're constantly behind?

KK: Um . . . yes. Scoring sessions are usually scheduled as late as possible so that there's a reasonable chance of recording to a locked edit. That means that the music mix is constantly chasing the dub. Also, when a director comes up with an idea at the end of the day, you're normally expected to have it ready to preview the following morning. Small changes are pretty easy, but big conceptual ideas can require listening to hundreds of tracks and constructing a number of different approaches to the same problem. Know what I mean?

KB: All too well.

KK: It's one thing to say, "Can you make this one cue end earlier?" It's another thing to say, "I don't know, I'm just not feeling it . . ." Hmmm, okay, I'll get right on that.

KB: That's the worse thing that any sound person can hear. Did you ever mix?

KK: No, not really. In the case of a temp dub, if I've constructed something with a lot of overlapping cues, I'll do some internal volume graphing. But no, I've never been a mixer and I'm not sure I'd be good at it.

KB: When you're sitting in the mix sessions do you ever have that urge to grab the faders and say, "No, no, it's supposed to go like this!"

KK: Not so much anymore, and that goes to your earlier question. Sometimes, if you've got a cross fade that is supposed to work a certain way and requires a delicate touch you can draw it in Pro Tools. It saves everybody time and grief.

In the past, I used construct some fairly elaborate overlaps on Mag (magnetic film). I'd practice my crosses using the trim pots on the Kem (Flatbed Editing Machine) until I was confident that they would work, and then watch nervously as the dubbing mixer struggled to duplicate the same move. It usually worked out though.

I think the question goes to an essential requirement of working in a collaborative business. You really need to be sensitive to the personalities around you and to be able to communicate with them effectively.

KB: What's the biggest change you have seen in post-production?

It's all about the technology. Computerized editing, automated mixing, and digital sequencers did not exist when I started in this business. They have all allowed for fewer people to accomplish more and to do increasingly sophisticated things. The same technology has also allowed for shorter and shorter schedules. The post process is in full swing almost from the first day of shooting, and continues until the last possible second.

I hate to keep dating myself, but it used to be the case that when the pictured was turned over to sound, it was locked . . . really locked, not merely latched. Now, picture changes continue through the entire dub.

In terms of music specifically, the importance and influence of the temp music track is the biggest change of all. By the time a film is brought to preview, it's taken for granted that it will be dressed up with a pretty evolved temp track, and, for better or worse, this track usually exerts a lot of influence on the final score.

KB: With all of these changes, what's the biggest challenge that faces you now?

KK: The challenges haven't changed. The time pressure can be an issue, but you're still trying to help determine the tone and structure of the music. You're still trying to make the composer's job as smooth as possible. You're still trying to collaborate with the post team to create the best possible sound track for the film. This requires an open mind and a willingness, on occasion, to take music out when it's not helping.

KB: If you were the director, what would you do differently as far as music?

KK: That's a little tough to answer. Every director is different. In general, I wish there was a little less reliance on the temp music as a template for the final sound track. The phenomenon of "temp love" has resulted in a kind of musical inbreeding of film scores. I'd like to see composers given an opportunity to approach the score in a way that doesn't mirror what the music editor happened to stumble upon in his library on a given day. We editors joke that in the future, and the future may be now, there will be just five CD's that you can use to score any film.

KB: Do a lot of directors get totally locked in to the sound of the temp dub?

KK: Oh they absolutely do, and it's understandable. Their schedules have been compressed as well, so the more exploration they can do and the more decisions they can make about music during the editorial process, the better prepared they are to communicate with the composer. The problem is that those tracks can really worm their way into your heart in a way that's hard to get out.

KB: Do you think audiences think much about sound?

KK: Well, I think awareness of sound is greater than it has been in the past, but I don't think the general public really understands how much of the film going experience is reliant on a good sound mix. I mentioned earlier my discovery of the Foley stage. I had no idea how much of what I was hearing in the theater was manufactured, manipulated or otherwise added to the original production tracks. Ironically, I think the lack of respect for sound is most noticeable on the set! Oh my god . . . production crews have no love for music editors traipsing around their territory. I've had to do playback on location a few times. It's every man for himself, at least until they get to know you. Production is like a runaway train. It's a miracle that production recordists manage to get anything usable at all!

KB: What do you think students need to know about working with music?

KK: I would advise using it with caution, especially while you're still in the early stages of editing your film. It's a little too easy to slather a scene with cool music and convince yourself that it's working when, in fact, the music is just distracting you from problems that should be addressed editorially. You've basically turned your film into a music video.

KB: Do you feel like less is better sometimes?

KK I think less is better most of the time! If a scene is working without music then why put a hat on a hat? Using a cue where it isn't needed devalues the music where it is needed. The same thing applies to sound as a whole. It's a matter of dynamics. If everything is at eleven the whole time, the audience kind of tunes out.

KB: Along those same lines, what is the most common music problem that you encounter?

KK: Well, when I bring the music tracks on to a stage for the final dub, I take it for granted that there is going to be a lot of negotiating for sonic space. For me, the biggest impediment to a transparent soundtrack is an over abundance of layered backgrounds. Usually, sound effects have been pre-dubbing for weeks before music gets it's first run through. It can take a lot of time, not to mention diplomacy, to really explore where those background ambiances are effective and where they are simply masking the details in the music. Again, this has become less of an issue in recent years because of technology and the generally cooperative atmosphere on the stage. Action scenes, in particular, require an objective inventory of which sounds are helping and which are just muddying thing up. If I find myself holding my ears on a dubbing stage, I figure we're not doing our jobs.

KB: A lot of film students want to know how they can get in to sound, what would you tell them?

KK: It's a little more difficult than it used to be because crews have gotten much smaller and, unfortunately, Hollywood is making fewer films. Anyone interested in a career in film post-production needs to know their way around Pro Tools and, because they're likely to start at as an assistant, it's important that they have some organizational skills as well. I'd be sort of helpless without an assistant cleaning up behind me, although music editorial assistants are not all that common. Most music editors only require them for a limited time, say, to help prep for a scoring session or final dub. Having said that, it's like getting any job, it requires patience and persistence. You have to meet and interview with as many professionals as you can and keep checking in with them regularly. Modern Music has several editors who started out as drivers or techs who now have careers. It didn't happen overnight though.

KB: When you're looking for a music editor what are the important things you'd want to know?

KK: Well, I just look in the mirror! Seriously though, there are two aspects of the job and they are equally important. Assuming that an editor, or aspiring editor, knows how to use the equipment, they still have to have a feel for the interaction between picture and music. Music can be used to help tell a story, to set the dramatic tone or to simply provide energy. It's also important to understand its limitations; music can't fix everything. It's not essential that you read music, but it does help. I don't, by the way. It is essential that you are musical in the general sense of the word, though.

From my point of view, the other imperative is the ability to coexist with other creative people . . . in the cutting room, on the dubbing stage, and in the production office. You want to bring a positive attitude to every film you work on.

KB: Isn't it strange that it sounds like we have to teach people to get along?

KK: I guess, but isn't that true of all human interactions, in all businesses, and all jobs? I know some really talented music editors who don't work as much as they should because they don't have a particular gift for dealing with people.

KB: It seems like Cinematographers don't feel like they have to be able to get along with people.

KK: Well, DPs are rock stars. I can't say that applies to music editing. No aspiring starlet ever came to Hollywood to fuck the music editor . . . at least that I know of!

KB: Good point. Can you think of anything else in sound, music, or post-production that you think would be good for students to know?

KK: Well, I think it's a great job. It can be creative on a lot of levels and if you see it as an end in itself and not as a means to another job, rock star cinematographer, for example, then it can be really satisfying and reasonably well paying. Not too many job involve the overlapping aspects of technology, psychology and creativity that this job does.

KB: Do you still like what you do?

KK: Very, very much, maybe more now than ever.

CHAPTER 6:

Why Do We Need Foley?

Foley Artist

Jack Foley started working at Universal Studios in 1914 during the silent movie era. When Warner Studios released its first film to include dialogue, THE JAZZ SINGER, Universal knew it needed to get on the bandwagon and called for any employees who had experience working in radio. Jack Foley became part of the sound crew that would turn Universal's upcoming "silent" musical SHOW BOAT into the vibrant musical we know it as today.

Because the microphones used for filming could not pick up more than dialogue, other sounds had to be added in after the film was shot. Foley and his crew would project the film on a screen while recording a single track of audio that would capture their live sound effects in real time. Their timing had to be perfect so that footsteps and closing doors would sync with the actors' motions in the film. Jack Foley created sounds for films until his death in 1967. His methods are still used today but with a difference.

In live-action films the most important thing you want from

your location recordist is good clean dialogue. When they are getting that they are also picking up things like footsteps, clothing rustle and anything that they happen to be doing, opening and closing doors, sitting down, shaking hands and things like that. Many of those sounds are "married" to the dialogue track. If people are walking and talking it can be difficult to cut those footsteps out. And we expect to hear footsteps when we see people walk in film.

There are times when you are unable to hear all of the footsteps in a recording so we add more footsteps. And if you are doing a mix for a foreign version of a movie (that is going to be dubbed in to another language) you need to pull all of the dialogue out and deliver to a foreign distributor a mix of the film with just sound effects and music so they can dub in the new dialogue in a different language. As part of the FX tracks you need to add in all of the footsteps and cloth rustle that you most often associate with the dialogue track to make everything sound real. It is easier and more efficient to actually perform certain sound effects to picture and that's where Foley truly shines. A good Foley artist can replace all of the footsteps much easier than an editor can cut each step individually.

Since animated films are recorded in a studio with the actors standing next to the mics, all of the common sounds we take for granted have to be added so that when characters walk and move the audience hears "natural" sounds like footsteps and cloth rustle.

Foley has become so much more than just doing footsteps and cloth. Foley Artists can create a character's signature sound through Foley effects. Foley, like most other parts of filmmaking is most effective when you don't notice it. All of the elements have to blend in seamlessly to create the over all sound track. The contribution of Foley artists is usually over looked.

Jana Vance

"We're like the ugly evil stepchildren in the basement."

Jana Vance seems to be the busiest Foley Artist I know. And if you look at her credits with her partner Dennie Thorpe they do the Pixar films, a lot of the Lucasfilms and tons of other things that come their way. Jana (and Dennie) do both live-action and animated films and everything in between.

I got lucky to catch Jana on a Saturday morning before she and I both had too much coffee. She had some great things to say about the importance of Foley and "signature sounds" when it comes to animated characters.

Jana's credits include all the TOY STORY films, HOW TO TRAIN YOUR DRAGON, AVATAR, WALL-E, IRON MAN, ZAK AND MIRI MAKE A PORNO, THE KITE RUNNER, THE SIMPSONS MOVIE, MUNICH, THE PRIZE WINNER OF DEFIANCE, OHIO, various INDIANA JONES and STAR WARS films, HELL BOY, PUNCH DRUNK LOVE and so many more.

If you want to know more about Jana Vance check out: http://www.imdb.com/name/nm0888527/

KB: How did you get into this crazy business in the first place? Was it as a Foley Artist?

JV: Actually, I started as a Foley recordist. I had a boyfriend that was working at Skywalker Sound and they were installing the mix stages at the time. Not that this is very pertinent, but he gave me a tour, and I went into the Foley stage, and looked around, and I was like, "Wow, what is this?"

They had an opening for a Foley recordist, I applied for the job even though I didn't have any film experience but I had management experience. At that time, we weren't working with computers it was more clerical. You were the liaison between the editors, the mixer and the artists. I was also the film projectionist. I striped tape, checked the Dolby cards and set-up the mics. So I was able to observe a lot of things. Chris Boyes was my first Mixer and I learned a lot about sound dynamics. While recording Foley, he'd have me note certain cues where he wanted to push up the sound levels during playbacks. The Sound supervisor and all the editors, and occasionally directors, would be on one side of the glass, during playbacks, while we'd be frantic in the engineer's booth trying to set levels on the fly. It was pretty intense shouting out numbers and levels as the picture played on, but in the end the editors were pretty impressed and never noticed the chaos on the other side of the glass! I learned a lot from Chris.

While Chris moved on to assist Gary Rydstrom, I worked with another Foley mixer and inspiring sound designer, Tom Myers. He had a chance to sound-design six, Japanese anime pieces, called, JOJO. These half hour intense animated films were very low budget. Tom asked me if I wanted to try my hand at Foley and of course I said yes. I ended up getting the repetition down, I had good hand-eye coordination, and I was making good decisions in terms of what I was using and my approach. I started off working with Marnie Moore and then eventually with Dennie Thorpe. Dennie and I have been a Foley team close to seventeen years. I think we compliment each other in terms of style.

KB: Can you tell me exactly, what is it that a Foley Walker/Artist does?

JV: We were originally called Foley Walker's because it was mostly known for replacing footsteps. Now it's changed to Foley Artist. We do much more than replacing footsteps.

Generally speaking, we are part of the over all composite of the sound track, and we tend to add what I would call the more "intimate" sounds. Shots that are close up, someone lifts their arm and they have a dangling bracelet. We would add that, if it was wanted. In animation it's everything - footsteps, wings, creature movement, body falls. Whatever anything or anyone touches, walks on, runs on, climbs on, and swims through.

In animation we do a lot of what we call "Signature Sounds" for certain characters. We just did TOY STORY 3 not that long ago (Jana has worked on every Pixar Film) and we have a bunch of things that we use over and over, because that's the sound of Rex or the sound of Buzz Light Year. You're helping to create a character with their own unique sound, particularly in animation.

In live-action you're enhancing the total sound experience. Foley tends to be used more in close ups and intimate shots or where the director wants somebody to stand out in a crowd. You can hear that person walking by, or the rustling of a jacket as he sits down into a leather chair or takes his cigarette and lights it. You're selling that character in a more intimate way, as opposed to larger effects, ambient sounds, dialogue, or music.

KB: Let's talk about animated films, like WALL-E and TOY STORY, do you approach an animated film differently than you do a live-action film?

JV: Definitely. Of course it all depends on the director and what they want. I don't know if you saw RANGO, it's an animated film. We actually flew to LA because the director wanted to meet with us, supposedly he had a lot of information he wanted to impart to us, but in the end he just said, "Make it delicious."

KB: Now that's an easy one to work with.

JV: Yeah, make it sound delicious. RANGO takes place in the desert and Johnny Depp is a chameleon and it lends itself well to Foley because obviously you don't have any production. You can't hear a chameleon walking by in real life . . .

KB: Probably not.

JV: . . . but on a big screen, when it's an eight-foot tall chameleon, you're gonna want to hear what it's feet sound like. What do you want it to sound like? What does the director want? So for the chameleon's footsteps he wanted them to be pretty fleshy, yet very distinguishable. When he was on hard surfaces I actually used my hands, but when he moved onto the desert sand that wasn't going to read as well. So I ended up putting on light shoes to give it more weight. Those are the challenges with animation, you're making things up as to what you or the director might want it to sound like.

In A BUG'S LIFE, what does an ant sounds like? I don't know. I don't have a microphone that's that sensitive, but we can imagine, and since it's also a comedy we want to add the cute element. Animation is generally for kids and it's comedy, so it's really a blend of having something sound funny, but also realistic, the audience needs to buy it. You have to sell that creature.

KB: A lot of people think that Foley is just replacing the footsteps or clothing rustle. But in animated films you're actually performing the characters. Do you think that's accurate?

JV: I think it's definitely a performance art. You're acting to the picture. Generally Dennie (Thorpe) and I divide up the characters. As we work on the film I'm watching Buzz Light Year for instance. I'm watching everything that he does, seeing how he moves, and thinking about ways to embellish him, make him as cute as possible, as funny as possible. But sticking to his signature sound that we have come up with in the earlier movies that kids recognize. I'd like to think if they heard the sound of Buzz, out of context, they would know that it was Buzz Light Year.

KB: What special skills does it take to be a good Foley artist?

JV: I think you have to be able to handle a lot of physical intensity in terms of holding your body in ways that . . . you couldn't call it exercise. You're running in place and you've got to do a lot of shallow breathing so you don't get your breath recorded. You have to have great hand-eye coordination, and more importantly you have to have a good sense of what things sound like. Not only what they sound like in reality, but also what it is you want the audience to hear.

When we worked on AVATAR the direction on the planet Pandora (where the Avatars lived) was to make everything sound really lush. So do you want it to sound spongy? Do you want it to sound drippy? It's a foreign planet. You need to be able to think, in terms of hyper sounds, going over the top, because you are fighting often with music and effects. Not really fighting with them but figuring out where do I come in?

As someone who wants to get into Foley, you really need to know your place and be realistic about that. You need to have a good sense of sound, then how to get those sounds recorded.

KB: When you use the phrase, "you need to know your place," can you expand on that a little?

JV: I often observe the approach to Foley is a "blanket" approach. And I don't mean this in a bad way with my editors cause I love them all and often they get caught in the mix.

Sometimes the director will say, "Where's that cup down?" And it may be in the middle of a wild music scene where you're thinking no one is going to hear that "cup down." You wouldn't hear it in reality but suddenly the director wants to hear it and its not there. They get in to a bit of a panic and race to us saying, can you quickly pull up the picture and do this sound for us?

I think a well-organized sound job is when you have a good relationship with the editor and the director. They know exactly what they want. They know where the music is going to be, the dialogue, and where the effects will carry the shot. Being an experienced Foley Artist, you generally know where to pay the most attention. You know you need to cover the more intimate shots, where you are trying to create a character. And you get that opportunity with close ups, like someone lighting a cigarette, fumbling around with their matches or walking with a limp. Foley helps to define their character. The quiet scenes and close-ups become your best opportunity. But as soon as he's thirty feet away and something else is going on in the shot, then why continue it? You need to be able to know when something is important and not important, because you don't have much time, generally speaking.

KB: You've worked on some huge films. How much time do you usually get to do Foley on a film?

JV: Well if I really thought about it and took all the films I worked on last year and added up the days, its probably somewhere between eighteen and twenty-one days.

KB: To do a single film?

JV: Yeah. Which I know can sound like a lot. But AVATAR for instance, was really three films in one. I think we went over forty days on that. It was the most we've ever had on a film, but we needed that time, it was a massive job.

KB: Sure, and since so many things were being created from scratch visually . . .

JV: Right, there was a lot of CG and rotoscoping in that film. And he (James Cameron) has been pretty kind to Foley, he tends to like Foley and he tends to know what he wants which is good. With that film we got quite a bit of time and we tried a lot of things. Like those military machines with the legs that go tromping through the forest. We did the sounds of the legs coming down in the forest and the mechanical movements of it. Now if you listen to it in the film there are a ton of sound effects with it, it was a real composite sound with Foley and effects. We often have opportunities to contribute to sound design and harder effects, which can be really fun, but it can also be very physically difficult.

KB: A lot of the films that I've worked on, we would get a day of Foley per reel. I was always fighting directors and producers who would say, "We don't need Foley, Foley isn't important." Why do you think Foley is important?

JV: To be honest I think that there has been a lot of poorly done Foley and I think because of that it doesn't have a great reputation. I think there are people doing Foley who aren't considering mic placement, for example, and trying to cover too much material in not enough time. They may not have a sense of what good Foley can sound like. Of course a great Foley Mixer helps!

Because of that, you get these sounds that are mic'd too close or too far, so they sound fake, or you're hearing too much of the room behind it. That's how it gets a reputation of not sounding good.

In a lot of shots, covering everything becomes annoying. If someone is talking, you don't necessarily want to hear someone next to them eating. Which is what Foley can do, but you're never going to play that because it's not about that person sitting next to them eating. To me it's about editing and being selective about where it's being used.

Because there is a lot of "blanket" cuing, it gets this reputation of, "What is that? I don't want to hear that! Lets just turn it down." So I find that a lot of people don't really understand the process.

KB: Right. I use to spend all this time cuing Foley, and as a sound designer I wanted to make sure that I was getting exactly what I wanted. I'm fairly anal too.

JV: I think you have to be.

KB: Do you still get cue sheets from the Foley Editor (or the Sound Designer), telling you where and how things should be placed?

JV: We do.

KB: How much more Foley can you add, how much input do you have?

JV: It's kind of nice because as the years have gone by, Foley is the department where a lot of people have been trained and then they segue-way into effects, dialogue, mixing, or sound design. Like Gary Rydstrom, he was in Foley, right? He recorded it and actually did some Foley. Tom Johnson did the same thing. The list goes on and on . . . these people like Foley and have respect for the art.

I think because Dennie and I've been doing Foley for such a long time and it has become such a training ground, that you get the opportunity to work with many new editors. We give them input on what is necessary. How we would like things to be presented, and split out or not split out. We like to be given a lot of detail mostly because we have to go fast. The more detail in the spotting session, the better. I'd like to know the character, what they're doing, what they're touching, and briefly what that action is. By knowing what's coming up, I can prepare for it.

It's like footsteps on gravel, if I don't know the distance or who it is or if they're walking or running, I have to look at the shot. Every time I have to look at the shot, that takes time away from performing. We can do up to 500 sound events in a day, and that's a lot! That's NOT our average to be sure, but we have been known to do that many, and those are our "kept" sounds. Not the ones you say, "Delete it or mute it", those are actually the sounds that are kept.

Because of that pace, the way things are spotted is important. It's all about time. Good spotting helps us to prepare as we shoot, because many times we don't get to see the whole film before we begin work on them. In some cases we haven't seen a single frame before we record Foley.

KB: You have worked on films like STAR WARS, HELLBOY, and the INDIANA JONES series. A lot of the shots in those films are still being composited when you're working. What are the biggest challenges that you face as a Foley Artist, on these films?

JV: It's true if there is a lot of blue screen it is difficult to know, what are they doing? What are they walking on? What is it going to look like? Is that my biggest challenge?

Really I think our biggest challenges are figuring out what is our place in the whole thing? What do they need from us? It's important to work with the sound designers and effects people to know what they have and what they want from us. What do we need to do?

And physically, action packed adventure films can be demanding. A really hard part of the job is staying fit and being able to physically keep up. It's like being a shoemaker, it's all hand made sounds. You're working with your hands all day.

KB: And your feet. You are the most physical portion of post-production. Most of the Foley Artists I've worked with do eight-hour days where everybody else does ten or twelve because of the physical concentration. Is that still true?

JV: We pretty much do eight-hour days unless we have to do more, which can come up for sure. Sometimes shows over lap or new shots have just come in and suddenly we have to go back to the show that we were working on to add a scene, or enhance something. It's difficult. It's like anything else, you're going to lose your productivity after a certain time and there's the frustration and point of no return eventually.

KB: I'm with you on that. Tell me something interesting about Foley?

JV: Foley takes time to refine your skills, you know it seems really simple from the outside but it's not that easy and I am still learning how to do it. I still pick up props and I never know if I'll ever use them.

I was in Iowa and I picked up this thing and I thought, what is this? I started looking at it and it was an old check writer. If you can imagine this big heavy adding machine, where you could set the numbers then you slip check paper into it and you can stamp up to $99,000. It's probably from the 1930s or 40s. It weighs at least fifteen pounds and I have no idea what I am going to use it for. I'm sure it would be great for stomping on a gas pedal or a brake pedal in a car. So I bought it. I had to give myself extra time to get through the airport because it was going to cost a fortune to ship it and I knew that they would really be looking at this thing. Sure enough they're putting it through the x-ray, they're going back and forth, back and forth. And I see the guy waving a couple of other security people over and they're looking at it and finally one of them looks up and says, "Whose is this?" And I started to say it's an antique, I didn't really want to say what it was, for fear that there may be some Treasury Agent around. So they're looking at it and checking it for bomb powder and they're putting it through the x-ray machine again. Then some wise guy says, "Hey I know what that is. They had one of those in that movie, CATCH ME IF YOU CAN, didn't Leonardo DiCaprio have one of those to print checks?"

And if looks could kill, I wanted to kill this guy. Cause now I'm thinking they're going to pull me aside and think I'm a counterfeiter. And sure enough I get it home and I hadn't tested it, but there was still some ink in it, and I guess I could have probably printed out some checks! I mean I could use another $30,000 a year. (Laughter)

KB: Oh boy, extra income! (Laughter)

JV: I am always looking at objects in terms of sound. Driving through the mountains last Fall, on the side of the road I kept seeing these giant pine cones so finally I pull over to get some. They are beautiful and wickedly sharp. I took about six of them, threw them in the car and brought them to work. I didn't know what I was going to do with them. Then a couple of the petals fell off and I thought, these make perfect claw sounds.

KB: What is the oddest thing you have ever used to create a sound? And what was it for?

JV: We were working on CARS, for Pixar. They wanted the sound of a race car chassis' because these cars are moving around and talking. How do you get the sound of a car chassis that won't interrupt the dialogue, and how do you get the sound of a chassis moving without a motor?

We had to come up with the sound of all these different car chassis'. We were pretty good at finding the 1940 Hudson. There's an old Model A, and we had a funny creaky thing for that. All that creaky stuff was easy.

Then it came down to the main character McQueen, the race car, What are you going to use for that? He's not going to be creaky. We tried a bunch of different things and John Lasseter (the director) was saying it wasn't quite working for him. I was thinking what am I going to do? I was driving home one day and I looked over and saw there was a garage sale, more like a parking lot sale, so I stopped. I see this couch, which turned out to be a mini two-seater couch with a hide-a-bed. It was $20. I said, "I'll give you $20 if you help me get this old thing into my car?" I have an old Saab where you can open the back. I was trying to be nonchalant because you never want to tell anybody what business you're in, if you tell them you're in film, then they would charge you $200 for that thing. Suddenly its got value! Now I have this thing hanging out of my car for the rest of the weekend.

I get it to work and unfortunately as my partner Dennie was helping me carry this incredibly heavy thing onto the stage, this iron bar under the front comes out and whacks her in the shin. She ends up going to the emergency room to make sure she hasn't broken anything. Turns out she hadn't, which was good.

I had this thought that somehow this thing is going to make the sound of the race car And sure enough it did, perfectly. I can't explain how I manipulated this fold out couch, but I was able to in a way so it gave this frumpy, cool big sound. It also sounded like it was coming from within, under the hood of the car. And John Lasseter was like, "That's it." So now we will have this 200-pound filthy, awful hide-a-bed on our stage forever.

That's kind of a big secret. They've been asking me for years how I made that sound. But I think I am far enough in my career that I don't need to worry as much. (Laughs)

KB: So I can put this story in the book?

JV: You can probably put that story in the book. But I'm not going to tell you exactly how I did it.

KB: Do you find that you can't tell directors or people involved what you are using to make a particular sound?

JV: Oh no! You never want to tell them what you're using, if they see what you're using they'll never believe it. They don't buy it. In fact on our stage there is that window in-between the engineer's booth and the stage? I have stacked up all kinds of pillows, backpacks and stuff so that our mixer can't see what we're using. Cause if he can see what we're using, often he isn't objective. It's a little like being a magician; you don't want to tell anyone how you've done it because once they know they'll be like, "Really? It sounds so much more complicated than that."

KB: I used to hate when a director would ask how I made something, I felt obligated to tell them but then like you said, they didn't think it sounded right anymore. They had just bought it a bunch of times while I was playing it back but now it isn't right because they know the truth.

I used to love to do snow stuff, a head of iceberg lettuce made the perfect snow crunching sound. Are there any secrets you'd care to divulge?

JV: What we use for snow right now is cornstarch. I don't know how much of a secret that is. People get surprised though. When you see someone walking on snow, you just assume that's it. Of course being from the mid-west has always helped me with that.

I was born in Minnesota. Not only do I know what snow sounds like, but what different kinds of snow sound like. Sometimes in my snow I may add a little rock salt, if it's a more crunchy snow.

KB: What is the toughest movie you've ever done, and why was it tough?

JV: AVATAR is one that comes to mind, and they knew what they wanted! I started telling you a little about Pandora being this "wet world". They wanted it to be really wet, we were trying all these wet things, make it sound lush, and of course lush plants don't sound like what we would think a lush plant would sound like. Tropical plants sound kind of papery, like plastic in a way. So how do you make something sound lush and wet? What I ended up doing was going to the beach and getting a bunch of seaweed. The seaweed sounded kind of slippery, kind of wet, kind of crunchy, and that was it. But of course it made our stage stink pretty bad. (Laughs)

KB: So there is a down side here isn't there? (Laughs)

JV: Definitely. But I think the physical demands in AVATAR were some of the hardest. Between the twelve-foot tall Avatars running for their lives, through many different terrains mind you, then you have the even bigger giant creatures running after them.

CAST AWAY was another hard one. There is a scene where he (Tom Hanks) is cracking and eating crab. You really can't fake that. I don't know what other people have used for cracking and eating crab. There are some things that you just have to use the real thing for it to seem believable. And man, that made our stage stink too!

KB: With all this new technology and the budgets getting smaller and smaller, how does that affect your work?

JV: I'll have people who approach me, "Hey, I have this low budget piece that I really want to do. And I really want you to work on it, but I only have five days." And I'll say fine, we can do it in five days, but you have to tell me exactly what you want and where you want it. You have to be very specific. Where are you really going to need and want Foley, it can't just be a blanket cover, cause you don't have enough time.

I tell people I could do your whole film in a day, give me a day and I could do it. But obviously it can't be everywhere; it has to be exactly where you want it. I would rather do fewer sounds of higher quality and be really selective.

KB: Exactly. I have worked with mixers who say we don't need to pre-mix Foley because we are going to hardly use it.

JV: Oh yeah. We're like the ugly evil stepchildren in the basement. Actually, I've worked with a lot of the same people for a long time now and I think we all have a lot of respect for each other. But if someone isn't going to pre-mix Foley or they don't have time to pre-mix it, it would have to be understood ahead of time then that you have to pick your moments and let me do the best job I can.

And I work with a really great mixer, (Frank Rinella) and now with Pro Tools we can do a lot of things like editing on the fly. We also work really hard at placing our mics so that it's almost pre-mixed. In that way, we make it so they don't have to do much pre-mixing.

KB: How often do you hear, "We need to do something with sound here? Can you come up with something to fix this scene?"

JV: Right. And you really think it's a sound that will save your film? I don't think so. I mean we can try. We can make it better. But basically you've either got a good film, or you don't.

KB: Absolutely. If you were looking for a Foley artist, what are some of the things you would want to know about them?

JV: I would want to know what they've worked on. Have they worked on animation, or live-action? Some people are really great with live-action but that's all they do. I think you would have to take a look at their credits and who they've worked with. And if you know anybody, talk to them and try and get a feel for who this person really is. I would probably talk to some of the supervisors they'd worked for.

KB: If someone coming out of school decided they really wanted to be a Foley Artist, what would you tell them?

JV: I would say send your resume around, try to make contacts with everybody you know. You probably have to work a lot for free, or very little, and be willing to apprentice. So you can get in that way. The bottom line is it's a really hard business to get into. There aren't that many people that do it and there aren't that many places to do it. I don't know, good luck!

I think the more things you can do in terms of sound for film, if you can edit, if you can go out and record effects and you've got good ears, then put yourself into an environment where eventually you will get to a place that is doing Foley.

KB: In a larger context, why do you think good sound is important in film?

JV: I think sound should be used as a big part of telling the story. When you think about the silent films, so much of it was dependent on people's facial expressions. The way they would look at each other. Their eyes would widen and then they'd open the door and a train was coming at them. The music would often help tell the story too. I think good sound will only enhance the storytelling in a way that's going to make it come across as a good piece of art.

If Foley is not used right, it just becomes more noise on the track. I think a really good sound track is dynamic. You want it to be loud, you want it to be quiet. When you have an intimate scene you want it to sound that way. You want to hear that person breathing, if it's a lovemaking scene you want to hear the skin on skin, it's going to put your audience in to your story. If you don't hear those details it becomes a little anemic or you're suddenly aware of that person eating popcorn right behind you. You just kind of lose focus.

KB: What is the one thing you would like to tell students and filmmakers about sound that you think is important?

JV: I think it really comes down to the art of filmmaking. What is the story you're trying to tell? In reality we are surrounded by sound. Sound helps shape our perception of whatever given moment we are experiencing.

You have to continue to think, what is your story? If it's an opening shot of someone in a hotel room, do you want to hear sirens in the background? Do you want to hear the fly buzzing around the window? Or do you want to hear someone in the next room laughing? What do you want to convey? So much emotional context can be conveyed through sound. And you have to think about sound as you are writing your film. Thinking in ways that you can, without words or music, convey the emotion.

KB: You know, you and I would get along so well if we ever worked together. I have been trying to tell filmmakers this stuff for years. Sound is so important. Do you think that films today are getting too dependent on music, instead of effects? Is music becoming wallpaper?

JV: I think so. I do think that directors in general tend to rely too heavily on the music to convey how they want us to feel. I think that music can be really great in a film but I personally love it when the music goes away. Then the dialogue and some of the light effects can carry that part of the scene or the development of some character whenever possible.

I feel like music directs how I feel in a movie and sometimes it's miss-matched. It's like the music has been picked poorly and I don't really like to be directed in that way, I may walk away from a movie and think, that wasn't that great. Maybe what it comes down to, is the fact that the music just didn't match my feelings? It's an easy thing to go toward, it's a really easy way to direct people's emotions. I think it can be kind of a cop out.

KB: Oh I love hearing you say that because I feel the same way.

JV: I am trying to think of some films off the top of my head where there wasn't much music.

KB: NO COUNTRY FOR OLD MEN had no music.

JV: That was a great film. And you remember the suitcase of money? I mean, that suitcase had it's own personality.

KB: Big time.

JV: In the film the suitcase was always heavy, kind of creaky, and it had this flabby front. Again I think that the average audience member isn't even going to notice that stuff, but somebody, subconsciously is going to notice that it actually is a character. And that's a lot like animation. We get characters that don't ever actually talk, but they talk with their character sounds, what we have created for them, their signature sounds. We're adding character through sound.

KB: *Do you still like what you do?*

JV: I do. I really like what I do. I think what's nice about it is, and you can relate to this, it's always changing. Just when you think you are ready to scream and run out the door, the project is over. And you're moving onto something else. It's not like somebody else's job where they're cutting out toilet seat covers or some same thing everyday. Because every film is not always the same shape, color and size, right?

KB: *Absolutely.*

JV: I love the fact that I have the opportunity for variety.

I love storytelling. I love stories, I love good literature, and I feel pretty happy to be involved in that process, even if it is in the tiny, tiny way of Foley.

KB: *Foley is not tiny. Foley completes the picture, and when I teach, I always tell students, God is in the details. It's all about the details in a picture, in anything. And that's where you find any piece of art complete. It's in the details.*

JV: Right. And Foley has been known as the glue in a picture. A lot of people think why do we need to do that? But when it's not there you miss it. It's that human element that we're always focusing on. It's really about, what are the people doing? It's the effects that are handling the car bombs and planes and the crashes and the explosions and the refrigerator hum. But it's Foley that's handling the personal, the person, the people, and the characters.

KB: *I like what you said, that Foley is the Human element. I think that's wonderful. Thank you.*

CHAPTER 7:

Probably the Most Incorrectly Used Phrase in Films

Sound Designers

The terms "sound design" and "Sound Designer" were introduced to the film world around 1972. The original meaning of the title Sound Designer was "an individual ultimately responsible for all aspects of a film's audio track, from the dialogue and sound effects recording to the re-recording (mix) of the final track."

Now anyone and their brother takes the title Sound Designer even if they were the composer, the mixer, or the person who brings in the coffee. There are very few people who are true sound designers, mostly because production companies don't want to pay a person to oversee all of the audio. The belief is that you don't bring the sound designer on until you've got a rough cut of the movie and you want to screen it for the studio or for test audiences. Very few audio people are involved from the beginning of a project where they could have a major impact on how the film is going to sound. They are brought in after filming and often have to clean up the mistakes that were made earlier.

I have listened to directors over the years talk about how

important sound is, but when they go out on location all of those amazing experimental ideas fly out the window. Sometimes when the film gets to the final stages of post-production the director (or the producers) get cold feet and are afraid to be experimental, to do things differently.

There are very few people in the sound business that are both sound designers and re-recordists. There are even fewer picture editors that also mix, Walter Murch being the first one that comes to mind.

To be able to create a sound track and then mix it takes a special personality. You have to put your ego aside. Just because you've created these wonderful moments in the movie with sound effects doesn't mean they are right for every scene. The movie itself dictates from scene to scene what audio elements should take precedence. Some scenes the dialogue is the most important, and in others it can be the music or the sound effects.

Is it a good thing for the sound designer to also be a mixer? I have done both and although I am not in the same league as some of these folks I have to say that I like to be able to present the sound as close as possible to the way I hear it in my head.

A good sound designer has to have a good overall feel of working with all the audio elements on a film, not just the music or the sound effects and the sooner they are involved, the better. They can do amazing things to help achieve the original vision.

Jane Tattersall

"When I look at a film or look at a script I think of what I'm gonna need to make that world."

Jane Tattersall is one of Canada's premier film professionals. With more than 135 credits in sound design and sound editing Jane's sound work has garnered her over forty awards and nominations, and her dedication to the art of film sound has earned her an international reputation for creativity and skill.

Jane has worked with such acclaimed directors as Istvan Szabo, David Cronenberg, Jaco Van Dormael, Fernando Mereilles, Bill Forsyth, Deepa Mehta and Clement Virgo, as well as many of Canada's new generation of directors - Sarah Polley, Richie Mehta, and Nathan Morlando. The work has seen her travel from Toronto to other parts of Canada and to London, Tokyo, Berlin, Budapest, Amsterdam, Seoul, New York, Hollywood, and Skywalker Ranch.

As an entrepreneur, a business owner, and a creative professional, Jane balances business and creative needs for her clients, her company, and herself. Through the company Jane and her partners continue their tradition of supporting independent filmmakers in the Canadian market.

Jane's credits include: THE FLY, NAKED LUNCH, BEING JULIA, LIE WITH ME, EDWIN BOYD, I'M YOURS and the TV show THE TUDORS.

If you want to know more about Jane Tattersall check out: http://www.imdb.com/name/nm0002938/

KB: How are things going today?

JT: Pretty good, thank you. I'm actually in a mix, but I just told them I'd step away for a while and there's no problem there.

KB: How did you get into this foolish business anyway?

JT: I got into the film business accidentally. I went to University and got a degree in Philosophy. While I was in University I saw lots of indie movies, 'cause I was interested in them, but I don't have a background in film school or anything.

I got a job as a philosopher on a television documentary series through a friend of a friend. For that I had to do a lot of research about gardens and how they related to the people who created them, it was very philosophical. The production team went around North America to shoot, then came back and started editing. They asked if I'd come in and help them write it because they didn't have much structure.

There was a scene in a garden in Santa Barbara. It was raining and there were drops of rain on all the foliage. The camera panned around the garden so you could see the extent of it. The editor said, "I know what this scene needs," and he rolled the reel back, he was on a flat bed, and he put up a roll of brown tape and the next time the camera slowly panned around the garden there was the sound of thunder. And I thought it was the coolest thing I'd ever experienced.

I suddenly realized the power of sound in changing the feeling of a scene. I thought "When this job ends I'm going to see if I can get work in post production because it seems really interesting." So I got a job as an assistant receptionist at a studio and eventually apprenticed with an amazing sound editor, Jeffery Perkins. Later in his career he got an Oscar for DANCES WITH WOLVES.

Jeffrey and I were working on these shows that weren't very good, they were two-minute commercials that played on airlines. But he always said, no matter what the content, we should do the very best sound we could possibly do.

I found I was good at it, and I liked it.

KB: How long have you been doing sound?

JT: My first official freelance job was in 1984. So, that's a long time.

KB: When I started cutting it was on an upright Moviola.

JT: I actually still have a Moviola; we have it on display here at our studio.

KB: (Laughs), That's all they're good for. Is there a particular film or films that were a big influence on you when you started?

JT: One of the earliest films I worked on was David Cronenberg's THE FLY. There was a sound effects supervisor and me. So I got to do a bit of everything. On that particular film I really learned about the power of sound in storytelling.

There's a machine in the film, the pod, which fired up and then the trans-morphing of the atoms, or whatever it is, happens. The machine had to turn on and wind up and so on. I had all these sounds that were created by the sound supervisor, but I didn't know what to do with them. He told me, "Just think of it like it's an engine starting up. There's a click and then a vroom and then a . . . " I suddenly realized that's how you build sound, layer upon layer, bit-by-bit, you create it.

That film really had a big influence on how I watched films. I always felt the sounds had to be believable. You can't disengage the viewer. That machine really had to work even though it was fake.

KB: Then you did THE NAKED LUNCH a few years later. And the sound is so, I'll use the phrase out of control. It's great. I love that film. How much input do you have on the films you work on? Especially with a film like that, that is so nontraditional?

JT: In general David Cronenburg doesn't talk very much about the sound. It was really more about what we would bring to the project and he either liked it or he didn't. He was very, very open to it. In THE NAKED LUNCH, we divided it into reels. I would do one reel and another person would do another reel and we had complete free reign. It may have not made it the most organized thing, but I think creatively it allowed everyone to feel like it was their world, that they could create it.

KB: Doing an entire reel is old school. Nobody does that anymore. Which I think is unfortunate. Do you prefer having an entire reel to yourself, or do you think it's better the way it's done now where you've got your dialogue editor, sound effects editor, ADR editor, Foley, etc.?

JT: The advantages to having one person do all the vehicles and one person do all the gun shots and so on is just pure efficiency. No one else seems to mind it, but I don't like it as much. I'd prefer to have my own world to create.

But now as a sound supervisor, I don't necessarily want someone to go off in a crazy direction and then have to reel them back in. There are advantages and disadvantages to both ways of working. What I've started to do is have other people do the first pass of editing and then I do a pass on my own where I get to finesse things and add things that I think might be missing. Or if I found something in Reel Two that's really great, then I use it again in a later reel. That's not necessarily as enjoyable for the other people. For them it's like someone's interfering with their work.

KB: How do you have time to do that anymore? The last few movies that I supervised, I felt like I was spending all my time in meetings or going to the ADR, Group and Foley sessions. I felt like I was doing everything but creating.

JT: Maybe you were working on more demanding shows than I do. I often work in conjunction with a dialogue supervisor so I don't go to the ADR sessions. And we don't have that many meetings.

KB: That would be nice.

JT: I have a friend, David Evans, who does a lot of big films, like Tim Burton's ALICE IN WONDERLAND, and he said that he opted out of being the sound supervisor and became the sound designer because he couldn't stand the fact that the sound supervisor did no cutting, all they did was meetings.

KB: I think that's really a US thing with Hollywood films. I totally burned out on all of it. Why do you think good sound is important in films?

JT: I think it's half the viewing experience. There are a lot of additional story points or mood points that you can create with sound so why not avail yourself of that opportunity?

KB: You're a sound designer, a sound effects editor, and a supervising sound editor. Have you ever thought about being a re-recording mixer as well? Is it easy to hand off your stuff to someone else?

JT: I would love it if I knew how to do it. I think it would be fun to control it all but I just don't think I have the skill and I fear that it would take me too long to learn it properly.

I have no problem handing my work over. I'm sitting in the room most of the time with them and I'm offering my thoughts on it and it's really great to have another person's take on it. I've been in a few mixes when I was frustrated, people just didn't do what I wanted, what I thought I was articulating and that's horrible. If that's been the case, then I haven't worked with that mixer again.

KB: I was talking with Ken Karmen, (a music editor) and he was saying every now and then you do get that moment where you just want to reach over and grab the faders from that guy's hands and say "No, damn it! This is how I want you to do it."

JT: (Laughs) Don't you understand? I want it almost silent! Don't just pull it down 2 db at a time.

KB: . . . that shit drives me crazy. When you first read a script or look at the rough cut, what is it you look for?

JT: I'm looking for setting and environment. I think of sound as a building block. When I work I start off by doing the ambiances, because then I've got my space. Then I work on the sounds that are in that space. So when I look at a film or look at a script I think of what I'm gonna need to make that world.

KB: And then you go with specific effects after that?

JT: Yes.

KB: Why don't director's spend more time on sound when they're on location?

JT: Because sound can be repaired or fixed or recreated after the fact. But that's not always true.

I just went through a mix with a director who only wanted to use production and her actors spoke really quietly. Now she's asking a lot of questions about her next film, which is a period piece. We tried to explain to her that you could get away with poor production quality dialogue in a film that's set in the modern day because you can have a bit of crap on it. But in a period film you just can't. You can't have airplanes or motors or air-conditioning. I think she finally understood and I know from now on she will be cautious of that.

And somebody commented to her in a pre-production meeting that if she wants to have certain things sound-wise in the film, it's good to establish that thing that's making the noise. She had a scene that started out with someone turning on a water sprinkler, and the sound of the sprinkler continues through the scene. If we hadn't seen her turn it on then nobody would have known exactly what the sound was. Some people learn about sound and incorporate those lessons into their films.

KB: What's your opinion of ADR?

JT: I think of ADR as being another tool. It's great to have the option, but if you're happy with the on set performance, you should always do the best you can with the production. When you get on the stage, it's nice to be able to slip an ADR word in because it wasn't clear on the production dialogue. I think the tools are getting better and better for making ADR sound just like the production, having it blend in as opposed to standing out.

I think ADR can be fantastic, but it's rare to see it done well. Most mixers haven't had the opportunity to play around with it enough, or they don't have time in their schedules to learn about the new software. Certainly for a student film they would never be able to make it sound like production.

I think filmmakers should be encouraged to get really good clean dialogue.

KB: You do a lot of television, so we'll start with the broader question, what are the differences working in sound on television shows and series as compared with working on features?

JT: The biggest difference is the schedule; you get less time to do your work, although some of the shows give you a pretty reasonable schedule.

Something one has to be aware of is, while many people have good quality sound systems at home, not everyone does, so you have to double check that the sound still works. You're not pushing the atmospheres or the music too close to the dialogue. You really want the dialogue to be heard, you can't obscure it.

I find in European films people are far more experimental with sound than they are in American films, and in television, even less so. People don't have periods of weird sound or no sound that just doesn't happen.

I think there's really good television being made these days. But I don't know that the sound in these shows is always given the opportunity to be good. I think that MAD MEN is really good television or SHAMELESS or WEST WING or THE SOPRANOS. I think THE SOPRANOS had really bad sound the first season. It got better over time. I think they probably spent more money on location recording or maybe they finally listened to the location recordist.

KB: They wouldn't actually listen to the location recordist, would they? Do you find there's a lot more ADR used in television than in features?

JT: Not necessarily. I think sometimes they're more willing to use it because they know it's really important to actually hear the dialogue. In some television shows I hear the ADR cutting in and out and I think, "Why didn't they fix that?" And I realized it's because they just didn't have the time to fix it and someone made a decision it was better to understand the line than not understand it, and they didn't care if it fit in acoustically that well.

On some of the shows I've been part of, the cast is quite hard to get hold of because they're shooting all the time. If it's a series, sometimes we don't get ADR lines until the final mix is happening and it's happening over three days and the actor's finally get their lines in, we get it the last day and then we decide not to use it.

KB: With a television series, you're doing multiple episodes at one time so you're supervising multiple episodes, how the hell do you mange a TV series?

JT: It's not easy. If you're trying to cut it and pay attention to all the other things, you have to be careful with your time. You have to manage your time and put that sign on the door that says "Do Not Disturb! I'm trying to cut". I have a sign that I stick on regularly. But the real key is to work with people who know what they're doing. You have to really trust them and give them lots and lots of rope so they don't need to be managed.

KB: But with television shows today, is it strictly you have one person who's just doing dialogue maybe two people on sound effects, is that how you also manage this stuff?

JT: Yes. In the case of something like THE BORGIAS, which we just did, or CAMELOT, I was doing sound effects, there were two people doing dialogue, they alternated shows, and one person who did ADR. I would have my assistant lay in all the backgrounds. When he'd done that he'd hand it over to me. I'd sit there for the evaluation when we'd figure out how much ADR we were doing and any kind of spotting. We took notes from whoever was in charge, usually the creative producer, never the director. I never heard the ADR until I got to the stage.

KB: Let me get this straight, you're going to the meetings and figuring out what's going to go into all these things and you're doing your cutting and then you're on the stage while they're mixing?

JT: Oh, you know I'm exaggerating. I don't go to the stage for the whole mix. I did for the first episodes of each show of those series, but after that they would just call me if they wanted me to look at something. Usually I'd be busy cutting the next show. They'd do a playback for our producer, which I would be at, and then I would do all the fixes that he requested. Then we'd do another playback for the broadcasters with all the producers notes addressed.

KB: Dare I ask, how many hours a week do you regularly put in?

JT: I don't put in the hours I used to. I start work around 8:15 and I leave pretty promptly at 6. And I don't work at home anymore. I used to, but I just stopped. The reason I stopped is my arm started hurting from too much editing. Now I'm very focused during the day. I notice a lot of people get their social life from work. They stand around and talk. I don't mind if they do that, but I'm not interested in being like that myself, I just want to go home.

KB: You and I would hit if off so well if we ever worked together. I put the "Leave me alone" sign on my door too. I want to get this done go home and spend time with my daughter. Although now she's in college and I'm by myself so it doesn't matter. I'll work all night if I have to. I just try not to have to.

JT: That's true. If I have nothing to go home to, like if my family's away and I've brought the dog in with me, I have no problem working until 8:00 pm and then go home. I've learned to compartmentalize.

KB: Do you find the people that you work with, expect you to put in long hours?

JT: They assume we're here all the time. I don't know if you ever got this, but you get emails from people at three in the morning, and five in the morning, and six in the morning, and I think, "Oh my god, do they think I'm really receiving all this stuff?"

KB: The part that always bothered me is you'd get a note from them saying, "Why didn't you reply when I sent you that email?" Well it's because I was asleep.

Do you prefer features to TV?

JT: Hmm . . . It sure is nice to work on a feature with a nice schedule and a good filmmaker. It's very satisfying but the stuff I work on is kinda indie, so often it doesn't get that many people watching it. There's something really enjoyable about people saying "Oh I saw THE TUDORS and I saw your name" or "Oh, you work on THE TUDORS," when people actually know what you do.

It really depends on the show. I used to love working on THE TUDORS and also THE BORGIAS. I really like period films because you can't hide anything. The birds have to be the right birds and the right acoustics and the horses going by have to sound authentic. A lot of television I don't really care for. It's not that I don't want to watch it; I just don't really want to work on it. Like anything that's set in a cop station - modern day. I get sick of cutting the car passes, I get sick of the telephones and the traffic. That's not very satisfying anymore.

KB: Yeah, I understand that one. In addition to doing all this sound editing you also run a company. How to do you balance the business part of all this with having time to be creative and to cut all these shows? Can you have a balance?

JT: First of all there are several partners at the company and there's one person in particular who deals with the money, sending out invoices, tracking studio time and all that. I don't do any of that. We don't have meetings about those kinds of things, but we're always talking about what's going on. We're kind of an informal company. I think the key to having a successful combination of creative work and business work is to have partners. People that you trust and can rely on. Everyone's looking out for everyone else's back.

KB: That's great.

JT: But in the early days, I worked so many hours. It was crazy how many hours I worked.

KB: Yeah, you and me both. I think everyone who's in this business has done that. I can't think of a single holiday that I haven't worked.

JT: It's true.

KB: I shudder to think how many all nighters have been done.

JT: Another thing is, I don't know if you've done the same thing, but whenever I do go on holiday, I'm always recording sound.

KB: I used to. I stopped doing that, but I used to.

JT: Even though it's fun to do it and it's been very useful because over time you get a big library, but for the people you're going on holiday with, it's kind of a drag.

KB: What is your biggest challenge now when it comes to post production sound?

JT: The biggest challenge is time. But then everyone in every business seems to be affected by that. Certainly they are during production. The second thing I'd say is I think directors are too cautious these days. I think they're not bold enough or they're too conservative or something.

KB: Can you elaborate on that?

JT: They come in for a meeting and they've got this show and they want to do really wild and wonderful things and it's exciting to talk to them.

For example, here's a film about two people driving in a car and it's a long journey and their relationship develops over the journey, so rather than being literal with the sound, having the car sound and things passing, why not put the sounds of some of the things they have been thinking about as it's going through their mind. We won't see the image, but we will hear the sound. That's the direction I was given and I start doing that and I thought, "Oh, this is really fun!" Here is an example, two scenes earlier the characters stopped by the side of a lake and watched the waves roll in. So now in the later scene I put the sound of the same waves and the wind and maybe a bird or two so you recognize the sound. I played it for the director because I was really happy with it and he said, "You know what, I think we're just gonna go with music here." And it's because the director was afraid to do something different. He was afraid the audience is going to think, "What's going on?" The shorthand for an audience to connect to a scene is just put music in. That's easy.

KB: Do you think more music in films has become the trend?

JT: Yes. That's one of the things I noted down for your questions that I wish there wasn't so much music.

KB: Why do you think they've become so reliant on music?

JT: With music, instantly you get a mood. It's a good way of communicating how the audience should feel.

KB: Do you think that has to do with directors not being bold enough? It's so much easier just to go to the music.

JT: I think so. I think they're also a bit afraid of not having music, they're afraid that people won't stay tuned in.

KB: Do you think music is in danger of becoming wallpaper?

JT: I think it probably is. [Though] people seemed to be more tuned to music than we give them credit for. People will remember a piece of music that was in a certain scene. I think they're really paying attention to this. And maybe it's me that's not paying attention because maybe I don't recognize the song or something.

With NO COUNTRY FOR OLD MEN one of the reasons it got so much attention was because people noticed that music wasn't there. That was a clever move on their part. I'm sure it was intentional, but I'm not sure what their reason for it was. Maybe you know.

KB: Everything those guys do is intentional, but I don't know why they didn't go with music. So if you were a director, what would you do differently?

JT: I would have more dynamic range with the sound. So it's not all wallpaper. I'd like to think I'd be bold, but funnily enough, I made a short film not that long ago and I knew what kind of score I wanted. I made a temp score using the style that I wanted, so the composer knew what I was going for, mood and so on. The film was only four minutes long so it [the score] pretty much went from the beginning to the end.

Originally, I had temped three different types of score, because there were different changes of mood. By it being only four minutes long, it was kind of chopped up by having three pieces. So the composer ended up making it all into one thing.

I didn't do what I'd like to think I'd do, which is cut some silences in. And then I thought maybe we should take music out all together. [I was] thinking, "I don't need music for this! It's really powerful without it." I took a friend of mine, a picture editor, with me to listen to the score because I wanted her judgment and she said, "You're crazy. The score is magnificent. It's doing everything you wanted it to do, so go for that."

So you know, I'd like to think I'd be bold and dynamic, but I wasn't. And I'm really happy with the film.

KB: What's the most common sound problem you run into?

JT: Noisy backgrounds. The world is such a noisy place. Whether it's streets or air conditioning or furnaces or refrigerators, those kinds of things. The other thing, which is very common is mumbling, low-level dialogue. Actors just not using their voices the way they should be trained to do.

KB: Do you have any suggestions about ways to get around some of the things you're running into? Besides making the actors talk louder.

JT: Sometimes I make a comment about it. You get to know certain actors and their mumbling so you actually make reference to that. And I'm not trying to discourage people from using them [the actors]. I just want to point out that they might have to do ADR to get some of it fixed.

In terms of background noise, let the [director] listen through headphones to the sound of that location. I think that they filter out the sound themselves with their own ears. They don't [recognize] how loud [the background] actually is, but once they've heard it, it could help them be more responsive to making a change.

KB: If you wanted to go out and find a sound designer or a supervising sound editor, what are the important things you'd look for?

JT: What I don't want is the person who acts like they know everything. And in a job interview, many many people want to tell you how much they know or what great stuff they've done in the past. What I'm interested in is knowing that person is going to listen to what the direction is. They're going to listen to me or listen to the director and be very open.

I want someone who is very flexible, someone who can listen, and not feel the need to prove how wonderful they are.

KB: Students are always asking me, how to get into sound? What would you suggest to them?

JT: You know I get the same question. We get lots of people sending resumes. First of all, I try to discourage all of them because there's just not the room in the industry for all the people who seem to want to do it.

My advice would be to intern or work for someone who would benefit from another pair of hands and then become indispensable. They could also do what composers do, which is attach themselves to up and coming directors. That's not a bad idea, but I think it might take a long time because I think it's hard for anyone to make it in the business these days.

What do you tell them?

KB: I tell them to find someone they want to work with and intern, volunteer, bother them. . . within limits. They need to ask, "Do you need help? I want to learn." Because I'm exactly like you and when people come in and tell me everything they know and how terrific they are, those are the last people I want to work with because they're not gonna listen to me.

When I was shooting my first feature, my script supervisor needed a day off and they brought in someone fresh out of film school. We're ten days into the shoot, setting up an exterior shot of this building. All of a sudden from behind me I hear, "This is the shot? God, it doesn't look very impressive." And I turned around and it's this young kid I'd never seen before holding the binder with the script. I said, "Who are you?" "Oh, I'm 'so-and-so' and I'm you're script supervisor today." And I said, "Okay. I don't want to be an asshole or anything, but I don't give a shit what you think and I don't want to hear you saying this stuff out loud. Do you understand?"

JT: That's awesome.

KB: Then I walked over to my producer and said "See that kid over there doing the script supervising? I don't want to see her after today." I had fifty-seven things going in my head. And having a kid straight out of film school make a comment out loud like we cared what they thought. I felt bad about it later, but they let her go after that day because you don't do that. I would never have done that when I was starting out.

JT: It's so insensitive.

KB: Can you think of anything else that would be good for students or filmmakers to know about sound? Is there anything we haven't touched on?

JT: Well I think it's worth pointing out there's a lot of drudgery involved. Like working in Pro Tools, there has to be a fade in the beginning and end of every piece of sound so it doesn't pop. That's just one tiny thing.

If you're doing dialogue editing, it's brutal work, listening and taking clicks out, trying to line up mics. It's not glamorous work.

I also think it's really important for people to travel and listen while they're traveling so they develop a memory bank of what different places sound like.

The other day somebody who's been around for a while was cutting a scene for me. It was set in the country and he put the sound of some sparrows chirping and I said, "First of all, acoustically the sparrows sound like they're beside a wall or in a school yard, and I don't think it's going to work here." He said, "Yeah, I know. I just needed birds and I couldn't think of anything so I just put these birds in." I said just put a marker that says, "Need birds" and get back to it. I don't think he knew what kind of birds there would be in that world. I think people should collect that information and know that in Europe, a lot of their cars are diesel. There are no crickets in the winter. You know, hundreds of thousands of things like that.

KB: Do you still like what you do?

JT: I do. I may have slightly less patience than I should have, but I really love putting sound to picture. It's really satisfying.

KB: Do you feel that way about your career in general?

JT: Yes. I think I'm really lucky.

Ron Eng

"I think the challenge for an animated film and also the beauty of it is that you really are building the sound track from raw elements."

Ron Eng is one of the most versatile guys I know. He does sound design on dramatic features, animated films, documentaries, television, you name it. He has worked with David Lynch, a personal favorite of mine and he has worked on some of David's most interesting films. Ron has a terrific range when it comes to sound design and he likes to work on a variety of projects. Originally a musician he brings a rhythmic sensibility to his work. I was a fan long before I ever spoke with him.

His credits include CORALINE, MULHOLLAND DRIVE, THE STRAIGHT STORY, THE HUNTED, STAR TREK: INSURRECTION, DARFUR NOW, CASE 39, DEATH AT A FUNERAL, many, many animated films, and Inland Empire.

If you want to know more about Ron Eng check out: http://www.imdb.com/name/nm0256995/

KB: How did you get in to sound?

RE: I back-doored in to this in the strangest way. The short story for me is that I was a musician in Florida. I graduated from Florida State and was working as a guitar teacher in Boca Raton and I saw an ad for this guitar finishing school called The Guitar Institute of Technology in 1979 or 80. I got accepted and came out here (to Los Angeles) to live and go to this school.

I came out with a good friend, a bass player. And you know

bass players always work more than guitar players. After two years of struggle to make ends meet, I got a call to get my original job back in Boca Raton. I was starving to death so I moved back. My bass player buddy ended up staying. About five years later he calls me up and says "Hey, you gotta come out and check out this new business, it's really cool. You make really good money, you get good benefits, and you have plenty of time to work on your music."

I said, "Oh, that sounds great. What is it?" And he says it's doing sound on movies. And it's really fun and cool. So he talked me in to moving back out here from Florida around 1989, and I got a job working on the first digital work station on a movie. It was a Wave Frame, at night for Dave West. And that was my first job in the industry.

I didn't know anything. I mean I just liked to watch movies, that's it. I'm not like some of you guys with film school, who study all of the history . . . One thing lead to another and I finally got in to the Union and I just kinda started at the bottom and worked my way up.

KB: When you started out, did you think about sound much when you watched movies or did that come later?

RE: When I first started working, I didn't pay much attention to it. I would look at sync and I would listen to the quality of the sound and then everything just came to me. I have "music ears" after playing music for so long, so I could really focus in on the sound. I got to the point early in my career that if something was off it really distracted me and took me out of the movie. I think over the years I've tried to ignore sound when I am trying to enjoy a movie. At least to a certain extent. I mean if it's really bad . . .

KB: We all hear the bad ones. Do you consider yourself a Sound Designer or a Supervising Sound Editor?

RE: I would have to say, both. I started as an editor. I came up as a dialogue editor and then got in to sound effects. Then I started supervising. I guess you could say the industry has almost forced people like me to be a "Sound Designer " because of the way budgets have changed over the years.

Budgets have shrunk and there are fewer people on a movie. The days of Chuck Campbell and Louie Edeman, the guys I grew up with are over. I would see these guys sitting in their chairs and delegate and actually "supervise," do no cutting at all. That's really on its way out in Hollywood if it's not already.

On some movies I work on, I would definitely say I am just a supervisor cause I don't do all that much cutting. I involve myself in some of the crucial sound moments in the film and I try to let my editors do most of the cutting. I would say on 70% - 80% of the other films I am pretty much involved with all of the sound design elements.

KB: You are one of the few people I know who does sound on both animated and live-action films, do you have a preference? Is there a difference in your approach between the two?

RE: I don't really have a preference. I know that when I do too much animation I want to see real lips once in awhile. It's happened in my career where I've done two or three animated films in a row. And I think "Oh God, give me a live-action one."

I enjoy them both but I think the challenge for an animated film and also the beauty of it is that you really are building the sound track from raw elements. Which is really cool and you don't have to deal with all of the production sound that you do on a live-action thing.

240

You definitely have to approach a live-action film, unless it's some kind of total science fiction thing, from your production dialogue. And that definitely takes you in a direction. Everything is built around your production track. And that's they way I usually approach a live-action film.

And you know that's the exact opposite for an animated film. All of your dialogue, your ADR is all sunk up and you spend a lot of your time worrying about lip sync. I think any sound job is a challenge no matter what it is, and they all have their own quirks.

KB: Isn't it true that in animation you truly have to create the universe?

RE: Oh yeah, and that's why CORALINE was so fun. The director wanted to go in all sorts of weird ways. There are times when directors or producers say, we want to go here and do this, we want to get a whole new sound design thing going on here. That's the fun part about it. Trying to figure out in a creative sense, I want this to sound like this. How do you figure that out, how do you do that? That's the great challenge.

KB: You've worked with David Lynch, a director who is very concerned with sound, and involved in the mix process. How is working with him different than working with other directors?

RE: It is a total blessing and a great rewarding experience because David is probably the only guy who is truly in to sound. I hear it from a lot of directors, "I'm really in to sound, I'm really in to sound." Then they get pulled in so many different ways and their intention is to focus on sound and then they can't. And that's why you're hired. And that's fine I don't get upset about that.

But David will definitely make the time to sit with you.

MULHOLLAND DRIVE wasn't a big-budget film. We did our pre-edit and we did our dialogue pre-dub and we came to this point in the final mix and I think it was January 3rd, right after the holidays and we were going to do the final mix. I believe there were fourteen reels. We had two weeks set aside to do a final mix, maybe three weeks I can't remember, but standard final mix time.

And after the second week the Post-Production Supervisor comes in and goes, "Okay where are you guys at?" We have just finished the first reel, and David goes, "We're doing great, really great!" and she says, "What reel are you guys on?" And David says we're on Reel One, and her mouth drops. He didn't have the budget to go another week. He said I don't care what it costs, we're going to keep Ron on and we're just going to keep mixing. We ended up final mixing MULHOLLAND DRIVE for three and a half months.

That was like the greatest thing. We were literally dubbing the film frame by frame. And he's there and he'll be sitting with you and you'll play a sound and he'll go "What's that? Take that, drop it down seven octaves and then add a forty second reverb on it!"

The other cool thing about David is he hears a sound and he'll go just go off with it. And two, three, four hours go by and then he'll say, "I hate this!" And then it starts all over again. He is really in there in the trenches and he's really creative and even though he doesn't really do the work himself, he has the patience to sit there and do it. Now that's fun!

KB: Doesn't David Lynch have his own mix studio?

RE: Yeah, he owns three houses in the Hollywood Hills. One is his living house. One originally was an office and he had his Avids and production people there. His third house has an art studio on top and underneath is a beautiful Dub Stage. It's like a medium sized Hollywood Dub Stage with all of the great gear in it and it's a really good sounding room.

And he has a Pro Tools set up. You know MULHOLLAND DRIVE was one of the first films that was done and mixed entirely in Pro Tools. Which was another interesting experience.

KB: Was there a different approach for you when you were working on THE STRAIGHT STORY as compared to MULHOLLAND DR?

RE: No. THE STRAIGHT STORY was the first film I did with David and when I interviewed with him for the job, he just asked me if I wanted to supervise it. They had already done some negotiations with some other people to do some of the other work. They had talked to Foley people and stuff like that. So we came on and started working.

I am trying to remember how long we mixed that. Probably a month, which is pretty long . . . there was a deadline and he had to have it finished at a certain time for showing it at Cannes if I am remembering it correctly.

That's a funny thing. We were mixing a certain part of the film, MULHOLLAND DRIVE, and I went to David and I said something about one of the characters. I think it was Emile and I think it was about whether that character was dead or alive and I said to David, what is it? Is she dead or alive , or . . . and I said how should we mix this? And he wouldn't tell me. He said "What do you think?" And that was it. He wouldn't actually explain it to me.

KB: Why do you think good sound is important?

RE: I think anybody could answer that question if they took any film and turned down the sound. If they watched it without sound I don't think they would enjoy it that much.

It's that whole thing where, if you notice the sound then it's probably bad sound. There is so much work that goes in to a sound track these days and a lot of people take it for granted.

What we add, when done correctly, enhances the whole movie experience.

KB: So how come sound gets no respect until Post-production?

RE: Those famous last words, "We'll save it in Post." That's a good question. I hate to say this but it might have something to do with our earlier sound editors. I mean I heard stories way back when I first got in to the business about the sound departments and how they used to have a particular guy come in on Saturday and Sunday and clock in for all of them while the sound crew was on the golf course, or with their families. They'd do stuff like that. And I think those horror stories kind of lead to our downfall.

I don't know, that's a tough one. Picture editors seem to still have a lot of respect in this business but we have absolutely none.

KB: Sound is at the back end of the whole process and producers and directors come to us and say you need to make all of this work. You have to make it great!

RE: Right. But the interesting thing over the last five years is that you have do it for less money and twice as fast. It's just the overall corporate mentality and a lot of people think that they can do it for cheap and it gets to the point where everybody is undercutting everybody else instead of banding together and saying "No!". We can't work faster and cheaper. But there is always somebody hungry who will do it. Technology has gotten better so people can do it by themselves at their house.

I am a perfect example. I am building a stage at my house now.

Over the last six or seven years, two major things have happened. The budgets have definitely shrunk and they keep getting smaller. Someone will say I can do it for this amount and someone else will say I can do it for this amount. And then a Producer will say well he did it last time for that. So you need to do it for that. It's a snow-ball effect.

The other downfall for our industry was that you used to have studios making twenty, thirty, forty complete films, which employed a lot of people for a large amount of time. Now they each make three or four a year where they have these huge budgets. Now you have all those sound designers and supervisors and editors looking for the medium and small budget films and they're not there. Tiny films are going through and there are so many people looking for a job, and that just keeps cutting the budgets down.

KB: Why should we worry about sound when we're going to replace all of the dialogue anyway? Who's going to notice?

RE: (Laughs) People don't realize all of the great dialogue work that we do, they don't understand that.

It gets down to respect for sound. I haven't talked to a ton of production sound mixers but the ones I have talked to, they always tell me that they spend hours and hours setting up a shot visually and seconds on sound. They don't ever get enough time to properly set up their mics. They will never re-do a shot for sound. If they get visually what they want they move on and that's the problem. If you don't take the time to set up sound for the shot in production then you're going to get crappy sound.

And the money has done the same thing to them. They are working for less, the equipment is cheaper, and once the equipment is better and cheaper and it does more things, then all of the producers and directors think you can do it faster and cheaper.

KB: What is your feeling on ADR?

RE: It's a necessary evil for sure. It's over used by some directors but it can help. Like on a comedy. All of the little walla stuff in the background can enhance and make things funnier. You know the perfect piece of ADR off camera can help explain a story without having to go to another scene.

I think ADR has its place. Then there are over uses, I did a movie a while back and the Director just stuck some words in the actor's mouth right on camera. I mean the guy wasn't even saying that. I am looking at it horrified saying, "That's okay for you?" and the director was totally fine with it. That's just the mentality that some people have.

KB: If you were the director what would you do differently as far as sound?

RE: If I am shooting a live-action film, when I say "Action" and remember this is coming from a dialogue editor, when I say "Action" I don't want anyone doing or saying anything for five or ten seconds. I want to get the ambiance of the scene recorded so that the dialogue editor doesn't have to pull his or her hair out trying to manufacture enough fill to clean up the dialogue. And I would definitely give my location recording person enough time to get set up so that they feel comfortable getting the dialogue correctly.

I would listen to my production sound mixer and they could say, "I know that last take was really good but the dialogue was over modulated and it's distorted. Can we do it again?"

I'd do those kinds of things. And I think if you do that then you're going to come away with the best sound. I know sometimes there are sound problems in places you can't control. Be that as it may, give yourself a fighting chance to get really well recorded dialogue.

KB: What is the most common sound problem that you encounter?

RE: The most common sound problem on the live-action side has got to be, not enough takes on dialogue. Also bad ambiances and bad mic placement. The stuff I was just talking about. The quality of production sound has gone way down in the last five, six, seven years.

The faster that everyone goes and the less time they give to the sound people, the worse the tracks get. That's the most common thing. Then you have to do much more work on the dialogue side, use ADR, that sort of thing.

The most common problem we have in animation is a lot of takes that aren't recorded very well. Not putting the microphone in the best places, things like that. But that's definitely not as common as the bad sound we get from live-action films.

KB: What's the worst sound problem you've ever encountered and how did you fix it?

RE: (Laughs) There have been so many, I can't think of where to start with that one . . .

I was working on LOST IN SPACE and that was the kind of film that there were changes every day. There were a ton of visual effects and we had this terrible schedule. We had a "hard date" that we had to make and we were mixing day and night. It was either reel four or reel five, there was this whole round of changes. We had just pre-dubbed the reel and there were a bunch of sound editors working on this together and we had just gotten a really good mix on the reel. It was a big action scene where the space ship crashes and it goes through all this stuff. It finally comes to rest. It was just this whole great scene and then they changed it.

The following night I had to conform it and I remember pulling my hair out. We took out all of this stuff and played the reel back, and I remember being so depressed because it had been this great sounding reel and when it was re-cut it just wasn't the same. It didn't have the same snap. They cut it all up and changed some of the angles and it just wasn't the same.

KB: We all have scenes like that. I worked on one film where they took out an entire scene and it was one of the best sounding ones we had done. You want to say, man you should have seen this before the director walked back in.

RE: Yeah there should be something like pre-nups between us and directors, we joke about that a lot.

KB: What is your best advice to filmmakers?

RE: I would say take your time. Definitely give yourself enough time for post and hopefully enough money too. If I was a director I would definitely fight for that. I would give my post crew enough time to do what they need to do. It makes for a much better and relaxing process.

I think when you get close to finishing your film you want to make sure that it's the best that it can be. Nine times out of ten you don't have the time or the resources to do what you need to do because you just didn't plan ahead. You want to make time so that you can relax while you're final mixing. It'll make the film sound better. And it doesn't happen too often.

KB: If you were looking for a sound designer what would be the important things you would want to know about them and/or their work?

RE: I would look for someone who is really going to sit down and bounce ideas off of others. Someone who listens. There are a few people I have encountered and worked with who are almost offended when they bring something in and it may sound great to them, but it's not what the director wanted. They get offended when the director doesn't like it. Or they try to push their ideas on a director whether they want to go that way or not.

I want to work with someone who wants to work with me. That is willing to work with me to try and find the vision that I hear in my head.

KB: A lot of film students ask me how they can get in to sound design, what would you tell them?

RE: Don't do it! Isn't that what we tell everybody? (Laughs) I'm serious. I swear to God now-a-days I see these young guys coming up and I feel so sorry for them. It's just such a dismal career.

I guess I would say get used to lots of rejection and just try and be creative. Do your own thing. Never burn any bridges and be nice to that assistant, or that first editor, or that guy who says he wants to be a director. They are all possible clients so be as nice as you can to all of them.

You never know, that person could be directing something and you want that job. Form those relationships and be nice to all of the people you come in to contact with.

KB: Do you think Hollywood is a small town?

RE: It is so small it's unbelievable. It may look like it's huge from the outside but it's very small. Especially the sound community. I have never, ever gotten a job that I wasn't referred to. I don't think I've ever hired anyone that I haven't gotten a referral on. "I am looking for a dialogue editor, who do you know?"

It's all about your relationships with your colleagues and the people you work for, that's how you get hired.

You can have the greatest resume in the world and you're not going to get hired unless you have done some work for someone and it went well.

KB: There are some guys who always seem to work.

RE: Tom (Johnson) is a perfect example of a guy that just has a way, he has a great personality, everybody likes to work with him, and he does great work.

I had never worked with him until CORALINE, he is the kind of mixer that just does the work. He doesn't leave the chair and he isn't real gabby, he sits in the chair and works really hard to get things right.

KB: Tom's whole thing is how do we get this to sound as great as possible. He works with you. I've worked with a couple guys who can hardly wait to point out all of your mistakes, especially when the producer or the director are sitting in there. That doesn't make it a pleasant mix.

RE: Unfortunately you have guys, especially here in LA, who came up twenty to thirty years ago with these "God-like" mixer attitudes. Those guys are out there and it makes it difficult for the sound editors. I've worked with a lot of them and it's not fun!

You want to go in for work, you don't want to go in for battle. It's like you're mentally preparing for this big kind of struggle that's going to happen.

KB: Can you give me a list of films that you think young filmmakers should see, and why?

RE: There are so many. I always watch the big action films just so I can see what I would have done different. How would I approach it?

There are so many films that come out and I look at them and think that was a really good sound job. There's APOCALYPSE NOW, that's a great sound film. I liked TOP GUN, I remember thinking about that one and saying that was a great sound film. THE HUNT FOR RED OCTOBER. There was a French film called AMILIE another a great sound job.

KB: Have you seen any films in the last few years where you say I wish I would have done that one?

RE: I see them all the time (Laughs) I probably don't see half the films I should see. After working all day on films, I don't want to go to the movies.

KB: Can you think of anything that you would like people to know about what it is you do?

RE: It would be nice if people, I am thinking of people in our industry, understood how creative we want to be. And it would be great if they would let us be as creative as we want to be. If only people knew how hard we work and how much we care about what we do. And how important it is to us.

KB: Do you still love what you do?

RE: I do. The business side of movies is awful, it always has been. It's very cut-throat and very political. Of course when I was an editor I didn't have to think about that as much. But being a supervisor you definitely get in to that world. But you know all about that too Kelley. How political it can be and how nasty it can be. We're all vying for the same jobs and we do the same things.

The creative side I just love. The hours just go by when I am doing that kind of stuff. If I could do that all the time it would be great. If that was all I had to do I would keep doing it forever.

Jim LeBrecht

*"Sound is kind of invisible, but when it's wrong
we know it immediately."*

I still remember the first time I met Jim. I was working on a film at the Saul Zaentz Film Center and Jim cruised in to my room. He said he had heard that I had worked with John Callahan (the cartoonist) and he wanted to meet me. He thought Callahan was funny as hell and loved his irreverent sense of humor. I soon found out that Jim was also quite irreverent.

Every time I'm in the Bay Area I hang out with Jim and when we're not laughing and making jokes at each others expense we're talking about our work. I was lucky enough to do a panel with Jim at SXSW (South By South West) a while back and I still believe that it was his name that got us in, because he and I both know how they feel about me at that place.

Jim does lots of social issue documentary work because he feels those kinds of films are important, but he also did one of my favorite dramatic films, he was the Sound Designer on THE SINGING DETECTIVE.

Jim's other credits include: THE DEVIL AND DANIEL JOHNSTON, SOLDIERS OF CONSCIENCE, FREEDOM RIDERS, THE MOST DANGEROUS MAN IN AMERICA: DANIEL ELLSBERG AND THE PENTAGON PAPERS, and lots of pieces for THE AMERICAN EXPERIENCE, and The Rock and Roll Hall of Fame.

If you want to know more about Jim LeBrecht check out: http://www.imdb.com/name/nm0495898/

KB: So how are things going?

JLB: I'm kind of busy, you know, little projects here and there. Everybody wants a piece of your time.

KB: It's great to have work, man.

JLB: Yeah, if we could just get everybody to pay their bills now that would be really nice.

KB: I'm the same way. I'm doing this small project for this guy because I got my daughter's tuition coming up. He's like, "Well, I don't know if I can pay you right now." And I want to say, "I don't know if I can make your deadline if you can't pay me".

JLB: Exactly. When did we become the Bank of Kelley Baker or the Bank of Jim LeBrecht?

KB: We get these people who need to have their movies done. You give them a quote and they say, I can pay that and then once you get into the job it's kind of like, "Can I give you weekly payments until we get this thing straightened out?" And you say, "Only if you can get all the payments to me in three weeks because that's when your deadline is."

JLB: Exactly.

KB: How did you get involved with this sound foolishness, Jim?

JLB: My father had a hi-fi down in the kids playroom and I'd be crawling around on the floor in there and there was this door that opened and it had this big speaker and I looked inside and I could see these tubes glowing and I kind of liked it And he used to tape Broadway Cast albums off the radio using his Wollensak reel-to-reel deck and play them back during dinner. This started my interest in sound.

I always loved music and appreciated it, experiencing the world around me through my ears. I think it was a way to reach beyond where you can see or get to. I fell into the drama clique in high school and since I had a reel-to-reel tape machine, and a turntable, and sound effects LPs, I could record some sound effects and play them back for theater and drama productions.

I went off to college to study acoustics, thinking that this was the way that I was going to be the next audio engineer for the Grateful Dead. I got there and realized acoustics was all math and science. I went down to the drama department and they were doing a big outdoor production and had speakers all over the place and they made me head of the sound crew. That's how much people were burning to be involved with audio. This guy rolls up in a wheelchair out of nowhere.

KB: Nobody ever wants to do audio?

JLB: I think most of the world is very visually oriented. One part of the reason I think is that sound is intangible. You can't really pick it up and say, look, this is what your sounds is going to look like. It's not as easy to quantify, we don't talk about all the great sound editors, we talk about the directors, we talk about the film editors that work with the directors, we talk about cinematographers or set designers. Sound is kind of invisible but yet when it's wrong we know it immediately.

KB: Do you think the people in film schools don't teach sound or don't approach sound correctly?

JLB: I'm not too up with what's happening academically but I would say with my background in theater that there is a slow but steady growth in sound design programs in theater departments - there are many more than there were twenty years ago.

I think with the improvement of audio in film, in general, that any good film school is going to have more than one class in sound, because they realize it's an essential part of the presentation of film. It certainly doesn't mean that silent films aren't wonderful, it certainly doesn't mean that you can't have a great soundtrack in mono, but the consideration that goes into making all these decisions is something that's just as important to discuss as theory and concepts as it is about lighting and camera angles.

KB: Why do you think sound is important in a movie?

JLB: You know, that's a surprisingly difficult question. Here's what I think, first off I'm a little bit biased but when you go to the theater, or when you go to a film, the lights go down but you still hear the people around you murmuring and you hear their voices unfettered by anything that is electronic or artificial. You hear the popcorn and you hear the kid giggling and you hear the noise of the door slapping the back of the theater and all of those things are very realistic. You have all of these different textures and I think that when you get into watching a film we have a good sense of what things sound like. I remember seeing some films from the 40s and 50s, the ones that were done on a low budget where people are in a wonderful apartment but there may be only one picture on the wall and it's of a couple of dogs playing poker. As opposed to the higher budgeted films that have the really excellent ashtray standing in the corner and the lamp and the kitchen set up just so and I think it's that kind of detail that, in audio, really fills in what's happening on the screen. Audio can supply a lot of the details.

KB: Do you believe that sound can improve a story?

JLB: Sound can do things like change the length of a scene. I worked on this independent film I really liked that didn't see the light of day but it started out with this woman sitting on the back porch of her house. The set up is that there's just been a wake for her brother and she's sitting in the back smoking a cigarette just kind of looking up a little bit. Without any extra audio just the sound of the traffic being picked up in production the scene is way too long you don't really get what's happening. But by adding the sounds of people's voices as if they're filtered by being on the other side of the house saying please let us know if she needs anything, hearing cars start and doors open and close and take off and other people responding to those kind of yelled questions at the end you get a sense of okay there are people leaving the house. Oh she needs something, oh this sounds pretty serious, and you start filling in the pieces in your mind about when she looks up, what is she thinking about? Has she discussed it with people? Is she thinking about the loss of her brother? Is she worried she doesn't have enough cigarettes to get through the night? You had absolutely no context before we started giving you some clues about what's going on and at that point that scene really became the perfect length.

KB: That's such a great example because everybody's going to be worried about the camera angle and the acting and all this other stuff because the camera's just sitting there, and yet by using sound in a creative way like you did, you started having the audience asking themselves a ton of questions.

JLB: You want your audience to be thinking, you want your audience to be wondering, and you want them to try to figure some stuff out on their own.

KB: And if they're watching a Michael Bay film. There's no time to think, there's no reason to either.

JLB: Well, there you go. So certainly sound can fill in for where finances fell short, it can certainly make things seem bigger than they are, even in a less obvious way. If you have an isolated character, if you have an isolated scene, carefully choosing your sounds can really improve or heighten that sense of isolation.

Particularly everything you don't hear, filtering through the windows or outside to how you treat the actor's voices, do you make it maybe just a little bit muffled so you don't hear any of these voices bouncing off walls? Do you feel like you're in a jar full of cotton?

I think people don't realize how much you can manipulate sound or use sound in so many different ways, what you use, what you don't use, what volume things are happening at and how thick or thin the soundtrack is.

KB: If we can be so creative with sound, especially in post-production, how come sound doesn't get any respect?

JLB: Why are we the Rodney Dangerfield or the poor cousin? I think it just comes back to people don't know what they don't know. And they don't understand what sound can do. I've certainly worked with people who said if I knew what you could do, I would have had you do more. I think everybody is trying to become a director through being a cameraperson and working their way up in the business. And sound people for the most part don't think, "God I really want to be a director some day and I'm going to do it through the sound department." It's not the road to directing.

KB: They don't like us until we have to come in and save their asses.

JLB: Yeah. But you know you won't be recognized for that. People pay attention to what things do get awards and it's usually films like KING KONG or SAVING PRIVATE RYAN and it was a shock to everybody when THE ENGLISH PATIENT got so many awards because for the most part it was a dialogue film or least that's what they were saying.

Look at David Lynch, or Francis (Coppola). They get it and

when I'm giving advice to filmmakers a few smart folks say I want to talk to you before we even start production. And the first thing I say is you've got to instill in your crew that the sound, the production sound person, has as much importance as the DP. That their work is as essential to you as anybody else's job. And that everybody has to respect everybody else's job.

KB: Do you find that they do that?

JLB: I don't know, but it is the advice that I give. I don't remember what that film was but I remember telling him that, "Look you're audio is going to sound a lot better if that person gets some respect." And it's better to hire somebody that you didn't just find on Craig's List yesterday.

KB: I just talked to this guy who put together most of his crew through Craig's List and these people don't know what they're doing. But they're cheap apparently.

You have a couple of different titles on the films you've worked on, sometimes you're listed as a sound designer, sometimes you're a re-recording mixer, how does that all fit together?

JLB: Some people think that if you call yourself a Sound Designer, you have your nose up in the air. Because of my background I based my goals and my standards on some really important sound designers and people who have blazed some trails. So that's what I choose to call myself and that's what I'm doing.

I believe a sound designer's job is to be concerned with the overall audio of the whole film. When I think of a supervising sound editor I kind of think of someone who's more in a managerial position making sure that everybody's got their work to do, and that people are delivering stuff on time, and they could conceivably be subservient to a mixer. Mixers tend to get a bit more artistic control than editors; I was kind of shocked at that at the beginning of my career in film. But they're the ones that are putting it together with the director.

This whole idea of a supervising sound editor doing a spotting session in LA with a director and a producer and then everybody going away for six weeks and coming back on the stage was shocking to me. In the theater, we talk about things together until we want to kill ourselves.

In film, it felt like the music's going to show up, the sound effects are going to show up, and they're going to have to sort through everything and see what works and what doesn't, and nobody's really talked to each other. I just thought this is the stupidest way in the world to do something artistic. And for me, being a sound designer, I can talk dialogue and I can talk about what we think we should be doing in a spotting session, or the mix. I can talk all the different languages of how we may or may not approach it, and I can work with a production sound editor, and get us all on the same page. I think that the title that I least identify with is the supervising sound editor.

I think that my job has really been sound designer and mixer. And they are strongly related. As I am sound designing a scene or adding sound to a scene I am mixing as I go. How do I know if something's really going to work unless I've got it dialed in properly? I prefer to wait until all the dialogue has been edited. That way the sound has all been laid out so that when I start my work, I've got all that material there as my base. And I prefer to have the final music. That doesn't really happen in Hollywood features, things are always coming in at the last minute.

KB: Do you think you get better results because you have your hands on everything throughout this process?

JLB: I think I do get good results, but I must say that having the dialogue in the hands of a wonderful dialogue mixer, who would do a better job than I do, is always great. Not that I'm a slouch or anything. I'm a really big believer in the power of collaboration and so I don't think I'm the only one that can do it.

But I think there is a lot involved with whether sound is going to work or not that happens in the mix. I would be thrilled if I was more of a sound designer who got to just sit back a little more because I had such a wonderful relationship with the mixers that were working with me that they knew what I want. If I couldn't describe it I could pop over there and just do it.

KB: You also do sound for games and computer programs, is that different than doing a movie?

JLB: Well one of the biggest differences is implementation. And it's only in this very linear world where every frame, every twenty-four times or thirty times per second where you know what's going to happen exactly. And in games there's so many things that happen that can be triggered based on what event has come before that the players initiated. You have to provide a lot of pieces that get put together.

The exciting thing about being a sound designer for games is that the tools have progressed to a point where with a certain amount of implementation we can do all sorts of things. They'll say they want bullets hitting a tank, so we'll give them four or five different sounds or variations and they'll set it up so that it randomly plays one but it never repeats one right after the other. You can get to the point where these bullet hits can be made up of four or five different elements that are being triggered at the same time and you build in all the variations. One variation will be just a little bit softer because we use the same pieces of audio but how it's triggered is contained within it's set of instructions.

We're in a situation where you're putting things into the game, seeing how it works and then a whole bunch of people you may or may not be talking to weigh in on it and you make a lot of changes.

You have to really understand the ability of the playback engine and be able to figure out how to get the most out of what you're dealing with. In the past you've had a limited number of resources dedicated to audio, so how do you use this amount of memory or this amount of disk space to get the most out of it?

KB: Is it more of a challenge to do the games than it is a film because of that?

JLB: In film, it comes down to everything's being mixed down in one stream. I think it really depends on the project. I think there are just some absolutely straight- forward films where nobody wants to be challenged and nobody's asking you to be challenged. They can be put together and the most difficult part of that is how not to be bored. There are games in which they're breaking new ground and they really want something incredibly creative and you're creating worlds that haven't been heard before based on something that you've thought about and it's clicking with the games. You're getting a lot of good support from the rest of the team which is difficult but it's really, really exciting. It really just depends on complexity and on expectations.

KB: It sounds like it's a much more collaborative effort.

JLB: Like any other process, sometimes it's very collaborative sometimes it's not. In the early days, you were handing a bunch of sounds to a programmer who also may have been doing the music because he has a synthesizer and production values were horrible. Nowadays, it may be more collaborative, but it may be just that there are a lot more people with their hands in the pot - producers, sound editors, and artistic leads.

I like working on games because they're fun, usually, and it's like just give me a game where I have to create some characters and an interesting universe.

You know there's nothing like making your own growls by ripping into a cantaloupe with your face . . . you know what I mean?

KB: I've never done the cantaloupe thing personally, but I'll take your word for it. I find that if you work with people you enjoy working with and they give you freedom, the jobs are a lot more pleasant. I used to do a lot of commercials, let's not go there.

JLB: It's like this guy hired me to do sound on some videos and they have a team of people they have to satisfy. "I really like what you do but we're going to turn it down."

KB: Exactly. Do you do sound design on documentaries? I mean, aren't documentaries put together just as they occur?

JLB: Oh please, I think you better sit down. (Shouting) Honey, can you give me the name of that priest because Kelley's going to have his whole faith in life shattered right now.

I was so surprised when I started working on documentaries. There's usually an awkward dialogue thing and you created a whole new line here and the director is like, "Yeah, but that's what he wanted to say." Okay. Wow! There's no Santa or the Easter Bunny.

Every filmmaker has an intention/bias in their film and every film has it's emotional content and how it's played out. I think really great documentaries are ones in which the filmmaker is not being heavy-handed about how they feel about something, they really try to show you a lot of different sides of what's happening and allow you to be intelligent as an audience member.

But the fact of the matter is that we've gone, in the last twenty years or so, from these really dry documentaries that were something you might have seen in high school, like driver's education films, to these films that are really quite incredible trips and romps and experiences. And that is done through creative use of photography, fabulous use of graphics, really aggressive use of music, all sorts of really wonderful ways to manipulate the image and sound. The opportunities for the audio to be creative, you're not going to do some kind of wild sound thing when it's a very straightforward documentary.

But that's not the kind of work I generally see nowadays. THE DEVIL AND DANIEL JOHNSTON is a wonderful example of a film, where there's a whole bunch of stuff shot in different locations, but there were more re-creations that were done and animation sequences and it was just a wonderful film for exploring a lot of different ideas in regards to audio. Where are we? Are we in Daniel's head?

We were doing a surround sound mix on THE DEVIL AND DANIEL JOHNSTON and the director and I starting to explore using an impulse response reverb to help us feel closer to Daniel. Where were we placing his voice in the room? Did we want to make him seem distant and far off? Well we'll put him in the center speaker and maybe add some reverb around the whole room so you want to feel like we're right next to him? Or maybe we'll pull his voice into the room a little bit by adding some left and right into the rear speakers. I was able to do these things because that's the kind of presentation the rest of the film was calling for. It was calling for the fact that there were a lot of different worlds that we were going to explore here.

There are a lot of films more straightforward than THE DEVIL AND DANIEL JOHNSTON. Like TRIMPIN: THE SOUND OF INVENTION. We had a wonderful surround mix and we set the sonic language up very early in the film. We were cutting back and forth in the title sequence between cinema verite shots of Trimpin in his studio, with the audio up the center. Then we'd cut to a title card and music would play from all of the speakers. Introducing the film this way is immediately saying to people, "Really open your ears." In fact the tag line for the film is, "Open your ears and your mind will follow."

We were trying to show people that they needed to pay attention to what they were listening to. You felt like you were hearing things around you and again it's a hard thing to do when you're seeing it on a two-dimensional screen. But we all get to this point where we kind of just let go and we're looking at images and in our mind the screen fades away and the room fades away and the audio really does just kind of feel like we're in these different art galleries or in these different installations.

KB: Do you think that because of where we've taken documentaries and because of the type of sound we're now able to do, we've been able to push the envelope that way with sound?

JLB: I think it's two questions that are there. What do you do and what don't you do? You don't use surround sound in a film just because you can. It has to be a logical part of the presentation. And for me it's often like, "Well gee, we need to add some ambiance to the scene but we're using mono audio for all these interviews and if all of a sudden I put a stereo farmyard background in then it's going to tip our hand that's it's totally fake." So I'll take these stereo ambiances and I'll take the left channel and just run that up the center with everything else. What I have to be careful with is that I don't destroy the documents, the documents that make up the documentary.

But audiences are now used to things like what Michael Moore does or other people are doing and so they accept it. It's like why do we accept the fact that all of a sudden there's music playing in the scene? Why doesn't that seem completely out of the character of the film? Well, it's a convention that we've grown to accept since we were kids. I still feel uncomfortable if I'm going to have a stereo ambiance in the scene but sometimes it's very subtle and I have good reasons for doing it.

KB: Right. But we're still manipulating the audience, aren't we?

JLB: Yes. You're absolutely manipulating the audience. But that is no different than what they're doing in the editorial process. When they're deciding what they're going to use and what they're not.

KB: My production designer, Teresa Tamiyasu, always tells film students every time you see something in a movie you see it because we put it there. Everything was put there for a reason. And that's something that a lot of film students and young filmmakers don't understand, they think you just go out and shoot.

JLB: And the same thing applies to sound. There's nothing that you hear in the film that wasn't thought about, discussed, and then added.

KB: How much control do you have over what you do?

JLB: It kind of depends. I think that when you have a good relationship with the filmmaker you have much more of an opportunity to experiment and try stuff. The director wants a couple of things from you as a sound person. They want to know you're invested in the work you do, they want to know that you care, and that you're focused on what's happening here. As you're working with them they'll know whether all of those things are happening. And if you actually do care, are focused, want to do a good job, and really work for them - then when you say, I got an idea, let me just try something. If they know what they're doing, they're going to let go and say, "Yeah do it, you have five minutes. I'm going to go and have a cigarette." Great! Go smoke your cigarette and when you come back I'm going to have the thing for you.

The exciting thing is that when you do work on an idea you bring it back and it's not all polished but it's in good shape then they say, "Yeah, I kind of like that." You get them involved in the process. I think everybody wants to be heard.

For a lot of people when it comes to sound, they do something in Final Cut Pro and they think that they're done, you know and I may be their first sound-man. They don't know what the process is. I make sure that everybody knows exactly what's going on and I also try to find out what hasn't worked for him or her in the past. If you actually look the person in the eyes and say what do I have to do to make you happy today on this project? What do you like? What do you want? And you actually don't stop listening until they've finished their sentence you'll really get yourself someplace. It's valuable information. I've had a good working relationship because I asked this filmmaker, what can I do for you?

So when something isn't going right I made sure that the filmmaker knew, but I also told her I thought we could fix it. And she trusted me and she knew I cared enough about the film and her project that I was going to work until I got it as close to what she wanted as I could. And I found her to be rather pragmatic when I said this is the best we can do with the amount of time we have. Usually she just accepted it or she'd try to do more work on the film. Sometimes I'd say look I'm getting concerned about getting everything right. Can we prioritize? I think it's these things people don't get taught in film school. I don't think they get taught about interpersonal relationships with the people you're going to be working with.

KB: With budgets changing all the time and people having less and less money, what is the biggest change you've seen in post-production sound in the last few years?

JLB: I started working in audio over twenty years ago, and the amount of equipment and the size of the crew is tiny now compared to what we used to have.

There used to be a lot of films where everything always had to be mixed on a big stage, a big room. You did your pre-mixing ahead of time also on the stage. Now you can save money by just doing the final mix for the print master on a mixing stage for a shorter period of time. All the pre-mixes can be done on Pro Tools.

The ability to manipulate and change things has gotten greater and that's a plus and a minus. In the old days if there were picture changes you would have to strike a new set of work prints and stuff and there was a certain amount of cost involved. Now it's, here's your new quick-time movie and the only cost really is the picture editor if they aren't on a flat rate. And with the constant changing of picture, the change note has gone the way of the fucking Dodo Bird.

I actually got a really good set of change notes on a film I was doing recently. It was awesome. The notes were like, I got rid of thirty-nine frames at this time code, and then at this time code I want you to do this. That's a freaking change note! Where I have had some people come back and I have had to conform an hour and a half documentary with no change notes. I had to put up the old guide track and the new guide track and it took forever.

KB: What do you think biggest challenge is working with a filmmaker?

JLB: Expectations have always been kind of a challenge, especially around changes you could say look my bid is based on a locked picture and these deadlines will be met. Look, if you have issues I'm going to roll with the punches with you as best I can. But in the long run if all of a sudden you decide that you need to put the show on a hiatus and you need to re-edit I can't guarantee we're going to be here. Or if you found you had to change a couple of scenes well either you need to do less work on your film or you're going to have to pay for the conforming on your track. I'm trying to keep people aware that there really is a cause and effect when they do things.

Certainly when I was growing up in the film industry a lot of us kind of cowered at the thought of, "Oh with this many changes we'll have to stay up all night." I think when you get older and you're a little more established you kind of go, "These things do happen and I'm here to help you, but I actually can not work past ten o'clock. I think that if you lay out your expectations or your limitations right at the get go - it's a smart thing to do.

KB: What would you do if you were the director as far as sound?

JLB: First off, I would hire the best location sound people I could. People who really have an understanding of what happens with their work, when they hand it off to us in post-production. I would want to know who my post-sound people are going to be and try to get them involved in the early stages of the movie, read the script let's talk about it, let's come up with a list of things we want to try to capture on location. Let's make sure the sound people are budgeted in such a way that we have time to make sure we have the microphone set up properly and have the sound people go out for an extra hour afterward to record some ambiances Get me coverage.

KB: What's the most common sound problem?

JLB: The recording of the audio itself. Either it's recorded too soft so that the track is kind of hissy or it's too loud so we're either getting distortion or lots of compression. A lot of times the microphones aren't always in the best location.

I worked on one film that was shooting on location and they didn't turn off the refrigerators because it was going to cost them $125.00 to pay for all the ice cream so it took us an extra ten hours to mix the film at $100.00 an hour because we had to work to fix the dialogue on all these different angles in their film.

The most common sound problem I see is really the fact that the different angles in a scene can really sound so different and fixing them is difficult.

KB: What are a couple of films that really influenced you?

JLB: APOCALYPSE NOW and THE CONVERSATION. Those are really huge. I think APOCALYPSE NOW set a tone and really set a bar for me as a sound designer. I saw it when it first came out in 1979 and I was just so blown away at how good the sound was in that world that they created. It was probably the first surround sound that I experienced, it was so amazing. I went back to see it two or three days later, and was still blown away. It had a huge influence on me.

Another film audio wise, CITY OF LOST CHILDREN. There are some really interesting visual effects, it's very highly stylized you know, this fantasy like film. So much of the sound relates to creating that world, it's really unusual. I remember there was this thing with this green plume of smoke and the audio that came along with that was just freaking awesome. I just thought it was really inventive and really good. I thought the audio on CONTACT was very good.

KB: If a filmmaker were going to walk into your studio what would you want them to know about what you do?

JLB: Let's talk about a student filmmaker. Let's say they scrimp together a thousand dollars. They say, I've got this five-minute film and I really want you guys to do the sound. I say, okay you really have to maximize the time that we spend together so I want you to be really well organized. Let's really think through some stuff and make sure that your work is prepared as best as you can do it, we're not wasting time doing other things. You need to have an idea of what you're doing. So maybe we start out by simply talking about the film for a couple of hours then you go away and get things ready.

I would tell you to really think about what's important to you, and please tell me what's wrong within your film that you think needs help. Why are you coming to me? What are your expectations? What does your film need? I think that with any director, be it a student director or someone who's been around a long time you have to develop a working relationship. What do they want out of a sound designer and mixer or sound crew? Are they looking for someone just to get the pieces all in place because they're going to create the magic on the stage or do they really need help on something? Are they looking for a water boy or are they looking for a collaborator?

I'm much happier when I've got a plan and we're on the same page. And I'm much happier when I'm using my brain and not just my fingers.

KB: Is it true you charge more to be a water boy than to be a creative collaborator?

JLB: Well, you should charge more because it's time you're never getting back. I worked on a film a few years ago, an independent feature shot in San Francisco and the director wanted to hear sirens and pile drivers in all the daytime scenes. And I said you're making me look bad. You're making me seem like I don't know anything better than to put sirens and pile drivers throughout the film. "But this is what I want." Plus he was going out into the parking lot and getting stoned every day which I don't think helped the artistic innovation.

KB: If you were going to hire a student what would you look for in someone you wanted to work with you or for you?

JLB: I look for someone who has a really strong reason for being here. In other words, NOT somebody who's saying well I can't quite find my place in film so I thought I'd try a little bit of everything. What's better somebody who says to me that I really love sound for film, I really want to be a mixer someday or a sound designer and I need to start somewhere and I've looked at what you do, the kind of work that you've done and I think this would be a really great opportunity for you to work with me.

KB: Nothing better than working with beginners with huge egos. Thanks man.

Gary Rydstrom

"Sound is an excellent carrier of emotion. And film is about emotion."

Gary and I have known each other since our USC film school days. We didn't know each other well but our paths have crossed a few times since then.

Since USC I have watched Gary collect seven Oscars for his sound work (fourteen nominations) and wished that I had gotten to know him better when we were both students. It might have helped my career.

Gary's list of credits is amazing. It includes: SAVING PRIVATE RYAN, JURASSIC PARK, STAR WARS EPISODES ONE and TWO, MINORITY REPORT, TOY STORY, A BUG'S LIFE, QUIZ SHOW, BACKDRAFT, SPACEBALLS and HULK. (Sorry Gary, I had to throw those last two in, they may have been stinkers but they did sound great!)

If you want to know more about Gary Rydstrom check out: http://www.imdb.com/name/nm0003977/

I have always been a fan of Gary's work and the fact that he goes out of his way to do different types of films. He always seems to be challenging himself, not trying to out-do himself like some in this business. He is a down to earth guy who truly has the respect of his peers.

He is up on the latest technological advancements and when you watch him work in either Pro Tools or at a mix console his command of the equipment is effortless. He also uses out of date equipment to achieve the sounds and the feel that he wants, which is pretty unique in and of itself, but more about that later.

KB: What are you working on right now?

GR: It's called WAR HORSE. It's the next thing that Spielberg is coming out with. It's got World War I and horses so from a sound standpoint that's pretty damn cool.

KB: Aren't period pieces harder to do?

GR: Well yeah, for the simple reason that we're recording in a world where you hear nothing but traffic, airplanes, and cell phones. The sound of the modern world encroaches in ways you don't realize until you're a sound effects recordist and then you realize how much of that stuff is out there.

KB: How did you get involved with sound?

GR: I didn't really have any expectation of which way I would go but I did sound at USC Cinema and Ken Muira, (Sound Instructor) recommended me to Lucasfilm in 1983 for a job in the sound department, which was pretty tiny at the time. So the first job offer I got was sound.

KB: So when you started school you didn't have this idea that you wanted to do sound. It was more about going to film school?

GR: I think one of the benefits of film school is that you try a little bit of everything. You don't have to necessarily decide what you're going to do when you get out and sometimes opportunities, surprising opportunities, present themselves.

KB: And I find this humorous that you weren't a sound teaching assistant. I always thought that you were.

GR: I got turned down. Kelley, you can put it on the record. I applied to be a sound TA and didn't get the sound TA position. I ended up being Ken Robinson's TA.

KB: We'll make sure those guys at USC know all about this. When we were in film school was there a particular film or films that were a big influence on you?

GR: It was a glorious time for film and for sound. While we were in film school, APOCALYPSE NOW came out, EMPIRE STRIKES BACK, RAGING BULL, Friedkin was doing great stuff and Bob Fosse, and David Lynch. Still some of the greatest sound work.

KB: Did you find yourself becoming attracted to sound because of those films or was it the whole film experience?

GR: The whole film experience, but particularly sound, at the time sound was getting some recognition. Walter Murch certainly for APOCALYPSE. I remember him coming to talk to us at USC and that was real exciting and then Ben Burtt was getting a lot of publicity for how he was taking real world sounds and turning them into science fiction sounds for STAR WARS.

I remember when we were doing sound for a 480 film (a senior project at USC), we tried to find natural realistic sounds around us that we could turn into really extreme and bizarre sounds. We had no idea how Ben did that, so we did a lot of scraping of things, scraping bananas on tables and trying to find the magic of realistic natural sounds all around us and turning them into exciting different things. It ended up being a lot harder than I thought.

There was a lot of talk about Frank Warner's work in RAGING BULL, using subliminal and point of view sounds, psychological sounds, and I remember thinking all that was very cool and trying to sneak it into our student films as best we could.

KB: Why do you think good sound is important in films?

GR: I think the main reason is that sound is an excellent carrier of emotion. And film is about emotion. Sound is sometimes neglected because it's so taken for granted. Everything from the sound of the human voice from the actors on screen to the music carries emotion and so the sound track to me is a huge component of film.

KB: What's the most important element in sound design in your opinion?

GR: To help tell the story. If you're supporting the story then I think that's the key to just about every craft in filmmaking, if you're not helping tell the story then you're doing something wrong.

KB: Do you want to explain the difference between a Sound Designer and a Supervising Sound Editor? Do you think there is a difference?

GR: I took Sound Designer as a credit early in my career because in Northern California that was the tradition that Walter Murch, Ben Burtt, Randy Thom, and others had started.

To me, Sound Designer is an overall position that included supervising. But I sometimes take the additional supervising credit to make it clear for the crass purpose of winning awards. (Laughs)

KB: I see so many films where people are taking sound design credits and there's no design. In your mind what is it that a Sound Designer truly does?

GR: In my mind, the sound designer is really the guiding force to the sound track, at least the sound effects part of the sound track. It's both creating sounds but also being the creative guide for the sound track from beginning to end.

I think the confusion is people think it comes down to someone using black boxes and trickery to make interesting sounds and then you make a hundred interesting sounds and you've designed sound for the movie. But sound design often comes down to really simple choices - where to put a sound and what kind of sound to put in a track.

KB: You work with the dialogue as well as the sound effects and the music. Can you explain a little bit about your approach?

GR: Dialogue, music, and effects are how it breaks down, but it's important to think of it as a totality. The audience doesn't think of it as three different things on a soundtrack it's really just one sound track so it has to work together.

KB: I recall many, many instances arguing with composers because it always seem to me if you were having a problem in a track some place their solution was always let's turn up the music and most of the time my response was, "That would work just fine but we can't hear the dialogue as it is."

GR: A lot of times people are looking for that one universal solution for a track. People saying the dialogue is number one, music is number two, sound effects number three, prioritizing an overall hierarchy in the track, or the solution to the scene is to just to raise the music.

Sound happens over time and true mixing and good sound work requires shifting what's in the track from moment to moment through the course of the film for the sake of being the most dramatic and the most emotional throughout. And it changes so there's no universal that since this scene is not working let's raise the music. It is raise the music in this section, but hand off to the effects for that little story point, and make sure this dialogue is clear, and then bring the music back to bring the scene to a climax and let our emotions have somewhere to go.

So the answer to what makes a good soundtrack may change from second to second.

KB: You're also a re-recording mixer, does this help when it comes to sound design?

GR: It probably helps and hurts I think. It helps because I know what we've put in to the track and I know what the plan was from the beginning. It is always a scary thing to hand off tracks to a mixer and then hope that they have the same tastes and thoughts you do. At least I know I'm doing what I planned on doing.

The hard part is that I have to get out of my own way and realize when something isn't working or I should weed it out and not be so precious about things. I've certainly been accused - and other sound effects editors who mix have been accused - of being protective of their sound effects. You have to be willing to take things out.

The key to sound editing to me is adding things in and seeing what combination works for the movie. The key to sound mixing is taking sounds out. When it comes to mixing, half the time you're finding what it is you want to remove. If I'm going to be the sound effects editor and the sound effects mixer I have to be really good about not holding on to something because I thought it was a good idea a couple of months before.

KB: Would it be easier to do one or the other?

GR: Not to me. I admire people who just do re-recording mixing because it's a hard job and it's intense to go from mix to mix to mix. I never liked the idea, I like going from editing to mixing. They're two different jobs and I like bouncing back and forth.

I never wanted to be just an editor because I was too controlling to get to a mix and not get my fingers on the faders.

In mixing there's something nice about sculpting the sound by moving a fader. There's so much work these days that happens in the digital realm, typing things on a keyboard. I still so much prefer grabbing knobs and faders and feeling it as opposed to typing it.

KB: How come sound gets no respect until post-production?

GR: You're saying sound gets respect in post-production? (Laughs)

KB: I don't believe the production sound gets respect.

GR: I think there are good directors and good filmmakers and everyone knows good production sound is key, but it is certainly taken for granted. It's something that on the set people assume can be dealt with later in a way that, say, the camera work can't, so sound gets kind of ignored.

It's amazing to me how many times filmmakers will complain about the production sound after production is over. You can't get good production sound back.

I think it's a seen but not heard fact of life for some people on the set. To be there but essentially not be a problem and hope to do your job as best as possible I think sound in general doesn't get a lot of respect for reasons I can only attribute to the fact that it's so central to how we experience the world that it's taken for granted.

KB: Do you believe that sound does get respect when you get into post-production? Because I'm used to getting my budgets cut and my schedules slashed.

GR: Well that certainly happens in post-production these days. The feeling is money could be better spent somewhere else, although sound people will vigorously say that you get more bang for the buck in sound, production and post-production. And money well spent there has a huge impact on the creative success of the film.

KB: I so want to believe you. Can you talk a little bit about how you manage a feature from beginning to end?

GR: I usually get a call from the director or the producer. Over time you start to get calls from the people you have worked with before. Ideally you get that call before they've started shooting, because it's nice to be involved from the very beginning.

The best case is that it's early enough that I can send sounds to be played on the set, to be part of ideas that can find their way into the script or the shoot. But alas, that doesn't happen too often.

Usually the first step, for me anyway, is to start collecting sound, while thinking about what the movie is going to be. The first steps are theoretical. The most fun part of sound is recording, so those early glory days on a movie are when you have time to record sound effects. Finding things that inspire ideas for the film.

For me sound design is taking a lot of these ideas and recordings and funneling them into categories. Sounds that I think will work for the movie and then organizing that so that once the rest of the sound editing crew comes on, they have a good starting point to cut the sound.

I've always thought of the beginning of the process as the big fat end of a funnel, where you throw all of the ideas out there and record everything you can think of. You don't even know what it's going to be used for, and little by little through design and editing and mixing you're reducing all that stuff to what really is working and helping the film. So when you get to the end of the process, it's just a little tiny funnel spout.

KB: You go out and record your own stuff? You don't just say, "Where's the sound effects library?"

GR: I use a lot of people to help record original stuff. It's hard and time consuming but I love recording. I think recording is the discovery part. I take that from the Ben Burtt style of sound design. He didn't use synthesizers, he found sounds in the real world and used them in interesting ways. The fun part of the job is recording and then coming back to the studio, listening to sounds, not caring what they really are . . . and then using them for something completely inappropriate. (Laughter)

KB: I'm always so jazzed when I see analogue gear still being used. Describe your workspace for me if you will.

GR: I have Pro Tools and digital access to my library. I have lots of ways to bring in recordings and record on digital these days but I also have a quarter-inch deck that I still use. It's nice for recording things, especially guns and high-energy sounds.

One of the key tools I've used for a long time is a Synclavier. I used to be on the cutting edge, now I'm a blacksmith. But the Synclavier is a way to sample and manipulate real sounds on a keyboard, using all these different dials to find the most efficient and quickest way to go through a lot of sound material and see how it works. Pitched up, pitched down, equalized, layered in interesting ways, played backwards. The Synclavier is a great tool for going through material fast and experimenting.

KB: I was going to say you're on the cutting edge of . . .

GR: 1983.

KB: Yeah. Do you think that sound can improve a story?

GR: Absolutely. You have those key moments where things turn in the story. There's a moment, there's a moment, there's a moment. I think it's very useful in sound to think in story beats and try to emphasize and clarify those turning points just like a writer would work out story beats in a script.

Sometimes you cover a story beat emotionally or subliminally, like Alan Splet did, shifting ambiances to emphasize a story point.

I try to be aware of the story first and then articulate the soundtrack so that it is guiding the audience through those story points.

There are wonderful things you can do with sound for the world not shown on screen, and tell that part of the story. I think it's really strong when filmmakers use the visuals and the sound to tell the same story but from two different angles.

And then there's the emotional part of it. You're always choosing and using sound to not only clarify story points but to underwrite the emotions that are going on in the scene. You can get into the minds of characters and you can say something about characters.

KB: Do you have your own particular style when it comes to sound? You've worked with people like Steven Spielberg and Ron Howard, two directors with totally different styles. Do you look at every picture individually because the range of your work is out there.

GR: Well thanks. Each film has it's own feeling. A key part of sound design is, what is the tone of this? What's the feeling of this? Is it naturalistic? Is it exaggerated? Is it stylized? Is it musical? What's that tone?

Each film is different. It doesn't shift with the filmmakers as much as with the film. And if directors are able to shift to make different style movies I certainly have to shift gears to fit a style to different movies. I'm glad I've done wildly different movies because that's what keeps it interesting. Sound can do so many different things. It can be funny, it can be incredibly serious, it can be tragic, it can be cartoony. It's fun to try them all.

KB: Do you ever get people who call up and say, "Can you do something like what you did on JURASSIC PARK, or what you did on. . . " or do they do they call you because they know you can do almost anything.

GR: I feel lucky because I never got locked into a certain style. Fairly early in my career I made a big effort to work on a Robert Redford film, A RIVER RUNS THROUGH IT, because after working on TERMINATOR 2 and movies like that it was about as different as I could get. If I worked the two ends of the spectrum I could essentially get offered anything in between.

KB: How'd that work out for you?

GR: Terribly. If I'd done the same thing over and over again it would have been a hell of a lot easier. (Laughter)

KB: You wouldn't have to go and record anything you could just use a library.

GR: Exactly.

KB: How much control do you have over what you do because you work with these really big people. Do they leave you alone or do they come in and sit behind you?

GR: Every film experience is a little different. Everything has to filter through the director and their vision for the movie.

It's good to collaborate with filmmakers, but to be honest, sound people get left alone in a way that, say, film editors or directors of photography don't. Each director has a different amount of involvement, but I've always felt a certain freedom.

I prefer directors that don't get involved in the nitty-gritty because they keep an overall sense of how the movie is working. And in filmmaking especially, you can get lost because you know the work that went into something, you know the source of something, you know the time it took, and that now makes it more precious.

One of the great things you can do as a filmmaker is turn off the part of your brain that knows all the details of the work you did to get there and watch your own film like an audience. And good directors are able to hear the movie in a way that I can't because I've worked everything up from the details.

Luckily it's incredibly boring watching someone do sound work so no director is going to sit over my shoulder for very long.

I've had many people over the years say wow I've never been in a mix before and they come and watch me and if they make it ten minutes that's pretty good. It's essentially torture to watch someone mix.

KB: With SAVING PRIVATE RYAN you did this amazing opening with all the gunfire and there's so much stuff going on. Did you have all this stuff in your head? You put it all together, you go on to the mix stage and you finally show it to Steven, and he's like whoa! Or was it one of those back and forth things, let's cut this and bring this down. How much of that opening audio is you and how much is you taking out most of the good stuff because somebody wants something quieter?

GR: Spielberg comes up with a lot of ideas about how sound is going to work in the scene before I've done anything. So he came up with the camera going under water and the sound of war disappearing and coming back and disappearing again, and the idea of Tom Hank's character getting shell-shocked and losing his hearing.

Also, Spielberg decided not to play the battles with score and to let them be naturalistic. The camera's almost entirely close on characters, on soldiers, on the experience. It's not grand. It's not wide landscape shots. It's intimate. Spielberg trusted the soundtrack to tell the story that was happening outside the camera view.

He set up the scene to take advantage of sound before I did a damn thing. We knew there was no music so we knew we had to carry the drama of the scene. We knew we wanted to be true to the memories of people who were in battle so we were naturalistic with the sound.

I'm always trying to articulate sound so that you know what sounds are for, but in PRIVATE RYAN we were trying to find the balance between being articulate and chaotic. The sound editors did a lot of cutting and it was incredibly detailed crazy premixing and mixing. But the exciting thing is that Spielberg set it up with all these great ideas and hooks and an approach for our sound job. And then when we showed it to him, really the first time we showed it to him, he loved it.

So the back and forth really happened conceptually. The concepts were built into the scene in the first place.

KB: My father was on a Higgins boat in World War II, he was in the Pacific. I saw the opening to SAVING PRIVATE RYAN, and it's one of the most amazing scenes I've ever seen both picture and sound-wise. I am in awe at the work that went into that scene.

GR: He definitely captured something and what he captured was a point of view. It's not a literal point of view. You're not a soldier going through from the Higgins boat to the Normandy Beaches but you get a sense of a point of view. If you think about that opening scene, aside from recognizing Tom Hanks, you don't know who anybody is. There are twenty minutes of battle where you don't know any of the characters, but it's still moving because it's experiential.

It's the cinematic equivalent of our fathers telling us stories from war, partly because of the way he shot it. He didn't shoot it like the LONGEST DAY with big wide shots to set up the scene. He did it intimately so that you would feel empathetic with the soldiers going through it. And from the point of view of the people being shot at as opposed to the people doing the shooting. That's primal and works too for the soundtrack. We hear fewer guns but more bullet bys and bullet hits, and artillery incoming, that kind of thing. It's the effect of war as opposed to the shooting part of war. There are so many things about that I thought were intelligently set up from the very beginning.

For that scene in particular, we didn't create weird new sounds. We know what an M-1 sounds like, we know what Higgins boats sound like, and we know what artillery sounds like. It wasn't about creating new sounds, it was about orchestrating the tracks so that it would have impact.

Occasionally I give a lecture about sound and I show a clip of a scene from DAS BOOT the Wolfgang Peterson movie and there's a . . .

KB: I show it too.

GR: Do you really? The one where the rivets pop?

KB: Absolutely.

GR: What I like about that scene is as the sailors try to evade being caught by a ship going overhead, it's all close ups of the men, waiting, in the section leading up to the rivets popping. There's a creaking of the sub that's going deeper and deeper and the pressure is increasing and the sonar from the ship that's coming near and passing overhead.

That part of the story is being told with sound and the camera is showing us the faces of the frightened men. The standard issue approach to that scene would be to cut to a wide shot of the submarine going deeper in the water and seeing the ship on the surface and show the ship and here's the sub fairly close and getting closer. Here they let the sound of the ship and the sub tell that story and use the camera to tell the emotions of the faces of the men, which is similar to PRIVATE RYAN.

KB: And what I tell people, because that's a huge film to me, the filmmakers turn that submarine into a character and you care what happens to the sub. You care about this giant hunk of steel. And to me the brilliant part of it is you care about the boat, you care about the guys on it and they're the enemy!

GR: That's true. And think about creaks and groans, what do they sound like? They sound like voices. It happens that those particular sounds are very . . . I mean I love sounds that evoke human speech, and sub creaks sound like human speech.

KB: You feel the pain.

GR: Yeah.

KB: You've also done animated films. How does your approach

*as a sound designer differ with animation as compared with
live-action?*

GR: Animation is wonderful for sound because everything has
to be created. Sound creates the base reality of what's going on
plus a more stylized level. Traditional animated film is more
abstract than live-action. You can get away with stuff. And I
love getting away with stuff.

Every sound person loves Treg Brown and the work he did on
the Warner Brothers shorts. It's brilliant, you know, putting in
inappropriate sounds to be funny and you can get away with it
in a way that you can't with a live-action film. You're
responsible for a lot more because there's no starting point from
a production track. That's wonderful. You have more control and
more possibilities. A lot of animation that I've done has been
computer animated Pixar films, which are a weird hybrid -
there's a reality to that style of animation that's asking for a
certain amount of reality with the sound. The characters have
footsteps and weight and there's a reality to them. I had to find a
way to use something that seemed real and grounded and still
have fun in a way a cartoon would have fun. If your going to go
into sound, do sound for an animated film, there's nothing quite
as fun to do.

*KB: It's fun but you're also carrying the weight of the world
because all you have is a dialogue track.*

GR: Yeah. Which is always fun. When we finished all of the
effects premixes, the Foley and the effects and ambiances, we
played it back for ourselves, the effects editors. It's satisfying to
watch the world you've created without the dialogue and the
music. It's like "Wow!" We created a whole new universe here.
For an animated film like A BUG'S LIFE or TOY STORY it
was a thrill to do all this detail work which created a reality, a
sound reality.

KB: How do you approach a film like TERMINATOR 2 where you're working on the sound and the visual effects aren't done yet.

GR: I remember in JURASSIC PARK the way it would work was there would be a big scene coming with the T-Rex attack, or whatever it was and for us on the sound crew we would have nothing. We would have nothing in the shot until it was done and then with days left in our schedule we'd get this massive shot.

These days in visual effects you're getting so many steps along the way so there's a fair guide of the direction that things are going even if the visual effects aren't completely finished. But certainly on movies with 2,000 visual effects there are a lot of moments you're going to have to guess at.

KB: With budgets changing all the time, and getting smaller, what's the biggest change you've seen in post-production sound over the past few years?

GR: I think the coming of digital editing changed the expectations of time. This is partially because when we were on magnetic film in the old days it took an army to get certain films done. You can do a lot more with digital equipment so the biggest change is fewer people and fewer weeks for those people. But at the same time the expectations of the quality of the work is still high.

KB: Do you think the expectations have gone up?

GR: I think the expectations have gone up because movies are getting bigger and production values are certainly getting better. So, I think creative expectations are high, but budgets are relatively lower. The excuse is equipment allows us to do more with less time, which is true. What digital has done is create this tension between high expectations and less time.

KB: That's a great way to put it. Now that you're a director what would you do differently as far as sound that other directors might not have thought about that don't have your background.

GR: The first thing is to think about sound from the very beginning and great directors do this anyway. I think Scorsese, David Lean, Hitchcock, and other great directors thought about sound from the beginning.

If you think about what sound can bring to the storytelling from the very beginning that helps. Also when editing the film, cut a good enough sound track with music and sound effects so that the pacing of it and the feel of it are heading in the right direction. Then you're getting a good sense of what the sound track can do.

It's really a matter of planning. Sound is something you can think about in parallel with camera and editing and all the other crafts, as opposed to thinking about it after the editing is finished.

KB: What do you think students and filmmakers really need to know about sound?

GR: It comes down to the emotional part of it. They need to remember their experience of going to movies, the moments in movies that work. How important the role sound plays. I don't know any other way to put it; film is not primarily a visual medium. Film is a combination, a unique combination of sound and visuals.

And sound is an amazing tool for conveying emotion.

Here is a question I ask when I give lectures. If you had only one way to remember someone who is dead would you rather remember them with a photograph or an audio recording of their voice? People think about it and a lot of times they say, "You know the voice recording would probably have more emotional impact for me," and I think that's true. Sound is such a day-to-day, moment-to-moment carrier of emotion that we take it for granted. And we take it for granted in filmmaking too. It's a huge powerful thing that's available to every film that too often gets ignored but when it's used, it can be extraordinarily effective.

KB: If you're looking for a sound designer, what are the important things you would want to know about them and/or their work?

GR: I think it's important to have a sound designer who thinks about the movie as a movie, as opposed to sound only or sound as a technical part of the movie. They should be thinking what's going to help the movie. They should have an overall sense of the drama of the film itself and how they can help.

It's also good to have a musical way of thinking. To me the soundtrack has to be orchestrated like music, so thinking musically and rhythmically and in terms of pitch is really important.

And it's good not to go down the cliché path. There's a lot of sound cliché's in movies, but it's nice to have people who think differently and want to discover things.

You want someone who's thinking outside the box and thinking in terms of the future that has the whole film in mind and is a very musical person . . . so there you go!

KB: You studied other sound people. You know what Walter (Murch) does you know what Ben (Burtt) does. Do you think that's important for filmmakers to know about the things that preceded them?

GR: Oh yeah. It's really important to see what people have done in the past and are doing now and be aware of it. There's something that I wasn't aware of until I got into sound. You know I went back and looked at a lot of movies that I always loved and I never realized that so many of them were great sound jobs. REAR WINDOW is a great sound job. I just thought it was a great movie, but as a sound person I'd go back and say, "Oh my God that's really good." Many people have thought about these issues for a long time and it's important to learn from their work.

You know it was that damn Walter Murch who worldized all the music in AMERICAN GRAFFITI and I remember at USC we did some movies where we tried to do some of that to our music.

KB: I tried that too.

GR: It's very hard to do. We studied and we struggled to do what they did but I think it's more important to see why Walter worldized the music in AMERICAN GRAFFITI. The music become atmosphere, this changing atmosphere as we move through it.

KB: What's the most common sound problem that you encounter by filmmakers these days?

GR: The biggest sound problem I see is people trying to do too much. Sound tracks need focus just like camera work needs focus. You can get much more impact from a more focused, simpler track. Out of the desire to make something really amazing people put in too much stuff and it's a real basic problem it happens to everybody but it's counter productive. Less is more.

KB: Can you give me a short list of films that you think filmmakers should see? Besides the ones we've already mentioned.

GR: The 70s and 80s were good times so I'm taken with those films, but I still think that it's important to go back to the foundation. See the John Ford, Hitchcock, and David Lean films.

Some great sound work was done in the 30s and 40s. KING KONG is still an astounding sound job. There's something so fundamental about what works about those old films. You know it's not all the bells and whistles laid on top, it is what's working at the most fundamental level.

KB: What's your best advice to filmmakers and film students just starting out?

GR: Whether you make a film or are working on a film, I think it's important to draw on experiences from life as opposed to watching films. A lot of filmmakers try to recreate the feeling they had going to another movie. I think movies are richer if people making them are drawing on experiences from their real lives not their film going lives. Filmmaking and film history are important to know, but what's lacking sometimes is the connection to our lives outside of film.

KB: That's one of the things I say all the time, but nobody listens to me.

GR: No one listens to me either.

KB: Can you think of anything that we didn't learn in school that would be good to have known?

GR: A lot of people go to film school and they say, "I want to be a director." They're not as interested in other aspects of filmmaking. I think it behooves everybody, most of all directors, to have experience with and know as much about the different crafts of filmmaking as possible. It's not just a matter of hiring someone to do that aspect of it. The Spielberg's and the

Hitchcock's knew enough about sound to make movies that took advantage of sound. So don't specialize so much that you're unaware or inexperienced in all the aspects of filmmaking.

KB: Are you glad that you went to film school?

GR: Yes. I think the mistake I made is that I went to film school for both undergraduate and graduate studies. I should have perhaps gotten one degree in something, oh I don't know, "real." If I could rewrite my personal history I would go to school as an undergraduate and study something not film related and then go to graduate school and learn about filmmaking. So I would have something more to bring to filmmaking when I got there.

KB: Did you get both your degrees at USC?

GR: I did. I got a bachelor's and I never finished my masters but I stuck around for two years in grad school.

KB: You and I are so similar it's scaring the hell out of me. I got my both my BA and MFA from USC and I sometimes think it would have been nice to have an English degree or Political Science or something.

GR: Yeah I mean it was certainly fun but I wish I had gotten another degree in something.

KB: Something that would make us bankable when we find out that this isn't going to work out.

GR: Exactly.

CHAPTER 8:

It's Getting Awful Loud in Here

Re-Recording Mixers

The re-recording mixers take all of the separate audio elements (dialogue, music, and sound effects) and put them together in a final mix. They are the ones who are trying to strike a final balance between all three elements so that the audience can understand the story and give it the maximum emotional impact.

There are some very low-key wonderful directors that know what they want and calmly go about the business of getting the picture done the way they see it. And there are the screaming assholes that make everyone's life miserable because of their own ego and insecurities.

They have a tough job, balancing the wants of all the various camps in a mix and yet give the director (or the person ultimately in charge) what they want.

They also have to have enough technical knowledge to know how much they can get away with as far as dynamic range on the entire sound track. They have to be able to strike a balance between the quietest and the loudest parts of the film.

A good mixer has to have superior people skills to navigate the minefield that is that final mix.

Dan Olmsted

"Good sound goes unnoticed, bad sound ruins a film."

Dan Olmsted was one of the first people I met when I started doing work at Saul Zaentz's Film Center in Berkeley. He is a musician who worked in the machine room and was always there when you needed something. Over the years he moved up, first mixing Foley or doing foreign mixes, or whatever no one else wanted to do. He seemed to be determined to move out of the machine room and by always being around he was given opportunities to move up. When it came time to mix my first feature I wanted two of my friends to help me, David Parker and Dan Olmsted. Dan has been the re-recording mixer on all of my features and I trust his ears and his mixing sense absolutely. We also spend a lot of time laughing while we mix.

Dan has done a lot of mixing, everything from short films and documentaries to independent features. I walked in to the mix stage once and Dan was mixing with Walter Murch on a special version of THE GODFATHER. It said a lot to me that Walter would have Dan working with him.

Dan's credits include: CECIL B. DEMENTED, DAUGHTER FROM DANANG, FEMALE PERVERSIONS, THE DEVIL AND DANIEL JOHNSTON, SALUD, LAST FLIGHT HOME, and projects for Independent Lens, P.O.V, the Rock and Roll Hall of Fame and THE AMERICAN EXPERIENCE.

If you want to know more about Dan Olmsted check out:
http://www.imdb.com/name/nm0647465/

Dan is a terrific mixer and an ever better friend. He has some pretty interesting ideas on sound, and why not? He's worked a lot with Walter Murch.

KB: How did you get involved with sound in the first place?

DO: I studied filmmaking in high school due to a lucky break where my school offered a pilot program to teach 16mm film production. They brought over a teacher from the Stanford Film Program and two of his students, and they taught us 16mm filmmaking. We had Bolex's and a Moviola and we made short films and it was a blast.

I decided to go to UC Berkeley where they didn't have any filmmaking programs. I studied English because I wanted to be a writer. Transferred to Santa Cruz, got a degree in English, and during that time of course I was learning to be a musician in a rock band and picked up a lot of knowledge of audio that way.

Tried making it as a musician, which is a pretty crazy thing to even think of. Didn't get very far earning my living as a rock and roll guitar player. So I decided I better go back to school and study something else. I applied to the graduate program at SF State for Film. Halfway through that program a phone call came in from the Saul Zaentz Film Center. They needed someone to do sound transfers 'cause they were working on a big movie, THE UNBEARABLE LIGHTNESS OF BEING.

I got the job, and I got sucked right in.

KB: And the rest is history.

DO: I thought I was gonna be an animator when I was in school. But the job came up and it was too exciting to turn down. There were a lot of big shots working on that film. People we both know and love now, Kelley.

KB: Oh yeah. Is there a particular film that was a big influence on you when you first started out?

DO: Not for sound. To be honest, I got into sound because I knew how to do sound transfers. But as you worked at that place, they were known for good sound work and it kinda rubbed off on me what an art it actually was, how sound design helps shape a movie. I really hadn't thought about it much before that.

KB: Why do you think that good sound is important?

DO: Well bad sound is important because it will take people right out of a movie. If people are annoyed by the sound, it'll really take you out of the story. Good sound I suspect goes unnoticed a lot of the time, but it actually has a powerful storytelling role in filmmaking, and that's what I love about it. It steers the emotion and in many subtle ways plays in the back of people's minds as they watch a film. And they don't always realize it.

And it should be that way. It should be about the storytelling, but the fact is - this is something I learned from working with all these brilliant people like you, Kelley - the way just simple choices about what kind of background sound you choose, even natural sound can have a musical quality that brings emotion to the story and to the movie.

There's a Jim LeBrecht quote, I don't know if he quoted you this, but he loves the saying, "Every sound has an emotion," and a simple choice like what kind of crickets you decide to put in a scene at night can either make the scene feel edgy or placid and comfortable.

KB: I talked to him and he didn't say any of that.

DO: It's one of his favorite sayings, "Every sound has an emotion Danny!" And I've learned to agree with that.

KB: As a re-recording mixer, how much input do you have in the final tracks and do you work much with the sound designer or supervising sound editor?

DO: In the final mix, ultimately the director has the final say, but the re-recording mixer is in a good position to offer constructive feedback because often they haven't heard or seen the film as much. They're like a fresh pair of ears and can give an objective perspective and be an advocate for the audience in a way because you're new to the show and you haven't lost sight of the forest for the trees.

I suppose the kind of relationship I always like to have is for the director to give me the chance to work things up to the way I think they should sound and then I'll ask for their opinion. And the same goes for the sound designer of course. You like to have the space to do the craft the way you think it should be done and then get feedback from them. Ultimately. Though, I really believe my opinion is not as important as theirs. It's their project, their film.

KB: When people ask, "How come you don't do sound anymore?" I say when I was doing sound for other people, no matter how cool something I might have created is, I have to turn around and say, "Is that okay? Do you like that?"

DO: And what if they don't?

KB: You re-do it. But when I'm making my own films, I never ever have to turn around.

DO: That's right Kelley! I'm sure that is better ultimately. You see a lot of tension in sound mixes over different people working on the film and how they've covered certain moments in the story.

KB: Oh God, yes.

DO: And you know, it's a mess sometimes. And I've seen people run crying from a mix stage because their beautiful work got either rejected or paved over by something else.

Basically the editor had come up with a beautiful sound design job of a village, and then they brought in the music cue on the first day of the final mix and it just paved over the whole scene. They turned all the sound effects down. I happened to walk by as he was bursting out of the doors crying.

KB: Oh God, that's horrible. I think we've all seen our work ruined by music. And that's not to say that music doesn't belong, but there are times when you just work like crazy and all of a sudden it's like, "Hey, we have this new song by this week's hot new artist, lets put this here instead." It's like what the fuck?

Do you agree that sound gets absolutely no respect until you get into post-production?

DO: And even then, it only gets grudging respect when it's absolutely necessary.

KB: Why is that?

DO: I'm not a location sound recordist, but I know that they always have a tough time on the set. I think it all boils down to the fact that we're visual creatures and people think of film as something you go to watch.

KB: I always tell people the three most important things in any movie are story, acting, and sound. You could have the most beautiful pictures in the world, but if the audience can't understand the dialogue, you don't have a movie.

DO: Yeah, that's true. Good sound goes unnoticed, bad sound ruins a film. It's a little like being a goalie on a soccer team; you can never score a point, you can only give them up.

KB: God, that's true.

You mix a lot of low budget independent films and you have worked on some really big films as well. Do you approach the big-budget films differently than you approach the small budgets?

DO: Yeah, I ask for a higher wage! It all boils down to time, how much time you have. big-budget films are generally feature narrative films, not documentaries, so the ground rules of working on sound in a narrative film are different and the needs and problems are different. Narrative films are fun because you really get to spend a lot of time on the details, bringing a scene to life. On the other hand, documentary films are truth and have the virtue of being educational and interesting and honest. They can also incorporate a lot of the same rules because they're stories.

With lower budget films, you try to give them the same polish and spin, but as a re-recording mixer sometimes all the ingredients aren't there. They haven't had a budget to do Foley or they haven't spent a lot of time gathering sound effects and creating the kind of layered effect that usually makes the richest sound quality.

KB: One of the things you just said which I find fascinating, is documentaries are truth. But we manipulate documentaries, especially the audio. So is it really truth?

DO: Well, I love that discussion, is it really fair game to add sound to a scene that wasn't picked up as you filmed even though you're portraying this as a real event? You know I just worked on a really interesting film about coal mining in Appalachia. And the filmmakers really wanted to convey the beauty of the woods that were being threatened by the strip mining operations and we put in all kinds of ambient tracks that were recorded separately, wind in the trees and birds and stuff to really connote the sense of beautiful open space. None of that of course got recorded as they were running their cameras down there. I think the typical viewer probably doesn't know that.

KB: Do you think viewers know how much sound gets manipulated in a documentary?

DO: I doubt it. I didn't until I started working in it. And that's fine you don't want people to think about that. You want them to get absorbed in a story and ultimately you want them to feel like this is all just really happening in front of them.

KB: You said that directors ultimately have control over what happens with a movie. . .

DO: Well yeah, except for the producers.

KB: How much control do you have?

DO: That depends a lot on the director. Some directors give you the space to let your own feelings dictate the process, your own feelings about what's right. Other directors really want to micromanage every little detail. I've worked on films where the director had a direction about every footstep in a Foley track. Turn that one up, turn that one down and so forth. But I like to think I leave an imprint on a film, at the very least by making it sound better in some way.

KB: What is the biggest change you've seen in post-production sound over the last couple of years?

DO: I'm thinking there's less assistance, doing more of it yourself. If I'm lucky there's somebody who's gone through and separated out the dialogue and turned off the tracks that didn't sound good and left the ones that did. But often I have to do that all myself if they don't have the budget.

Compared to the big-budget films I used to work on, a low budget feature just doesn't have as much work done on the sound before it gets to me. Foley is a perfect example, a feature film of the level that we worked on at the Saul Zaentz Film Center would Foley everything, and you could really make choices, is this helping the film or not? Now you're lucky if you've got ten little Foley cues done.

KB: When you have the big budgets and you have the resources, they allow you to do a nice job on the sound. Whereas all these independent people don't believe in sound like you and I do. When you say that just adding footsteps to this particular scene here is gonna help the scene, and you get asked, "Well how can it do that?" Trust me, it's gonna do it.

DO: Yeah, but it's expensive.

KB: It is expensive and young filmmakers would rather spend money on new cameras then actually making their movie better through sound. What is your biggest challenge when it comes to mixing a movie these days?

DO: The biggest challenge to me is always making the director happy and working within the time limits. Sound mixing is a really expensive operation. It requires a complicated studio with a lot of equipment, so we never really have all the time we could wish for. I was always jealous of sound editors because they work on their own and if they need to put in twelve to fifteen hours a day to make the sound just the way they want it, it's fine. But sound mixing is done by the hour or by some kind of bid for a certain number of days and you have to finish in X amount of time.

When you're sound editing, you're not dealing with an apparatus that has infrastructure like a machine room and operators and people who are also on the clock while you are. That's one thing that I always noticed about re-recording is that because of the studio that you have to use, the mix stage, everybody has to work quickly, if you go to the bathroom too much apparently you get in trouble.

KB: Yeah, that's what I've heard too. You and I are big coffee drinkers.

DO: Plus we like to chat a lot and shoot the shit.

KB: But you and I are really good at mixing and talking.

DO: Right, good point.

KB: 'Cause I don't think we ever slow down, every now and then there will be a nice pause, but it's amazing how many conversations you and I can carry on.

DO: While we're mixing.

KB: You know what is still my happiest moment mixing with you?

DO: Oh no.

KB: It was on THE GAS CAFE when what's his name came into the room pissed off.

DO: Berger!

KB: Berger! 'Cause we blew out that speaker.

DO: Because our futzing was too loud. We were trying to make a jukebox sound really lively and we blew that speaker.

KB: He was so pissed off at us. I loved that!

DO: We got the neighbors mad at us!

KB: He was and he was really condescending to you and I.

DO: Of course he was.

KB: I never liked that guy. Anyway, you're a teacher and a musician and you've made films in the past, what do you think students need to know about sound?

DO: What I always try to impart to students first and foremost is the idea that sound can help tell the story. Most of them have never thought about that. The kind of stuff I was talking about earlier, how natural sound chosen carefully can have an emotional impact on a scene.

And the other side is that there's an awful lot to worry about to avoid problems as you're filming and not later, hoping to fix it in post. I would say if students are making films, they need to learn that if your filming in a noisy location and you don't quiet it down, or if you're shooting in a room that's really echoy and you don't try to deaden it, or if you don't choose your locations carefully for how they sound as well as how they look, those are problems that cannot be solved later. And often you have to learn by being burned by this.

KB: Why is the original production dialogue so important?

DO: Because every actor in the world wants to have their natural performance preserved.

First of all ADR is tough to make sound natural. I guess it depends on the style you want your film to have. God knows, Fellini's films don't disagree with ADR and it's part of the charm to have everything a little unnatural and studio-y, but if you want to tell a story and have the action played out naturally, it's the real performances that matter.

Not to mention the fact that ADR is expensive and actors hate doing it and it's tough to get a good performance again months later in a little room with headphones on when you don't have your other actors to play off of.

I worked on a low-budget film last year where they had a couple of scenes that the sound couldn't be used for various reasons, not that I'm blaming anybody . . . but all the characters in the film were actors in their early twenties and the director pulled them all in for ADR. After a full day of ADR he came back to me sort of crestfallen because he was saying these people don't have experience doing this, they don't even sound like the same people anymore.

We couldn't use any of the ADR because the actors could not get back into character. In a rainstorm in the movie, they're all huddling under ponchos freezing and in the shoot of course they really were wet and tired and cold. In the studio, none of them could get that back again. They just sounded kind of nonchalant.

KB: That's a really good example. What's the most common sound problem that you encounter when you're mixing?

DO: Room echo and location background changes on every cut. The room echo can be avoided if you get the mic close enough, but not everybody does. Location noise that happens on cuts is bound to happen especially if you're shooting outside. And you know this from experience. I can be tough to smooth all those angles out.

KB: Big time. What's the worst sound problem you ever encountered and how did you fix it?

DO: I did a movie that took place almost exclusively inside a grocery store. They shot in the grocery store for seven or eight days and they didn't turn off any of the refrigeration because they couldn't "expense the ice cream" as the sound guy told me.

So I was dealing with four or five different refrigeration devices that would come and go from each shot. At one point they're standing by the meat counter and another they're by the soft drink cooler, then they're over by the cash register with the cameras pointing toward the window and it's quieter. It was a really interesting test of my ability to de-noise dialogue. I de-noised it pretty well and then of course we added more refrigeration sound that was continuous over the whole scene, so that was pretty tough. Especially because one or two of the actors didn't really know how to emote with a full voice. In other words, they were kind of doing the, what do you call it, the Mickey Rourke thing and that makes it really hard when you try to raise the volume of dialogue and up comes the refrigerator.

The editor asked me later, "How is this film, how did it rate?" and I said, honestly it was one of the toughest jobs I've ever had to do. Top five.

KB: With all of those different refrigeration units, it's going to sound different on every angle. I mean you can use notch filters and some EQ, but there's only so much you can do.

DO: It was really tough. I've always thought this was kind of unfair, as we watch a scene, we see cuts where the view changes abruptly on the screen. You go from a wide to a close-up to a reverse angle and we accept all those edits visually, but you can't do that in sound. The dialogue has to all sound like it happened continuously in real time through the whole scene.

It's not fair Kelley. Sound has it tough. On the other hand, it's that smoothness that ties all the edits in the picture together so it sounds really continuous. Sound makes us accept all those cuts.

It's rare to hear a sound edit unless it's really intentional, like to jar people into a new scene. Or you're Jean-Luc Godard, who I love actually.

KB: Yeah, I have my moments with him.

DO: Well I love the way you hear the sound edits, it's kind of goofy. I just got to see a little bit of this Mexican film, Y TU MAMA TAMBIEN, have you heard of that?

KB: I've heard of it, but I haven't seen it.

DO: Well it's interesting only in that the filmmaker uses a technique in sound where there's a narrator who will come in and narrate the story from time to time. When that happens the guy just cuts the sound track off. Everything. All the natural sound just goes click and turns off so the narrator can speak for a minute and there's really no attempt to fade out or make it so smooth you don't notice. It's really kind of unusual.

KB: Well, speaking of styles, you've done a bunch of work with Walter Murch. What have you learned from Walter, as a re-recording mixer?

DO: He's actually been a great inspiration to me.

When I first got a job as a teacher back in 1995, I was working with him at the time. I was his mix tech while he was remixing THE GODFATHER movies and when I told him I had just gotten a job as a teacher, he came in the next day with a whole stack of books for me about film sound. And honestly reading through all those books formed a lot of the background of what

I understand as my philosophy of sound design now. Including a lot of things we've already talked about, sound bringing emotion, and use of natural sound. I mean if you look at his work, he does that all the time in so many interesting ways.

There's a scene I love in THE TALENTED MR. RIPLEY. Tom and Dickey go boating, and a murder ensues - spoiler alert! As I remember it, Walter was very particular about the sound the boat's outboard motor makes - the production-sound motor had a quality that sounded like a small animal growling. And he really wanted the motor to play a role in the scene. There's a fight, the boat is pitching up and down, the motor's going out of the water and kind of accelerating and it ends up being a little like a Greek chorus for the scene. The motor becomes this spectator going, "oh, oh no!" It escalates the emotion of the scene even better than music could do.

KB: Oh yeah, he's amazing at that. Do you still have any of his books that he gave you?

DO: I sure do. Sound on Film by Vincent LoBrutto, Audio-Vision by Michel Chion,

Film Sound: Theory and Practice edited by Elizabeth Weiss & John Belton.

KB: Can you name a film that you think has outstanding sound and tell me why?

DO: I've been thinking about MASTER AND COMMANDER, which won an Oscar for best sound. It's interesting to me because it's not a big blockbuster sound film, but the attention to detail and the sort of beautiful natural quality of the sound of that film really impressed me.

KB: If you were looking for a re-recording mixer for one of your

films, what would be the important things you would want to know about them?

DO: Hopefully they know how to solve the sort of problems of location noise and they'll ultimately do what I ask them to and not have a big head about how they think the movie should sound.

KB: A lot of film students ask me how they can get into sound, what would you tell them?

DO: Honestly if people ask me that, I'll tell them they'll probably have pretty good luck because very few people who study filmmaking really want to concentrate on sound. A lot of sound work needs to be done on films and I suppose the best advice is to just simply do it all you can. First of all, learn the craft and second of all, get everybody in your community to know that you're good at it.

It's the same as any of these disciplines I suppose, you have to work on a lot of films. I got started by working on the films of my fellow students. First for free, then when I was getting too busy I had to start charging people. I always felt that getting a job in sound was easier than getting a job doing other things in films 'cause nobody wants to do it.

KB: Do you like what you do?

DO: You know, I'd have to say 75% of the time I can't believe they're paying me to do this. The other 25%, it sucks. Can I say that for your book?

KB: Of course. Why does it suck sometimes?

DO: Because a lot of it is problem solving and you don't really feel like you're doing anything creative. You're just getting out camera noise or some other noise in a scene and after it's done you feel good because the movie does sound better. It's fun when it's creative, but when it's just problem solving, an eight hour day can feel like a long time.

KB: No shit. Since you are a teacher, can you think of anything else that would be good for students to know about sound?

DO: It's worth the trouble, ya know. It's worth the trouble as a filmmaker. It's worth the trouble to worry about it. And a lot of people, I think, shy away from worrying about it because it's sort of scary and you don't know how to fix the problems right away. But you've got to if you want to be a good filmmaker, even if you're not a sound person. You've got to know what it takes to make a film sound good, both technically and artistically.

KB: Well that's a wonderful conclusion, I mean your statement, "It's worth the trouble." That says it all.

See this is why I wanted to talk to you because you do all sorts of different stuff. You're down in the trenches with the small filmmakers.

DO: Yeah baby! I know. I like it better.

KB: You don't have the resources that these other guys do, so sometimes as a re-recording mixer, you do have to be more creative. You know you can't call back to the machine room and order up some fancy piece of gear to notch out one frequency. You're using those old dip filters from the 50s.

DO: Hey don't go badmouthing the old Urei dip filters.

KB: I love those old dip filters.

DO: They're a honey, even if they do scratch a little.

KB: *Hey you want to buy any patch bays? I got one I'm trying to unload.*

DO: You still got your Sonic Solutions?

KB: *That's the one I'm trying to unload. I'll give you a helluva deal on a DA-88.*

DO: A DA-88.

KB: *It doesn't have a lot of hours on it. A couple of famous films were backed up on that. Happy to sell it to you cheap, 200 bucks.*

DO: 200 bucks? That's a pretty good deal Kelley, but realistically I don't think so. It's just, it's useless Kelley, you're just gonna have to face that.

Tom Johnson

"How many times in your life do you even get to meet a hero of yours let alone work with them?"

I have known Tom since my USC Film School days. He and I met and immediately became friends. We were roommates for quite awhile and spent hours discussing the kind of films that we loved and wanted to make. We shared a love of westerns, foreign films and good literature. We were also the only two guys in the department with really long hair and beards. Tom's resemblance to a certain messiah is still the stuff of legend.

When we graduated Tom moved up to the Bay Area and I headed for Oregon. We kept in touch and I watched as Tom carved out a career working both big films and small art films. He seemed almost embarrassed by the two films he won Oscars for (TITANIC and TERMINATOR TWO), they were not the kind of films he normally enjoyed working on. It was the smaller films and the films that he worked on in Europe that he always seemed proudest of. He has made a living mixing in studios all over the world and was among the first of a handful of mixers who would travel to wherever there was an interesting project. He is usually the hardest of my friends to track down but I finally caught up with him at home in Dublin, Ireland.

Tom's credits include, SWEENEY TODD: THE DEMON BARBER OF FLEET STREET, THE DEMON BARBER OF FLEET STREET, THERE WILL BE BLOOD, CHILDREN OF MEN, KING KONG, a couple of HARRY POTTER films, HOTEL RWANDA, CHARLIE AND THE CHOCOLATE FACTORY, STEALING BEAUTY, FORREST GUMP, QUIZ SHOW, TITANIC and TERMINATOR 2, and REQUIEM FOR A DREAM.

If you want to know more about Tom Johnson check out:
http://www.imdb.com/name/nm0426348/

KB: How did you get involved in sound in the first place?

TJ: I started at the USC School of Cinema. I became a sound TA in there and at that time it was a great way to get through school because not only did they pay tuition but they paid me a salary too, so for a poor kid at a really rich school it was the only way I could get through. It was through that process I fell in love with sound and found out that that's what I really wanted to do.

Once I got out of school I moved to San Francisco. I knew I didn't want to work in Los Angeles if I could help it. One of our professors, Ken Miura, was helping build George Lucas's first mix studio where they were going to mix RETURN OF THE JEDI.

I went by for an interview and then put it out of my mind thinking I was going to become an experimental filmmaker. I remember this well, I had fifty bucks left to my name and got a phone call saying, "Hey, would you like a job as a machine room operator?" I took the job and the rest is history as they say.

KB: How long did it take you to go from the machine room to actually mixing.

TJ: At that time, San Francisco was one of the best places for me to be because everything was just starting out. George was mixing his first film outside of Los Angeles and Francis had already mixed APOCALYPSE NOW in San Francisco. RETURN OF THE JEDI was going to be the next big one that was done in the Bay Area. Everybody was moving up really fast. The guy that ran the studio asked me, "What do you want to do?" and I said mix. It took about four or five years for me to start mixing, which in the Hollywood film business is a pretty fast rise.

KB: Do you think that starting in the machine room then working your way up to recording Foley, then doing Foreign mixes (separate DM&E mixes so that the films can be dubbed in to a foreign language) has helped you as a re-recording mixer?

TJ: Absolutely. Being in the machine room I could watch how people mixed and how editors brought their tracks to the stage, so it was totally insightful. The best way to lay out pre-mixes, the way you want editors to cut their tracks. I could see all that happening, it was great because I would talk to the editors and to the mixers.

KB: When you were starting out was there a particular film or films that were a huge influence on you?

TJ: When I was an undergraduate student in San Diego I took a film course from the film critic/painter Manny Farber. He passed away a few years ago. Manny's method of teaching was to show parts of films, he would never show us the whole film. Often it would be a middle reel, or he would even show a reel backwards. His goal was to get us to watch the frame, to learn how the language of film worked.

This film came out called DELIVERANCE and Manny said, "This is a new young director, he's English, and I think he's someone to watch. He's going to be pretty fantastic and his name is John Boorman." He did a film before DELIVERANCE called POINT BLANK and when I saw POINT BLANK I said, "Oh my God, I really want to get involved in making movies." It's still one of my favorite sound movies too. It's very low budget and very crude in terms of sound.

It was years later that I first got to work with John Boorman, and when I first met him I told him that one of the reasons I went to film school was because of POINT BLANK. I've never been brave enough to ask him if the approach to sound was

315

intentional or was it just a matter of it being a low-budget film. It's an amazing sound track. That's probably one of my biggest influences.

KB: Being your former roommate I know a bit about your taste in films and you have mentioned two names that I know were influences on you, Boorman and Bertolucci. You studied their movies and enjoyed their work and you've gotten the opportunity to work with them. Do you want to talk about working with someone like Bertolucci who is an icon in foreign film?

TJ: To be honest I don't want to talk too much about directors if I can help it because it's not like I know them on a personal level. I have to say to work with both Boorman and Bertolucci were dreams come true, its like how many times in your life do you even get to meet a hero of yours let alone work with them.

With Bertolucci's films, I still look at them and say to myself, "This is a filmmaker that knows how to direct a film, get good performances from actors and tell a story." And it's the same for Boorman. They definitely know how to construct a story and get good performances.

KB: Yeah, I'm with you on this. Your official title is re-recording mixer, what is it exactly that a re-recording mixer does?

TJ: Its called re-recording because we take previously recorded materials, the dialogue recorded on the set, the sound effects that have been edited, and the music, and we mix all of those together. We re-record all of those elements into one soundtrack, the final presentation of the sound part of the film.

My job is similar to the director of photography in the sense that as they choose a lens or choose lighting for the shot to help the audience know what you want them to be focused on in the frame, we do the same thing with sound. We decide the balance of all the sound elements in the soundtrack. What is the main thing that you want to hear, what is the main focus of the film, what is the emotional content of the film? My job is to balance all that so it's presented the way the director intended.

KB: When I worked on the larger mix stages there were two or three re-recording mixers at the console. Is there a hierarchy?

TJ: Traditionally there was the three-mixer setup. This was often the method used in Los Angeles, although that is less common these days. One person does dialogue, one mixes sound effects and the other person mixes the music. The way they work in New York and often in Europe is just one person will do the whole thing. A lot of that has to do with budgets. In San Francisco, we work with two people, which is more common these days. Normally the person that does dialogue will also mix the music and the sound effects person will do the effects and the Foley. I think that was the method in San Francisco because San Francisco is well known for its sound effects work.

In FX heavy movies it seemed like the dialogue person didn't have as much to do so why not do the music as well. We don't always work that way; there are times where the effects person does the music. It depends on the film.

In terms of the amount of people mixing it depends on the budget more than anything else. In terms of hierarchy, in Los Angeles, the dialogue guy is often in charge. In San Francisco, it's usually the sound designer or sound effects person who's in charge. I'm lucky enough to work with people where we see each other as partners working together. We can split the job equally and discuss back and forth what should be done. There's no one really in charge.

KB: Why do you think good sound is important?

TJ: Good sound is really important to present a clear idea of what the story is all about, in the same way that a good image is important or good acting. In narrative films, it's all emotion based. If you can't present the emotion in a clear concise way, if you can't tell the story clearly, then the film becomes muddled and as an audience member I sit there and don't know what's going on. I don't understand what you're trying to tell me.

A sound is technically "good" when it is clearly recorded, not distorted, and contains a full range of frequencies. But a "good" sound may not be a technically good sound. Sometimes we choose the sound that tells the story best, not the sound with the best recording quality. This is true for all aspects of the sound track (dialogue, effects, and music). We would never reject an original recording of Caruso singing a beautiful aria, if that is the performance that tells the story the best, just because it is grainy and distorted.

So the rule of thumb for good sound is - does it tell or promote the emotional content of the scene, does it support and/or reveal the story.

KB: If that's true, how come sound gets no respect until post-production?

TJ: It's not a black and white thing. There are some directors who do understand that if they spend the time on the set to get well-recorded dialogue tracks (which means, without a lot of traffic noise, airplanes flying over, fans, or generators running, lights buzzing, costumes rustling, hard soled shoes clomping about, etc.), it will make things clearer.

Some directors make sure the actors aren't wearing noisy pieces of clothing or the steps aren't creaky, things like that. In the long run that seems like a lot of work, but it actually ends up saving the director and the producer lots of money because if they don't get good sound then they have to replace all of it with ADR and that can be really dissatisfying in terms of performance. It can produce a soundtrack that feels lifeless. A lot of actors hate doing ADR and this can often be felt in the ADR recordings. It can become a serious problem in the end. The directors that understand all that will actually spend the time and the effort to get good sound.

I suppose the reason sound can get such little respect is that a shot can take a lot of time to setup. The last thing anyone wants to hear is the sound guy say, "Can we hold the shot, there's an airplane going overhead?" Most people (directors, cameramen, producers) will say, "Forget that! Let's go, let's move!"

If you go out and scout locations and you don't bring the sound person along and it happens that your doing an 18th century drama and your shooting right next to a highway you're going to have cars running through your dialogue all the time. Which means your going to have to throw it all out because cars didn't exist in the 18th century. You're going to regret not having spoken to the sound guy.

A lot of people say, "We'll just fix that later, we'll clean it up somehow," and the thing that a lot of directors don't understand is, not only is it going to be really expensive to do that but, they won't get what they thought they got on the set.

KB: Have you heard the rumor that 80% - 90% of all of the dialogue is replaced in films these days?

TJ: On films I've worked on it's not true. I've worked on a lot of films where I'm actually embarrassed by the work I've done because I've had to spend so much time cleaning up dialogue. I'm processing stuff to get rid of all the junk that you don't want in the dialogue, to the point that the quality of the voices starts to suffer. Then everyone goes, "Well, it sounds better than it did and the performance is still there." But in the end even directors understand that the film itself has suffered.

A lot of the films I've worked on we don't replace all that much. Most of those directors that claim they're going to loop it later in the end don't want to do it because they hate ADR. And I think that most of these young directors will find they ultimately hate ADR too.

I did work on a major Hollywood film where 90% of the dialogue was replaced, it was all looped, but in the end we only used about 50% of that because the performances weren't good enough and you always have to go with the better performance.

I'll get in trouble with actors here, but there aren't a lot of actors that are really good at doing post-sync or ADR because they find going into a looping stage not only are you replacing all of your dialogue without the actor that you're playing off of but you're also spending half of your time trying to figure out how to get it all in sync. You're concentrating on sync, you're concentrating on line to line to line so you never get into the flow of your original performance. You are putting an actor into one of the hardest situations they would ever be in, trying to repeat a performance that they got. I can almost count on two hands the number of actors that I've seen that can actually do a really good job with ADR.

KB: Any actors who read this will think that they're among those ten people who can do it really great.

TJ: Well, I could be exaggerating.

The reason a lot of ADR gets thrown out is the director will often go, "Well, I don't want to loop the whole scene so what do we absolutely need?" And they'll end up doing half a sentence or something and I would say at least 50% of the time you're going to throw that ADR out because it's really difficult for an actor to match the performance they've already done.

KB: What's your stand on wild lines on the set right after they finish something as a backup?

TJ: I think that's the most ideal situation if you can get actors to do that. A lot of actors don't want to do wild lines, they're like, "God, I just went through the most difficult scene in my life and now you're asking me to go through it again?" But if actors can be convinced that if you don't do it now you're going to have to do it later and while you're in character its probably going to be easier for you ultimately.

If you can do wild lines absolutely do them. And the best time to do them, if you can get everyone on the set to be quiet for five minutes, is right there. You just have to convince the director and the producer you can save them so much money if you can do that.

KB: You clean up the dialogue in the mix but the tracks that you get are usually prepared by a dialogue editor first, are they not?

TJ: Yeah. And a lot of times when we're in a final mix a director will say to me, "God, you really cleaned that dialogue up." I'd say, an editor has cleaned up 70% of it. Editors can do amazing jobs just going in and cleaning up a lot of the dialogue clicks and hits and bumps. They find alternate takes that can be substituted in for unintelligible dialogue, things like that. A really good dialogue editor can do so much work to save a lot of the production dialogue, they're the unsung heroes in these situations.

If a great dialogue editor goes in and finds alternate takes, that's probably the major reason that we end up not using ADR. Often a really good picture editor will do the same thing.

KB: Do you approach the big movies differently than the small movies? Is there a different mindset you have to get into when you work with a Tim Burton as compared to a Robert Redford? They have totally different styles, how do you negotiate that?

TJ: It's a mind-set. I sometimes find going into a low-budget film with editors who are used to working on multi-million dollar films, they will present me with millions of tracks. I go, "whoa what are you doing" and they'll say, "I just cut all this really wonderful stuff." "Yeah, but we've got three days to mix it. How am I supposed to get through all this?" So the mind-set has to become, I need to do the most important things in the least amount of time on a low budget movie.

The way I approach the dialogue is, I go through scenes and clean them up the best I can. I don't spend a lot of time finessing things and just hoping by the time we get to the final mix we can cover up problems. You don't fine tune things, you don't spend as much time with detail as you can on a big-budget film.

With big-budget films I can spend a lot more time with detail, a lot more time making everything sound better. We can often make the track more complicated with things like Group ADR, and the effects people can make the effects denser and more detailed. To put it in terms of music, it's the difference between garage bands where people just go in and record their stuff with one microphone in one take and you'd go, "God, these guys are really good but it's just a bunch of unfocused noise." Then when they finally get in the studio they're able to control things and do over dubs and suddenly the music sounds a lot clearer and a lot better.

On the other hand, when you have more time it can also cause the music to suffer because you spend too much time screwing around with things that aren't very important, or you smooth out rough edges that were giving the music life. There have been times when we spend a lot of time on a scene and then you watch the whole movie and you feel the scene or reel or whole film has lost its life; it has become too controlled.

In general I'd say you get to deal with a lot of detail and richness in big-budget films. There are more chances to choose performances, be more subtle with the sound track, and much more refined with the emotional content of the film.

KB: Generally what kind of hours do you put in and is there a big difference between the lower budget and the bigger budget films? If you have seven days to mix or eight weeks to mix, does that affect the amount of hours you put in on a daily basis?

TJ: It can. If a film hasn't been budgeted for sound correctly but the director still wants all of the detail and all their subtle stuff, you end up working lots and lots of overtime so an eight-week mix could turn out to be really sixteen weeks of hours. And it costs them a lot more, they're paying overtime, double-time, triple and quadruple time, meal penalties, short turn around, etc.

On a low-budget film really good directors and producers will stick to their budgets and you work an eight or nine hour day everyday. They're really good at saying we've got to stop we don't have anymore time and if everyone's really conscientious and pays attention to the time you get through on budget.

In the end, if the film is budgeted properly, and the expectations of the filmmakers fit that budget, then you can come up with a pretty nice sounding soundtrack. That goes for both low and high budget films.

Well, budgeted films are always the most pleasing to work on as they understand the work that needs to be done, and the direction is usually much clearer. Therefore there is little wasted space or time.

KB: You try to be efficient.

TJ: You try to make every single minute worth it.

In big-budget films you're given more minutes. This gives you more time to work the dialogue so that it's clear and you hear every word; you get to work the music so that each note that can possibly be expressed well is expressed; you get to work the sound effects so that they can work with both dialogue and music and still have a chance to support the story. Essentially you are given time to present as full a track, as humanly possible, with a clarity of story and emotion that is pleasing to the ear; or not pleasing, if that is what you are going for.

In low-budget films you use your experience, intuition, and seat of your pants to come up with the best track that you can produce in the minutes given.

KB: And speaking of luxuries it seems like budgets are, for the most part, getting smaller. I mean you've still got your big blockbusters obviously but for most films what's the biggest change you've seen in post-production sound in the past few years?

TJ: I recently worked on a low-budget film right after coming off a huge budget film. When I walked into a spotting session for the low budget one the director said, "We know you just came off this multi-million dollar thing and you've had all this time and it is in 3-D, but we don't even have a tenth of the budget those guys have." It seems like Hollywood movies cost 200 to 250 million dollars which is enough to feed half the world probably, or they are somewhere around fifteen to twenty million, there's nothing in between anymore. I'm sitting here in Ireland and I know of at least three directors here who could easily make ten to fifteen movies off that 250 million dollars and they'd be a lot better movies.

Where we used to have six or seven weeks on a low-budget film to mix we now have three. And even big-budget films are usually eight weeks, we used to have twelve or fifteen. There are only a few directors that are smart enough to say, "No, I want the same amount of time for my sound as I used to get." Most of them are just like, "Yeah that's fine, we'll do it in six weeks." And these are the films that we put a lot of overtime and weekends into. In the end I have to ask, "Are you really getting a better soundtrack? And is it costing you any less?"

In my opinion, a lot of that has happened because the people who are selling sound technology, or even visual technology are saying, "Look you can go with an HD camera, you can walk out on the street and start filming right now, and you can make the whole movie for a tiny amount of money. Things are a lot faster, a lot cheaper, you can cut at home on Final Cut Pro you can do all your sound at home. It is going to be cheaper and faster." But quality takes time in my opinion.

KB: You're one of the few people I know who works in Europe, New Zealand, Ireland and places like that. Is this big budget mania purely American or are you seeing this happen in other countries too? And I would consider THE LORD OF THE RINGS purely American.

TJ: I would say its mostly American films. The big budget stuff's all American films, which is causing the little films a lot of trouble. It seems to me when a top non-American director can't get a budget together to make a movie that's insane. And the same thing is happening in the US. Some of the great American directors just can't get money together to make a movie because in terms of the studios, they may not be seen as moneymaking filmmakers. The studios are often saying, "They still want to make those stupid political dramas or . . . courtroom dramas or . . .?"

KB: Do you have a lot more control on foreign films?

TJ: Not really. Post-sound people are still being hired at the very end, so by the time I get to the mix the producers are saying, "We don't have any money left but we want everything we can get." But you don't have any money left, so I can't do anything. And so I end up doing things for free, or for very little money, and this creates a whole new kind of beast that we probably don't want to discuss at the moment.

I'm being really negative but you do have films like THE HURT LOCKER that come along and it's a very low budget sound job and they do a really good job. So it is possible people are doing that sort of thing.

KB: Did you work on HURT LOCKER?

TJ: No.

KB: I didn't think so. You are a rarity in that you're not affiliated with one studio. Most mixers used to work at one studio and you work everywhere. Are you different or are you part of a new breed of mixers who travel and mix at different places?

TJ: I'd say most mixers these days aren't tied to studios. Even a lot of the LA guys are moving around more and more, working in London and other places.

I'm more unusual in that I work in the US and I don't live there. I suspect it'll happen more as people are more capable of doing sound on non-traditional mix stages. I suspect that the big mixing studios are going to become things of the past just because movie theaters are smaller. And people can do a lot of that stuff at home, or in a small room. THE HURT LOCKER was basically cut and mixed in a small editing room.

I'd like to point out one thing about films like THE HURT LOCKER, however. I feel that the film has some really interesting and wonderful sound moments and ideas, but I also feel that the film feels a bit flat in terms of space. It sometimes feels almost two-dimensional; it lacks depth of space. Those are the kinds of things that can be done in a larger mix room with a traditional film-mixing console. Or, perhaps, it is a matter of experience? I'm not sure. I do worry that more and more films these days are losing the richness and depth that they used to have. And I'd posit that this holds for picture as well as sound!

KB: When you come on to a project, because you're freelance, does the producer call you or is it the director? What are the steps you go through from beginning to end when you come on to a project?

TJ: I'm usually hired either by the director or the studio.

Usually people start talking to me once they're cutting picture. Every once in a while I'm brought in on spotting sessions to talk about what they want to do with the mix. I sit there with the picture and sound editors and we talk about how it's going to work, how we're all going to bring things to the stage. We break things down, who's going to do what. That's the ideal situation for me.

It's more typical that I walk in on the first day of pre-mixing, I'm the hired gun in the factory kind of thing. Those are not the more enjoyable films but it's a living.

KB: With all the different stuff you've done over the years is there a certain type of film that you like to work on?

TJ: I enjoy films that have a lot of depth. I have an undergraduate degree in English Literature so I really like words, I like thoughts and I like depth. A lot of films these days, if you start to look below the surface, you find that things fall apart really quickly. There's no second or third or fourth level. Films with real depth are very rare. When I get to work on one of those that has a really good message like HOTEL RWANDA, or a film that has a very interesting story, I really enjoy that. I really enjoy watching actors. Sometimes I work on a film and I watch the movie and go, "God, this isn't a very interesting story, but it's interesting just to watch these people act."

KB: If you could be the director what would you do differently as far as sound?

TJ: The first thing you want to do is hire a good sound person, and the way you find a good sound person is to ask sound people or other directors. I always refer to this guy here in Ireland who's from New Zealand. He's a great production recordist a super nice guy. He's really attentive, and tries really hard to get good sound. He becomes really good friends with the set designer and the camera people and the costume people in a sort of self serving way so that he can go to the costume people and say, "Could you maybe use cotton instead of silk?" or something like that. He explains to them that then we won't get all this cloth sound. Or he'll talk to the set guys, "Instead of just throwing down some boards do you think you could nail those down so they don't clank and creak?"

If you can, get a really good production sound person, somebody who has a good boom operator and is really attentive and really concentrates on sound. Once you get that person, you need to listen to them and when they say, "Can we do this or can we do that?" at least consider what they're saying and ask them questions like "If we don't do that, what's going to happen?" That way you can start to understand the ramifications of what happens if you choose not to do that.

KB: What's the best advice that you would give filmmakers?

TJ: It's interesting, I was at a film school a couple of years ago and these kids were just making their first film. They had written their scripts and I said to them, "If you really want to start thinking about sound you need to think about it when you're writing, and you need to be aware of it; and if you're always thinking about sound, then you'll trust the scene to play. If you put in an interesting score or something that's going on off-screen, those things sound wise can tell the story rather than having people constantly talk and tell everything that they're feeling and everything that's going on. If you can find other ways of doing things with sound, your film is going to be much more powerful because you're allowing the audience to use their own imagination and become involved in the whole thing rather than them watching a stage play."

Then in the picture editing process if you feel like a scene is playing slow your first reaction is going to be to start cutting the picture, cut heads and tails off the shot and all that sort of stuff but if you start to think, "What if we add some sound in there or do something sonically that supports the story and helps speed up the pace, then maybe we can let the scene breathe."

KB: It seems like we have a habit in filmmaking these days, if you want an actor to really emote, say an actor's supposed to be sad. Filmmakers tend to shoot a quick shot of the actor, then they put on a sad piece of music instead of letting the actor's performance carry it. I think a lot of filmmakers don't trust actors. Have you noticed that?

TJ: Absolutely. I worked on a film which is going to come out soon, I won't tell you what it is, and luckily I wasn't in the room because I would've started crying. What happened was we did a whole mix that the directors were all happy with. The producers came in and said, "Oh my God, the music all needs to be louder, louder, louder." What we were calling a dialogue driven movie suddenly became a music driven movie. And one of the producers actually said in a scene, which was a heartfelt scene where the actor was giving a tear-jerking speech, "the music needs to be a lot louder here because that's where all the drama is." And I was like, "What?" And when the director told me that I said, "Well, don't tell the actor that."

And in the producer's defense they've been watching the movie for two years so they knew it inside and out and the new thing was the music and that was the thing that made it exciting for him again. But it's an easy trap to fall into.

KB: I feel like I hear way too much music.

TJ: Definitely. I think the main advice that you can give directors in terms of sound is, all sound is music. Everything sound wise in your movie has emotional content, the dialogue, the music, and the effects. It's all the same and once you see that it's all the same that it all has emotion then you liberate yourself and you don't need to support it with anything. The sound effects will play it or the music will play it.

KB: Definitely. If you were looking for a re-recording mixer, what are the important things you would want to know?

TJ: First of all you don't want someone who's a tech head, you know what I mean? If you're hiring someone to put sound in your movie, they certainly do need to understand how to get it printed, but that shouldn't be the main concern.

Most importantly you want somebody that understands your story, someone you feel you can connect with, and definitely someone who understands what you are saying when you describe something you want.

Somebody asked me once, "Can you describe something that you contributed to a film in terms of being the mixer?" I thought about it and said, "Well, everything I do is contributing to the film." I know what they meant was, "Was that explosion yours?" But everything we do is contributing to the story and to the filmmaking process. So, you want somebody who can speak to your film, communicate with your film and understand your film.

You certainly don't want to hire somebody who doesn't understand you or the film or what you're trying to do because all you're going to do is fight with them constantly. And I've worked on films like that too.

KB: Me too.

TJ: All this stuff is pretty basic. A lot of people, let's say the young kids in film, understand the technology really well. They can work around Pro Tools so much faster than anyone I know and certainly faster than I could ever do. They can talk about the science and be a lot more articulate than I can. But the thing a lot of them don't understand is the story. They don't understand why one sound is better than another. You start talking about door closes and go, "But that's the wrong door close", and they're like, "What do you mean it's the wrong door? It's the door close." And you say, "But the guy's mad and that door close isn't mad." "What do you mean mad?" That demonstrates to me that person has no idea what sound does at all.

KB: But do you think that's a product of the film schools and the way they're being taught now with an over emphasis on equipment and not on technique and content?

TJ: When you and I went to film school, and this is no criticism to my two sound mentors because both of them were great technicians, they taught us everything we needed to know about sound, but we never had any education about what sound could do for a movie.

We somehow learned how to do it on our own. Look at a film like TITANIC an incredible tour de force of technique. Technically it's absolutely amazing but story wise not very interesting in my opinion. I think that's what's happening with our culture too.

KB: When I'm talking about sound design I still show the opening to ONCE UPON A TIME IN THE WEST.

TJ: A very effective scene.

KB: Besides the six badly dubbed lines of dialogue, it's all sound effects. There is no music until Bronson shows up with a harmonica and that's not score that's an effect.

TJ: . . . and I thought that was kind of interesting. . .

KB: It's brilliant. Is it long? Yeah. But we learn so much about the characters through the photography and sound effects. Jack Elam and the fly, Woody Strode with the water dripping on his hat. It says so much about who they are and where they are.

TJ: Yeah.

KB: I just watched Walter Murch's version of TOUCH OF EVIL. I've always loved that opening even with the Henry Mancini score, but seeing it now based on what Welles wanted was phenomenal. Hearing the music and backgrounds from the different clubs as we pass by, and that was what - 1961? There were people who were doing interesting stuff and nobody shows or talks about those old films. Better get me off my soapbox here.

TJ: Grab my hand and come on down.

KB: Thanks. What are the most common sound problems you encounter?

TJ: Several things in terms of production sound. Lights. They have these high frequency tones.

Any time oriented sound that happens while you're shooting. Cars going by, waves in the background, even wind. If you're not aware of that stuff it is going to cause you problems as soon as you try to cut two shots together that were shot two hours apart. They're not going to match. Your backgrounds are going to be totally different because of different rhythms. You have to smooth them out. There's a lot of plug-ins in Pro Tools and I have some outboard equipment that we can use to clean a lot of stuff up, but none of that can help with these time related problems.

There's a film I just worked on about the Lincoln assassination and they shot it all in Savannah, Georgia. Even though the dialogue was really well recorded it all had traffic and city noise all over it. We had to clean all that out because none of that existed then. It had electrical hums and light hums and things that have to be dealt with, so anything with electricity you need to deal with.

KB: A lot of film students are asking me how can they get into sound, sound design, and mixing, what would you tell them?

TJ: Luck. I don't know. Do they want to work in Hollywood or just in general? I wouldn't even start on the phrase sound design because that would just make me really mad. A lot of people these days talk about sound design, "There's that scene that has that weird tone in it, that's sound design." Wrong!

A sound designer is a person who is the director of sound and should be hired from the beginning. The person who oversees the production recordists, who is on the set to see what's happening or records interesting things that are happening. The one who talks to the director and develops the soundtrack.

These days I think a lot of young people want to be sound designers because they think, "I can use Pro Tools and use a lot of plug ins and come up with some really cool weird sounds." That's NOT sound design!

Originally when Walter (Murch), Alan Splet, Richard Beggs, and Ben Burtt started calling themselves Sound Designers it included the entire soundtrack, all this stuff we've been talking about. They didn't just sit in a studio and try to come up with cool and weird things to add.

Anyway that's my soapbox.

Probably the best way to get into sound these days would be to connect up with a friend who wants to be a director, or find a filmmaker who needs sound people. You have to start at the beginning in low-budget films. I think the people in LA start out working in TV or on really low-budget films. If you understand Pro Tools, if you have a computer you can often sell yourself as an assistant to a sound editor because you can help them. Fill in the spots that they aren't quite up to snuff with.

Having said that, even if you're really good technically you're not going to go very far if you don't understand the rest of it.

KB: After all these years, do you still like what you do?

TJ: Usually. I'm a fairly negative person. It's funny because I'll be on a mix and I'll start to say to people, "Oh man, this is going down fast, it's going to get bad," and everybody's like, "Man, you're so negative." And within three or four days I'm right, I just see it quicker than most people do.

I work on films sometimes where by the end of it I never want to do this again.

And just at that moment along comes that film, or that director, or that group of sound people that revitalizes me. There are some very, very good films being made. There are also some really great directors and sound people out there. And to work with them is a joy.

Yeah, I love what I do.

CHAPTER 9:

Learning Your Craft

Teacher and Innovator

So how do we learn our craft? Colleges, universities, film schools, the Internet, or on the job training?

What I got out of film school was working with a lot of different people and having my work critiqued by professionals. Many film programs use working filmmakers and specialists in their fields to teach. For me that was great.

Not everyone can afford film school or they don't have the patience. You can watch how-to-videos on line to learn different pieces of equipment. The problem most beginning filmmakers run in to is one of, re-inventing the wheel. You are going to be making a lot of mistakes others before you have made, over and over again because you don't have any guidance.

You need to find out who are the innovators. The people who know the rules of filmmaking and are breaking them. Those are the people I want to learn from. You aren't going to get what you need listening to the director's commentary or watching the behind-the-scenes videos. Those things are commercials, marketing pieces.

You need to do your research (and buy books). Find the people you want to learn from and check out everything they have made and written. Why did they do what they did? Just watching movies isn't enough.

You need to learn film history and stay up with new innovations. Why make the same old mistakes when you can go out and make new and different ones. I respect people who know why they're breaking the rules. They may fail, but they're the ones that are taking the chances.

Tomlinson Holman

"Movies are my church. We go every Sunday." [Laughs]

Tom's distinguished career in audio, video and film spans over thirty-three years. He is Professor of Film Sound at the University of Southern California School of Cinematic Arts and a Principal Investigator in the Integrated Media Systems Center at the university. IMSC is the Engineering Research Center for multi-media of the National Science Foundation. He is founding editor of Surround Professional magazine, and author of the books Sound for Film and Television and 5.1 Surround Sound Up and Running, both published by Focal Press. He is an honorary member of the Cinema Audio Society and the Motion Picture Sound Editors, a fellow of the Audio Engineering Society, the British Kinematograph Sound and Television Society, and the Society of Motion Picture and Television Engineers. Tom holds seven U.S. and corresponding foreign patents totaling twenty-three, and they have been licensed to over forty-five companies.

Tom was chief electrical engineer at Advent Corporation, founded Apt Corporation, maker of the Apt/Holman preamplifier, and was at Lucasfilm Ltd for fifteen years, winding up as the company's corporate technical director, where he developed the THX Sound System and its companions the Theater Alignment Program, Home THX, and the THX Digital Mastering program.

If you want to know more about Tomlinson Holman check out: http://www.imdb.com/name/nm0391642/

KB: How did you get started in sound?

TH: I started doing lighting and sound in high school for plays and when I went to college, I wanted to concentrate on lighting. There was a lighting professor, but nobody to do sound. So I started doing sound for plays and stage management. I did it for several years as an undergraduate and then kind of migrated over to the journalism-broadcasting curriculum at the University of Illinois. I started working in the television station, in the film department. A job came open in the summertime to cut some utterly awful film that some professor of veterinary medicine had shot which consisted of alternating shots of cows standing in a field in Egypt with equine encephalitis and slides of their brains after they'd been dissected.

KB: [Laughs]

TH: It was absolutely the world's worst movie and nobody else wanted to touch it. I did some of everything on that. Then the Motion Picture Production Center at the University was being rebuilt, so I was hired on as a technician. I kept that job for five years after graduating.

I became the sound person, mainly, but I also edited and directed. I did a lot of things - kind of USC-style. The program at Illinois was very small but it was modeled on the USC program because we had three people working in that unit that had come through USC. I'm sort of USC once removed.

KB: You know, there's a lot of USC people out there and a lot of once-removed folks as well.

TH: Yeah. My film school partner was Andy Davis who went on to direct THE FUGITIVE and UNDER SIEGE and all those movies. We're still close friends after all these years.

KB: You make friendships in film school that stay with you forever.

TH: Absolutely. So, I got into sound because it was my fallback position. [Laughs]

KB: [Laughs] A lot of us did that. Now you've been a re-recording mixer, an audio engineer, an inventor too . . . What is it you really do when it comes to sound?

TH: I put technology in the service of art. I could not see a path to doing what I wanted to do, which was to provide infrastructure for the arts. I know I'm not a big artist myself; more like a midwife for the mother. I knew I could push the engineers to solve problems that would be placed in the service of the story, shall we say.

KB: Um-hm.

TH: There's hundreds of examples, one of them was they came to me a few years ago with a system for running high-bandwidth video and audio across the internet. This is high-definition video and ten-channel audio and so forth. And they said, "We've got it down to six signals which is how engineers always talk. That means one bit in a million drops out. And I said, "Well, that's not nearly good enough. I can hear one bit in a million." And they said, "You can't hear one bit in a million." And I said, "Play it for me." And then I pointed out where all the dropouts were. [Laughs]

KB: [Laughs]

TH: They had no clue! And this resulted in a patent pending for the university called Selective Retransmission, which fills in the gaps by asking an IP system for the missing bit in the time that it's reconstructing the image. So there are advantages to being a son of a bitch with the engineers. [Laughs]

KB: [Laughs] Right. When you look at different sound programs like Pro Tools, it was obvious to me, that film sound people didn't design them. Engineers designed them. They're not very intuitive.

TH: It's not only not intuitive, but all of Pro Tools was based on a whole trend that we piggyback on top of in the film business. The trend was toward the home studio. It's really toy software that came at a very low price compared to what was built for the industry. So people started using it, as clumsy as it was, and then it got overlaid and overlaid in time. How many more midi things can it do? Not very interesting to us.

KB: Not at all. What is it you teach at USC specifically?

TH: They all think it's engineering but it isn't. It's purely descriptive.

It's a series of lectures that are based on my book. Actually, the book is based on the lectures, Sound for Film and Television. I do more science-oriented stuff than they might expect.

I do a lecture on objective sound. I tell them about diffraction. When I tell them about diffraction, I tell them how that influences a story.

I always try to make tie-ins so they understand the world better. I do three pretty abstract sections called Objective Sound, Subjective Sound, and then Audio. And then it's from microphones through recording, editing, mixing and so forth. There is lots of input from the class. The favorite of the class is the first twenty-five minutes of LOVE ACTUALLY. I watched many movies to come up with the content for the class and LOVE ACTUALLY uses every scene-change method known to man.

KB: *Really?*

TH: It's all there in twenty minutes.

KB: *Wow. I gotta check that out.*

TH: It's got the fade out-fade in. It's got the dissolve. It's got the bang cut. It's got the J-cut. It's got everything. I put what's coming up on an overhead projector. Listen for this, listen for this, and listen for this. And that's a twenty-five-minute demo.

KB: *Wow.*

TH: That's probably the best-known one in the class.

KB: *[Laughs] Do you find that students, when they come to film school, are not interested in sound at all?*

TH: Typically, yes. But in the last twenty years we've taught about sixty people who now have full-time careers in sound. It's about one to two a semester, out of sixty. It's not many, but hey, how many students want to direct? And how many of them are directing?

KB: *Very few. Is there a particular film or films that really influenced you when you started?*

TH: I thought FORBIDDEN PLANET was just magical when I saw it . . . in mono, in a small-town theater. And of course the big ones like LAWRENCE OF ARABIA and 2001: A SPACE ODYSSEY where I know what seat I was sitting in, what I had for dinner that night and who I was with. [Laughs]

KB: *Kubrick is a personal favorite of mine. 2001 and CLOCKWORK ORANGE, to me, are two of the most amazing films ever made. Anyway, why is it you think good sound is important?*

TH: It's probably the least well known of the trades. Everybody says, "Look at the costumes, they're beautiful!" We just saw THE TEMPEST and, "Oh my God, the special effects were unbelievably good."

Everybody can tell a table and chair apart. Nobody can tell Foley and ambiance apart.

This is Walter March's answer, developed over many years. Sound comes in the back door. It can move you, it can cause emotions in you that you don't quite have control over because you don't quite know how you're being manipulated. And manipulated is a good thing, in this sense. The filmmaker gets to work on a method that is not so obvious to you. It takes in the whole thing as a big gestalt. And one of my main things to do in class is to get people to start tearing the sounds apart and figuring them out.

It's the difference between the classical and the romantic. It's there in Zen and The Art of Motorcycle Maintenance, where we take it all in as a one big romantic thing as a child, but as working professionals we have to know what each component does, how it works. A number of people have come to me over the years and said, "You've ruined the movies for me!" [Laughs]

KB: [Laughs] I've been told that too.

TH: That's my job! To figure out how it works so you can do it yourself. Of course, the trick is when it all comes back together . . . I probably have the highest level of suspension of disbelief as anyone around for technical problems in soundtracks.

There were two faults at Arc Light this week when I saw THE KING'S SPEECH, which I could report to them, to get fixed, but the film was wonderful!

I can get it on two levels at once. It took me a very long time to get there. At first, as a kid, it's all the gestalt; growing up as a professional, you learn everything that's wrong, so I would filter all the content out.

I still do this in our doc class. I'm a terrible filter for content because I'm listening to the backgrounds, I'm listening to the boom hits, and I'm listening to everything under the sun to be able to make a clear channel for the story to proceed. I was really not on the story. I was on everything around it to make it work. But it does come back together at the end of the day.

I tell the story in my book that my conversion reaction from being a strict professional was watching Steven [Spielberg] sitting in a dub stage, watching I think it was JURASSIC PARK. He's rocking back and forth in his chair. Oh my God, this guy's really into this movie. Hell, he made the movie! He's got the highest suspension of disbelief of anybody and yet he can take the roller coaster. You have to get on the roller coaster at the end of the day.

KB: That's true. I talked to Gary (Rydstrom) a couple days ago. We talked about JURASSIC and PRIVATE RYAN, and that's what Gary was saying too. It's fascinating that Steven can do that.

TH: Well, that taught me a thing or two. Now I can look at movies in two threads at once. I can tell you that the soundtrack was printed wrong on reel 5AB. I can go to the manager and tell them, "You got a problem with your Dolby decoder in reel 5AB. It's not your sound head, it's the print. You have to change the reel of the print." You know, stuff like that.

KB: Do you believe that sound gets no respect until post-production?

TH: Oh, that's very dependent on the director. You take a picture like ALMOST FAMOUS by Cameron Crowe. Jeff Wexler did that and it's virtually all production sound. He was given the right on the set to control what he needed to control and when the director's behind you, you can capture wonderful things on the set. You have to maintain control. A lot of the young, starting filmmakers don't know how to do that and they're a mess. That's why I wrote this other book Sound for Digital Video. It's for single-system, low-budget productions. And I've been criticized on Amazon on Sound for Film and Television for spending so much time on production sound. There are three chapters on production sound. And the reason is if you start with good production sound, you're not going to have to do very much. The book is heavier on it than it is on editing or mixing, because of that.

KB: There's a rumor that I've been trying to smash for years and I ask everybody in the book this very same question. On most features and television shows, how much of that dialogue is replaced, that you know of?

TH: It varies enormously. I know, Gary would have told you, going from RAIDERS to INDY III, it went from something like twenty percent production sound to eighty percent production sound, on the same general picture.

DESPERATE HOUSEWIVES, I happen to know, is absolutely, completely boomed and it's all production sound. And the reason it's all boomed is they have so many costume changes, they can't possibly radio mic them.

KB: That's an interesting fact.

TH: I know Aggie, and I'm on the board of CAS and I've chatted with him about it. Basically, he is well respected on that set, and he knows he can make those decisions. He's been on the show seven years. They all talk to him and listen to him. When he calls "airplane," they know they gotta stop. There aren't too many like that.

KB: *When I was doing sound design on Gus Van Sant's films and with Todd Haynes we used 95% of the production audio. It was rare that we would use ADR.*

TH: Well, it all depends on the genre. If you're doing THE STORM, you pretty much have to do it, but . . . I teach that the performances are often better on the production audio. I teach that there are people who cannot loop. I teach that there are people whose career went up and then disappeared from view because they couldn't loop.

There's nothing looped in WAR OF THE ROSES. Nothing.

And that Cameron Crowe picture. There's very, very, very little looped. I use that as a reference because the scene in the bedroom where the rock star goes back to see the kid to apologize at the end of the movie. It's just a Schoeps hyper-cardioid on a boom, and I know everybody in the entire chain, I know every person who touched that film. [Laughs]

And it's perfect! I just tell them, "Do it like that!" [Laughs]

KB: *[Laughs] Well let me ask, and we're skating around this issue anyway, do you think sound can improve the story?*

TH: Oh it certainly can, without a doubt. The problem is that it's so interactive with the picture edit that, today the trend is toward more and more sound editing in the Avid by the original picture editors. They're not cutting two tracks anymore they're cutting eight to twelve tracks. And up to a temp mix they don't use any sound people.

The taking apart, scrubbing it, cleaning it, putting it back together has become more an industrial job. People in Hollywood used to divide it up by reel. On GRAND PRIX - you hire ten editors, give each one a reel. There was no sound designer idea at the time of a movie like GRAND PRIX.

Today it's a whole different approach, and it came from the 70s forward. It started with Walter (Murch) and Ben (Burtt) and people like that. It came out of Northern California and, unfortunately it got diluted by the time it got to Southern California. Now you have these characters calling themselves sound designers running around and they weren't all that good. Regrettably, the name never got a registered trademark.

KB: I see all sorts of films, especially student films where people are taking the sound designer credit and I don't hear any sound design in their work.

TH: Yeah. A few weeks ago, we must have looked at thirty student movies to pick out a sound award. We did pick one, and it was quite good . . . and everything else was pretty bad. So, one in thirty.

KB: I could see that. With budgets changing all the time, what's the biggest change you've seen in sound the last few years?

TH: I think the biggest change occurred with the conversion from analog to digital. We can look at two films: CON AIR was done completely on film and, PUBLIC ENEMIES was done digitally. Now calculating out inflation, they are similarly budgeted. CON AIR had I believe seventy people for sound. PUBLIC ENEMIES had fewer than thirty. It's a nearly three to one reduction.

There are two things going on here. Its editorial workstations and console automation. Those two things have not only reduced the number of people but they've sped up the process. So the budgets have actually followed the technology rather than the other way around. Because they can get it done in less time and less money, they do.

Of course you could say they are compromising sound quality and there's no doubt about it in some movies.

KB: What do you think the biggest challenge is now when it comes to doing sound?

TH: Everyone in post complains to me about young first-time directors, they don't have enough sound savvy. Of course, that means they didn't come from USC, [Laughs] cause we beat it into them.

The biggest complaint I hear in post is, the three-camera shoot, it's the shoot with no master, it's the shoot where they shoot the master at the end - have you heard of that one? You shoot all the coverage first, then the master - what!? [Laughs]

It's this sort of stuff that's out of control. And crossing the stage line, forget about it. I've spent more time on sets talking about the (stage) line. I mean besides lighting, the second most common thing is crossing the stage line. Nobody worries about it anymore. People are just confused therefore the pictures are confusing.

But then you get a picture that's very well put together by an obvious journeyman director like THE KING'S SPEECH. The acting is superb. But the coverage is journeyman. It works. It's not confusing.

I tell my kids to turn down the sound and watch reruns of

SEVENTH HEAVEN. SEVENTH HEAVEN is very well shot. The coverage is the coverage. They get the master - it always starts on the master, it always goes into the close-ups - and then I say, "Okay, count the setups." They don't even know how to do that. I'm working with beginning kids but they don't know coverage, pages, setups and we're trying to turn them into artistes. You gotta know your coverage and pages and setups.

KB: Absolutely.

TH: There was an interview on television some time ago with Elia Kazan and he asked the rhetorical question, "Who is the first person to the set in the morning?" And the answer was "the director."

The director comes in, blocks out the action and makes the shot list, figures out how to do the coverage. Hello.

KB: Fritz Lang used to say the same thing. He was always the first one on set and the last one to leave. Those people took it seriously. They were absolute professionals. And sometimes I think a lot of these new guys are in love with the glamor of the film business but not the working aspect of it.

TH: Yeah. You asked what's the biggest problem in post? The biggest challenge in post is directors who are very ordinary. A lot of the sound designers tell me that directors are so conservative. "What's that sound? What's that?" They don't go for atmospheres or for Walter Murch-thinking. They just want to cover what you see on the screen, and it becomes a manufacturing job - not terribly interesting.

KB: What do you think of this whole single-system thing? Has single system solved or created problems?

TH: I'm sure for those who can judiciously handle it, it has solved problems. However, the trend is toward more tracks, toward four and eight tracks. This is at one and the same time the savior and the terror of post-production. The savior because, if he's a good production-sound mixer and he does a good mix on track one, then picture post can ignore everything but track one and cut it, show dailies, everything works. Of course, there are no dailies anymore. That's another problem.

Then if everything's kept with the right file names, the sound department can go and split out the tracks and fix a radio mic fritz and things like that easily. So double system has a super advantage. Unfortunately our kids go off and change file names and file extensions without knowing what they're doing.

With single system, I saw some data years ago where the Sony PD150 had one dynamic range and as you moved up to the 500 it got considerably better, at least 12 or 15db better. And then you moved up to the F900 and guess what it did.

KB: Got worse?

TH: Yeah. It's like a PD150. Because what was on the F900 was meant to be a scratch track. They never treated it as real high quality. It did not have the dynamic range of the 500 and here you're spending four times the money and you're not getting it.

KB: I try to tell students that basically camera manufacturers could care less about sound, if they cared about sound they wouldn't mount the mic on top of the camera. In film, the camera was the camera and the Nagra or the audio gear was the audio gear. Trying to put them together in one package has always been a bit of a problem for me. I can see single system when you're doing documentary.

TH: Yeah. The kick in the head is that Sony came out with a small mixer to compete with the Shure mixers at the time, (now

Sound Devices). It has an AES digital output. Their camera does not have an AES digital input.

If you could have the converters in the mixer and run an optical cable to the camera, or a high-reliability digital link, which would probably have sync problems, that would be a good thing possibly. No syncing, not even auto-syncing, you'd be okay. But that's not happening.

KB: If you were looking for a sound person, what would be the important things you'd want to know about either them or their work?

TH: Collaborative skills. Standing up for themselves. Not having been beaten down too much by the vagaries of the business. Credits. Personality. And whether they held any really crazy technical ideas that are wrong. People make observations and the observations may very well be true; unfortunately, they often come up with a reason for the observations, which is not true. Their engineering skills are zero. [Laughs] I'm groaning, that's not the why.

That's part of why the objective sound and subjective sound chapters of my book were written. This is a test question of mine - "Why do we divide the world up this way? Why do we look at it this way?" And the answer is because in order to fix something subjective you have to fix it in a subjective domain; it may not be an objective problem.

Conversely, if you get too much reverb on the set, no amount of subjectivity is going to fix that. You better hang up some blankets, you know? [Laughs]

KB: [Laughs]

TH: Fix the problems in the right domain.

KB: A lot of students anymore ask me, "How do I get into sound?" What would you tell them?

TH: Develop an ear. I can state the frequency and sometimes the level of problems pretty quickly. I recite these to them in the mix. I'm hand holding students in the mix. In the documentary class they're doing production sound recording, Pro Tools editing of documentaries with no outtakes, and no wild lines, and no ADR - and doing re-recording (mixing) and they're doing all three skills in one semester. A twenty-six minute film, it's pretty friggin' amazing.

They can't yet nominate the frequency of a problem to treat. I've had systems where I've had to, in developing products, go through this incredibly hairy programming routine just to change an equalizer. So, I had to do it by ear and then have them run off and do a whole bunch of programming and it took one day, basically, to get a knob moved. You've got to be able to nail the frequency, level and Q of equalizers. And that, of course, is why they pay the big bucks in post-production to a re-recording mixer who can do that on the fly rapidly.

So learning that skill, for which I have a method. It's to use blind equalized pink noise A-B'ed with pink noise, which you get to equalize. And so you go back and forth and back and forth until you can get the two to match. And that test can be run by everybody. It's really hard and it's easy, in a sense, because compared to a movie it's not dynamic, it's a constant noise. Conversely, you can hear half-db errors in it so you gotta be really good! It's a great exercise.

KB: Absolutely. What's your best advice to filmmakers?

TH: Of course, it would have to be "pay attention to sound." Low-budget films always have a look. Everybody knows that, okay your look is "I'm grainy and out-of-focus." But what they don't think about is it also has sound character and if that sound character is particularly bad, it won't go anywhere.

I went to PARANORMAL ACTIVITY because it had such hype. And you realize that PARANORMAL ACTIVITY was completely and utterly made in sound post-production. Whoever decided to pick it up obviously paid for the sound post-production. That's the major ingredient to that movie because all the scary bits are just grumbles. Except for one shot . . . There's only one shot that's a special effects shot. And the rest of it are rumbles. [Laughs]

Cheapest movie ever made! We shot it for $5,000. Yeah, and you sound-posted it for what? They didn't say that part.

KB: No, and that was they same thing with EL MARIACHI and BLAIR WITCH, all those films. They dump a ton of money into post on those things and then they market that it was made for $1,000 and a hand full of magic beans.

TH: Right. Certainly PARANORMAL ACTIVITY is one where sound is telling most of the story.

When you go to Sundance or other festivals and you sit through a bunch of films, it's obvious that the sound is the worst element. [Laughs]

KB: I wrote an article for Filmmaker Magazine a couple years ago called "Why Does the Sound in Independent Films Always Suck?" I have worked on a lot of low-budget stuff and I've always said, the sooner you bring me in, the more success you're going to have as far as audio, and the better it's going to sound.

TH: So I'm having dinner in West Hollywood several years ago and a guy at the next table turns to me and says, "Didn't you teach me sound?" And of course, I've had about 3,000 students. [Laughs] And he was unremarkable and so I had to say, "Well, I teach sound, but I don't know." And he said, "Yeah, you taught me sound. I hate sound." "Why do you hate sound?". . . "Cause I'm directing my first feature and the sound guy makes the most money on the set!" So I tell every student that. [Laughs]

KB: [Laughs] That's a lucky sound guy. Usually they're an after thought.

Tell me Tom, is there anything that I'm missing? Is there anything that you think would be good for students, independent filmmakers, and young filmmakers to know about?

TH: Well, one thing that occurs to me is that cutting on the Avid is a very different experience from projecting movies full screen. What everybody tends to do is to cut too rapidly. They don't give us pauses to digest, to not sit on the master and let it build. Cut-cut-cut-cut-cut because they're trying to get some kind of energy or action into the scene on a small screen.

Unfortunately, when it translates to a big screen, it just gets to be frenetic. And this affects first-time filmmakers more than it does more experienced people. Steven's editor Michael Kahn cuts on a Moviola still, but he knows the translation. So he can cut on a small screen and make it work on a big one.

Well, likewise with sound. What are the most common words in post-production? "It sounded all right on the Avid."

KB: [Laughs]

TH: Right? Which means that with a burned out tweeter in a Fostex two-way in a room full of computers running you didn't notice all the bumps and horrors at the edits.

"You guys are too picky." Well, it's because the monitoring is so screwed up and of course those people are paying attention to the story rather than to the sound as they cut, as well they should.

But they cut too fast and they cut without an eye on what the sound is going to sound like.

I developed a system called MicroTheater that was used on TITANIC and CHAIN REACTION and CONTACT, a bunch of films in the late 90s and it was actually fielded too early. And that's because, at that time, digital editorial workstations were run by editors who didn't know how to run plug-ins. Today, the world has changed. The lines between editing and mixing have blurred. And while they're still working on workstations and maybe not doing as much with plug-ins as they might be able to do, the main limitation there is their monitoring.

They can match the background of a word that's dropped in. Let's say you have to drop one ADR line in and you can match around that. So, okay. I understand that, I have headphones. But the whole experience can't be had until you get it onto a large screen and get it into a dub. And really it is the tragically bad monitoring conditions of editing rooms that lead to that statement, "It sounded all right on the Avid." That's got to be the most common phrase heard.

KB: Thanks Tom, it's been great talking to you.

CHAPTER 10:

Putting It All Together

Storyteller

I am a Storyteller. I think about all the various elements (especially sound) that make up my films and I approach other people's films in the same way. When you are creating sound you have to find a way in to the story and characters and make it accessible to the audience.

I have done wonderful work for other people but I feel like I've done more interesting work on my own films because as a storyteller I am taking personal things from my life and trying to infuse those things in to the lives of the film's characters. I want an audience to feel like they can identify with my characters and a great way to do it is with sound.

As a working filmmaker I am in a tough bind. I can never find anyone willing to do sound design for me. They all tell me that I probably know more than they do, and since I can do it all myself, I should. I think they really don't want me to critique their sound work. So I end up doing my own sound design.

In 30+ years I've learned quite a few things.

Kelley Baker

"I am a filmmaker who has made a living doing sound."

My name is Reka Yellek. I got the job of interviewing Kelley for the book because I'm his long time editor. He wasn't going to include himself but people kept telling him he had to be in it. He made his living and part of his reputation working with people like Gus Van Sant, Todd Haynes, Will Vinton and a host of others. He never refers to himself as a Sound Designer. He is a filmmaker who has a great sense for sound.

Kelley has a natural ability when it comes to sound. Not many people know that when he writes the scripts for his films he listens to the types of music he thinks his characters would listen to. He always knows how he wants things to sound long before he shoots. I've watched him in the editing room try different sound approaches to various scenes.

One of the things I learned early on is if he comes up with an idea that sounds outrageous don't tell him it won't work until you try it. The only time I've seen him lose his cool is when he was working with a mixer who would dismiss his suggestions without trying them. He gave Kelley a condescending, "That won't work." Kelley then showed him that it would. If something doesn't work he is the first one to admit it and move on to something else.

The two things you never want to do around him are misspell his name, and refer to him as a sound guy. Trust me, when that happens he's not pretty to be around.

If you want to know more about Kelley Baker check out: http://www.imdb.com/name/nm0048634/ but don't believe all of it, some films he's never even heard of, let alone worked on.

RY: *How did you get into sound?*

KB: I started as a picture editor when I got out of USC. The great thing about USC was that you had to do a bit of everything to get out of there, so even though I wanted to be a filmmaker I had to take classes in all aspects of filmmaking. When I was doing 480 (an advanced production class) you had one crew position but you had to have a second position in something else. I was the picture editor on our film and I was the "second" for sound. That meant I had to go to all of the audio classes and I was even taught how to use the ancient mix console there, which came in handy later on.

RY: *What do you mean, "came in handy?"*

KB: Later on my roommate (who was one of the sound teaching assistants) and I mixed some "outside commercial projects" that other students were doing to pay the bills. We would sneak in to the mix room late at night, mix a commercial, short film, or whatever and be gone by 5:00 am. We got paid to do those gigs and since we were poor students in a rich school it really helped out. If we had been caught I'm sure we would have gotten in a lot of trouble, so we made sure we didn't get caught.

Anyway, on the 480 I was working on, our sound person turned out to be kind of a flake and I ended up cutting most of the sound for the movie in addition to cutting the picture.

When I got out of school I moved back to Portland, Oregon and was hired as the co-picture editor on Will Vinton's THE ADVENTURES OF MARK TWAIN. Once the picture editing was finished I asked Will who was cutting the sound. He asked me if I wanted to do it, and since I was afraid I was going to be laid off I said yes and spent the next year and a half creating and editing the sound on that movie.

RY: And that was an animated film?

KB: Yeah. I was dumb enough to cut my teeth on a film where I had to create everything from scratch and since the film is also a fantasy I really had to create a universe from scratch. That film was hard and as an editor I was a second class citizen as far as Will was concerned so there was a lot of other bullshit I had to put up with, which turned out to be good practice for when I started doing it on other films. Sound editors are always considered second-class citizens in the film business.

RY: Then you started working for Gus Van Sant?

KB: I did MY OWN PRIVATE IDAHO, we ended up working together on seven movies. It was a good run.

RY: Was there a particular film or films that had a big influence on you when you started?

KB: When I was working on MARK TWAIN, THE DARK CRYSTAL came out so I went and saw that figuring that the Muppets were pretty cool and figured I could learn a lot about how they approached sound.

I thought the movie sucked! The sound was flat and pedestrian, it was like they blew all their money on the puppets and did a very minimal sound job. That was a huge influence on me. Being young and cocky there was no way I was going to do such a shitty job.

I was creating these really complex sounds from organic materials, going out and recording all sorts of real things and then playing them back at half speed and backwards, which I could do on those old reel to reel tape machines and then transferring it all to 35mm magnetic film and cutting that one track at a time.

In the storm scene I had something like 120 separate FX tracks and I cut everything on a Kem flatbed so I didn't hear everything all together until after we had pre-mixed that reel for a couple days. I was flying blind hoping that all of these things I had created would work and move the story forward.

I used to argue with Will all the time because I was cocky enough to believe that I was always right, but I kept forgetting it was his movie. I'm not sure how he put up with me back then, but they did have me come back and do sound on I think four of their CBS specials over the years.

RY: Did you ever argue with Gus?

KB: Probably. Like I said, I was pretty cocky back then, but I also think my work backed it up. I think I did some pretty unique sounding stuff on all of the films that I worked on.

RY: Like What?

KB: The clockworks scene in EVEN COWGIRLS GET THE BLUES. Don't bother looking for it, the scene was taken out of the movie before it was released. It was this giant Rube Goldberg contraption that was built in a cave and when it went off it did all of these crazy things and I got to come up with sounds for it. The machine was designed so that when it ran it didn't make any noise so they could record the dialogue with it running in the background. So I had to create the sound of it running normally as the dialogue occurs, then a flying bat hits it and starts this whole other thing. It was pretty wild. As I recall they shot most of the insert shots without sound so I got to create this entire thing from scratch.

I think the fight scene in GOOD WILL HUNTING has great sound and I really got to push the envelope on that one. I know we ended up throwing out at least fifty percent of the sound I designed for it. By creating and then cutting out you learn what works and what doesn't.

I still think about scenes like that when I'm writing my own scripts. How can I give a character an inner life without using dialogue. How can I tell you something about their past?

RY: Do you think that your sound background helps you with writing and directing?

KB: Absolutely! I can think in pictures as well as anyone in this business but when it comes to thinking about sound on my films I have a real advantage. I see and hear the movies as I am writing them. I know what kind of music the characters listen to and what their neighborhoods sound like. I use sound to tell the audiences things about character, environment and emotion. How a piece of equipment works doesn't interest me, I want to know what can be done with it!

If you want to tell the audience about a character you can use sound effects instead of explaining it. In my film BIRDDOG, Tommy the thief lives in a bad neighborhood, he's a criminal. The house we found to shoot the scene in was a real dump that was about to be torn down but it was in a neighborhood that was pretty nice. So I only shot a tight exterior of the trashed front of the house and used sound to fill in the gaps. If you lived in a shitty neighborhood, where would that be? I used backgrounds that were industrial and even had it on the landing pattern of an airport, and there were some big barking dogs next door and a loud motorcycle that drove by. Even though you never saw the neighborhood you know it was bad by the way it sounded.

Sound is such a great storytelling device that filmmakers either overlook, or don't want to learn.

RY: You've also done some mixing but that has mostly been un-credited. Why is that?

KB: I didn't get credited because I wasn't in the union. I'm actually not allowed to even touch the mix console. Some of the mixers I've worked with over the years knew that I could mix and depending on the situation would just let me do it. Other mixers have ego problems and don't want anyone else touching the console. The good ones always knew that I had designed the FX to be mixed in a certain way, so it was easier for all involved if I just did it instead of trying to explain how I want it.

To be fair, some of the studios I have worked at over the years have been more restrictive than others. I never took it personally if I was told I couldn't mix, I never wanted to get any of the folks I worked with in to trouble. There were times on some big stages where we would put signs out stating that it was a "closed session" and no one was allowed in. That was mostly to keep the union reps out so the mixers wouldn't get in to any trouble.

I have a lot of respect for mixers, but sometimes when you create something you just want to put it together yourself. I mix all of my films with either Dan Olmsted or David Parker. Those guys are great! Mixing helps me concentrate on the sound of my films instead of just sitting there watching someone else have all of the fun. I never worried about taking a credit for mixing, it was more important to make the film the best that I could.

I know some mixers who will never admit that I was a mixer on some of the films I worked on, and there was one mixer who hated the fact that I mixed at all. Whatever.

RY: You've always said that sound gets absolutely no respect until you're in post-production. Do you really believe that?

KB: Not on my films! If you ignore sound until post, you're screwed.

You don't want to be trying to fix things in post, you want to make them better. By the time most films get in to post they have spent most of their budget so you get paid less, work longer hours and you spend your time fixing the screw ups that happened on location. I don't want to do that.

I would rather spend my time being creative and adding things to the overall feel of the film then trying to fix the dialogue so people can understand it.

On my films I always try and give myself enough time for sound. I take my time during this phase because it's truly the last time I can get everything the way I want it. It's one advantage to self-funding your own work I suppose.

RY: How do you avoid sound problems when you're shooting?

KB: First off I check all of my locations a couple times before I shoot. I want to know as much as possible about the location, not just how it looks, where's the power? I want to know what it sounds like and are we going to have any problems. When we shoot I always wear a pair of Comteks (wireless head sets). I want to know how the dialogue is sounding as it's being recorded. I don't use a video monitor on the set, I try and get as close to my actors as I can so I can feel their performance. If I can feel it and hear it clearly I know I have it. If not, we do it again.

I also give my sound crew a few extra minutes if they need it to set another mic or whatever, that can be the difference between good clean dialogue and hours of trying to fix stuff in post.

RY: What about the worst sound problem you've ever had?

KB: As a sound editor, probably the restaurant scene in MY OWN PRIVATE IDAHO. They hired some guy who didn't know what he was doing and he had mics in the restaurant to record the actors and then he hung a mic outside the place to get the traffic sounds and then he mixed it all down to a mono Nagra track. All of the dialogue had a ton of traffic background on it and sometimes you could hardly make out what they were saying. Add two young actors who didn't believe in doing ADR and we were kind of fucked! We worked a lot on that scene to try and make it sound decent. I think we did an okay job of making it work, but I still think it sounds like shit.

As a director, I still kick myself over the strip club scene in BIRDDOG. We shot the scene with the guys sitting at the rack having a discussion while this woman dances. They are talking in normal voices because the music wasn't playing while we're shooting. When I got the scene in to the editing room and put the music to it I realized that they should have been talking loudly so they could be heard over the music. I really liked the performances and didn't feel I could improve them in ADR so we kept the original. I look at that scene and it still drives me crazy.

RY: Tell me how you really feel about ADR.

KB: As a director I think ADR screws the actors mostly. You're asking an Actor to come in to a recording studio weeks or months later and become that character again without having anything to truly draw from. The other actors are not there, they're in a sterile recording studio staring at you and you're asking them to go back in time and re-inhabit this character without giving them much help. You surround them with technicians and tell them to try and read it the same and have the new read match their lips on the earlier take. That's just stupid.

There are some actors who are great at it. Matt Damon was amazing! So was Minnie Driver. There are some really big actors I worked with who were awful. Their stuff was unusable. And I worked with one famous actor who showed up to the session so fucked up that he was useless, and so was his ADR. I've heard from other people that this guy has shown up many times to ADR sessions messed up. Go figure.

I like to work with good dialogue editors because many of them can piece together words from other takes and fix a bad line and still keep the performance intact. I can also listen to a couple of takes and hear the problems and have a good idea how to fix it. I know when I'm going to have no choice but to ADR. Remember ADR isn't just about matching the lips, it's about matching the performance and that's really hard.

In one of my films I had a scene that was shot on a busy street (we had a location fall through and this was a back up location) and within a few minutes I realized that I was going to have to ADR the scene. What I did was bring both actors in to the ADR studio and have them do their lines together. The actually re-performed the scene in the studio. I had the mic between them just like the boom on location and I directed them and talked to them about the same motivations that we used on the set. I was able to re-create the feeling of the location inside the recording studio. It was a lot of work but most people have never spotted the two scenes that were completely ADR'd. I can and it still drives me crazy. I really wish I could have used the location audio because their performances were so good.

I ADR'd the entire scene not just the bad lines! That way the whole scene sounds the same. I didn't have any matching issues between the location and the ADR session.

RY: Have you had an experience where something you did in sound really improved the story you were telling?

KB: Absolutely. Look at the Madison Square Garden scene in

FINDING FORRESTER. Forrester (Sean Connery) has a panic attack when he goes to a basketball game with Jamal. When I first saw the scene with out the FX it was pretty lame, you see Connery spinning around, falling, there really wasn't much to it. After a discussion with Gus we decided to do the panic attack from Forrester's point of view. Everything the viewer is hearing is what is going on inside Forrester's head. I put in the sounds of a baseball organ, marching feet and some other things that are part of his past, things he remembers that shaped him. None of that stuff was in the script, it's what a sound designer adds. It really made the scene memorable, especially when you saw some of the things I was alluding to come up later in the film.

In the fight scene in GOOD WILL HUNTING I did the same thing. The fight is all from Will's (Matt Damon) point of view. You hear what he is hearing and a lot of the sounds relate to things in his past and things that he's feeling.

I first started using sound in that manner in MY OWN PRIVATE IDAHO when River Phoenix would have a narcoleptic fit. He would nod off and have these visions. The questions I asked myself were not only what do these visions sound like, but how can I use them to advance the story or to tell the audience something about the character. I am not putting in cool sounds to just put in cool sounds, I am using those sounds to tell the audience things that relate to story and character.

I've never understood why more filmmakers don't do this.

RY: You do these things but deny that you're a Sound Designer. How does that work?

KB: People like Gary Rydstrom, Jim LeBrecht, Jane Tattersall, Ron Eng, Walter Murch, Ben Burtt, those guys are all sound designers to me. I did it to support my own filmmaking.

What drives me crazy these days is to see people take a Sound Designer credit but they really don't know what it means. Walter and Ben really invented and defined the term. They were in charge of sound from the get go on a film and they had some kind of control over all of it. They had discussions with the directors before they started shooting and all the way through the mix.

Now you get these people who might do music, or make up some really bizarre sound effects and call themselves sound designers. I'm not saying they're not talented, actually a lot of them aren't, but they aren't in charge of the sound. They come in after the fact and fix things.

I always tell people that big action movies are pretty easy to do from a sound stand point. You pile on lots of sound, gunshots, explosions really loud shit and mostly they do that to hide really lame dialogue. If you want to really be challenged, do a quiet dialogue driven movie. That's really hard because you have to keep the track alive but you can't let it get in the way. It can't overpower the dialogue and the story. That's hard to pull off.

RY: If you were looking for a sound designer what are the things you'd want to know about someone and their work?

KB: I'd want someone with a sense of humor! They're going to have to put up with so much shit that they'd better have the ability to laugh.

I want a sound designer that knows about story and character. What can they show me that is going to advance the story or tell me something more about the character in a way I haven't thought about.

I want someone that is going to bring a lot to the table in terms of creativity. I want someone who will listen and try to translate my ideas and my vision in to reality. I never want to work with someone who is unwilling to try new ideas and who says, "That won't work," before they try something. Tell me it doesn't work after you've tried it, because I'm going to want to see it and decide for myself.

RY: When you used to sit in the mix how much control did you get over the things that you'd done?

KB: It totally depends on the director. Ultimately it's their film and I'm just a hired gun. You are there to do what they want. You can make suggestions and try to shape the mix but if the director disagrees you have maybe one shot to convince them you're right in a nice way and then you do it their way.

There are a lot of politics that go on during a mix. On one film, we had this horrible music editor that would argue with everyone about the music. She even argued with the director basically saying that his ideas weren't right and the way he wanted to mix the music wasn't right. It was a very tiring and uncomfortable situation and when that film was done we never worked with that music editor again. There are some music editors that are wonderful to work with and bring a lot to the mix, this woman wasn't one of them.

The mixers have their own points of view and some of them can go behind your back to get what they want and there is nothing you can do about that. I've heard of mixers bad mouthing editors and sound designers to make themselves look better. You hope you don't have to deal with those people but there are times that you do and you just grin and hope that they don't try to push the knife in your back too far in.

The director sets the tone of the mix and you are all there really working for them and working together for the good of the film. People really have to keep that in mind. You need to be a part of a team and do the best that you can.

When I'm doing my films I'm the guy who's in charge and I want the mix to be relaxed so mostly I work with people I trust. I keep it very low key.

RY: What are some of the biggest changes you've seen in post-production over the last few years?

KB: Before I stopped doing sound for other people I felt like half my time was spent arguing with producers about getting things I needed for my crew. There was always a fight about paying overtime, which to me was always ridiculous. I hate working overtime! I always have. I would rather be hanging out with my daughter, taking a walk, reading a book and just generally enjoying my life.

Somehow producers always think that we want to gouge them and we're not working that hard or maybe they think that we can work faster than we do. They always take the overtime thing personally. They make up the schedules and they really seem to think we can do all this work with fewer people in a shorter amount of time and all of our work will be genius.

I got so sick of fighting for what we deserved. That was one of the reasons I walked away.

I like doing the sound on my own films, I know the guy I am working for pretty well and he knows a thing or two about schedules. I make my own deadlines and I don't have someone sitting behind me.

RY: What are the most important things students need to know about sound, both location and post-production, from a director's point of view?

KB: They need to think about sound from the beginning. Forget about cameras and all of the other equipment that they all seem so concerned about. Think about what you can do with sound while you're writing you script, think about it while your shooting. Make sure you get good clean recordings of your dialogue and then use it really creatively when you're editing.

Make sure you hire an experienced location recordist and let them do their work. If the DP says we need to do another take because they think they can make a smoother camera move or there might be a problem with the last shot you always do another take for them. Why don't you do the same for the audio person. The Coen Brothers seem to and their stuff always sounds great.

If you want to be a great filmmaker you need to learn how to use all of the tools at your disposal, why are you ignoring sound? Great sound is the difference between professionals and amateurs. What do you want to be?

RY: Do you miss working in sound?

KB: Do you mean do I miss working for other people doing their sound? No! I burned out and it wasn't fun or creative anymore. I still do it on my own films and I love it then.

I feel like for the rest of my life I am going to fight this "sound thing," which is okay I guess. Doing sound gave me the opportunity to learn an awful lot about film and how the business is run.

I am at a point in my career where I don't play well with others. Actually I've probably never played well with others, but now I just want to do my own stuff. Sound is a wonderful thing and it works best when you've thought about it from the beginning. It's why I love films by the Coen Brothers, or David Lynch, people like that. They're complete filmmakers. Their films are interesting story-wise, visually and with their use of sound.

RY: Can you imagine a situation where you would go back and do sound again?

KB: I try not to.

RY: What do you tell students who want to get in to the business?

KB: Only do it if you love it. Only do it if you can't imagine doing anything else with your life. There are times when you're going to get screwed over, you're going to work crazy hours for some real assholes, and there are times when you wonder why you do this at all. It all has to come back to why you do it. You do it because you love it and you can't imagine doing anything else.

RY: I have heard you ask all of these other people if they still love what they do. Do you?

KB: I love working in film. I always have. Even on my worst days I am one of the luckiest guys in the world. I get to work doing something I love every day and in this society that is rare.

CHAPTER 11

Five Scenes in Five Films You Need to Watch

Deciding to make a list of five scenes you need to watch was not an easy one. There are so many amazing films with good sound that have been made. Do I include an action-adventure film, a horror film, a drama, and a comedy? Everyone is going to have their own opinions on this subject so I figured that since it is my book then I would pick five scenes that I find interesting and I would list a bunch more at the end of this section.

I had my own criteria for these scenes. They are from films I like and that I teach. These are films that I believe are innovative in their use of sound at the time and they have a point of view. The filmmakers and their sound people used sound in an interesting way to tell the story.

I decided against space epics and fantasy films. Yes they have to create an entire universe which is very hard to do, but I wanted films that were of a live-action variety that dealt with real people in different and unique ways. I have included some of my favorite science fiction and fantasy films in the later list.

ONCE UPON A TIME IN THE WEST

C heck out the opening to ONCE UPON A TIME IN THE WEST. There are only a couple of (badly) dubbed lines in the first twelve minutes of the movie. Everything else is sound effects, no music, just effects and this is for the opening title sequence!

Without using dialogue Leone sets up the entire film and let's you know what the themes are going to be.

Three men are waiting at a train station in the middle of nowhere. Are they waiting to pick someone up, or kill them?

The West is a really hot, boring place. We hear the sound of the windmill throughout the scene. It moves slowly and it squeaks like it needs to be oiled. It never stops. There is a wind track running but the breeze is not enough to cool anything off. The men are wearing long dusters which will come in to play later in the story. They are sweaty and they have a minimum of movement throughout this opening.

One of the telling moments when it comes to the character of these men is that they lock the Ticket Seller in to the vault and run off the Native American Woman. They don't shoot or torture any of them like many modern directors would (talking about you Quentin Tarantino). It is apparent these men are professionals not psychotics.

As they wait for the train, Jack Elam sits on a bench, puts his hat over his face and tries to get some sleep. He is disturbed by the sound of the telegraph machine so he slowly reaches over and pulls the wires out of the wall using very little effort. Then a fly lands on his chin. He spends the next few moments trying to blow it off his chin without using his hands. He is trying to expend very little effort, saving it for whatever is coming up. Finally he does use his hand to get rid of the fly and it lands on the side of the bench next to him.

I ask students what the fly sequence tells us about this character. What types of things are flies attracted to and finally someone will chuckle and say "shit!" I then ask what these characters probably smell like? They probably smell awful! The west was a dirty stinky place and through the use of the fly in this scene we are told that.

With the fly finally off his face and on the bench Jack Elam slowly pulls his gun out and in a lightning fast movement, catches the fly in the barrel of the gun. He puts his finger over the barrel and keeps the fly trapped in the barrel occasionally shaking the gun to irritate the fly inside. He smiles as he tortures the fly, a look of contentment on his face. What kind of a man is he and how fast and good does his hand-eye coordination have to be to catch a fly in the barrel of his gun? The man is a professional gunman with a sadistic streak.

Woody Strode finds shade under a water tower. There is a slow drip that hits him on his head. Instead of moving he puts his hat on, using it to collect the water and when the train finally shows up he carefully removes his hat and drinks the water from the brim. Water is scarce here and must be savored.

The third member of the gang sits by a water trough and cracks his knuckles, loosening them up as he prepares for the upcoming gunfight.

Finally the train comes in to view, we hear it before we see it. The first shot of the train is from below as it passes over us. It is huge and the presence of the railroad will be huge and a theme throughout the movie. The three men snap to attention and move in to place, and wait.

When the train pulls in and stops the steam locomotive sounds like it is breathing as it takes on water. The train is a living, breathing thing. This comes in to play later.

The three men see no one get off the train and as it exits they turn to walk away. The train pulls out to reveal Charles Bronson who has gotten off the other side of the train. He starts playing a harmonica, and in this instance the harmonica is not used as music, it is an effect, and it is laced throughout the film. It is a character in the film in the same way that the train is.

Until the sound of the harmonica there has been no music what so ever. The music doesn't come in until the Bronson character stops playing the harmonica and has a short conversation with the three killers. The music first comes in as the tension builds and we know that there is going to be a gunfight. Brilliant!

And by the way, Henry Fonda is fantastic as the psychotic bad guy in this film. Check it out!

SAVING PRIVATE RYAN

What can I say about the opening of this film that hasn't
already been said. Gary Rydstrom has done a fantastic job to
keep the opening of this film personal. This is a huge battle that
has been featured in a lot of films and usually on a grand scale.
Not this time. Spielberg and Rydstrom keep it small and personal.

The story of the storming of Omaha Beach is told from the
point of view of the troops being fired upon.

The storming of the beach takes almost twenty minutes and
there are so many amazing moments it would take an entire
book to describe them so I am going to write about the scene in
a much more general way.

We see very few wide shots in this sequence, the story is mostly
told in close up. Close ups of men's faces and hands. We are not
introduced to anyone (except Tom Hanks of course), all of these
soldiers are anonymous which is the point.

The scene starts slow as the men are in the Higgins boats and
moving towards the beach. We hear a few bits of dialogue but
mostly we get the sounds of the boats and the waves. We see
and hear men praying and puking. It is when the door of the
boat drops that the scene really takes off. We are hit with
gunfire, but not what you would ordinarily expect. The sounds
are muted. We are hearing very few shots from the point of
view of someone firing them, we are hearing it from the POV of
someone on the receiving end. A very different idea in a film,
especially a war film.

Certain things stick out in my mind, the sounds of the men
when they are under water, because there are still sounds. They
are muted and truly sound like what you might hear under water

and as the camera bounces between underwater and above water the sound transitions with it.

The sounds we hear throughout are the sounds of impacts, not rounds coming out of the barrels. We get some of those but at the beginning of the scene those aren't the predominant sounds. It is the sounds of bullets hitting the men and their equipment. We hear bullets bounce off helmets, back packs, the tank traps, and bullets exploding into bodies. Very graphic but also under played.

An interesting sound moment is when there is so much noise that Tom Hanks loses his hearing. It doesn't all go away but a lot of it does and he looks confused. We are totally focused on the Hanks character and what it must be like to be in the midst of all of this. As an audience we also need a break, we have become used to the sounds of battle and here we are getting a breather. This allows the sound track to start building again once he gets his hearing back.

Remember if this was just twenty minutes of loud explosions and guys shooting guns we would soon tire of it. But by changing up how they are handling the sound there are so many things coming at the audience that we don't have time to get bored. An audience can only take so much loud sound for so long and then it just becomes noise.

Throughout this scene we are given tiny interactions between soldiers. Some are dying, some are trying to save others, some are trying to instill order and keep moving things forward.

There are gunshots, bullets flying and explosions but everything is on a small personal level as well. Highlighting individual moments. The filmmakers are telling us that war is not grand or glorious, it's personal.

It is the details we are shown that make this scene so effective.

DAS BOOT

Check out the chapter marked "Payback" on the Original Uncut version. It is right after the sub crew has attacked the convoy and the destroyer comes looking for the sub. The scenes with the depth charges going off are wonderfully executed as the men get knocked around the sub and there are machines breaking and exploding and catching fire, in general everything you want from a good action scene.

The interesting part of the scene is in between the depth charges when it is quiet in the sub. There is very little musical score, it's almost atmospheric effects and backgrounds. We never go up to the surface to see the ship dropping the depth charges, we stay in the sub and this scene is all about sound.

The quiet of the interior sub is punctuated with the sound of the sonar coming from the ship. It is very sparse and effective. You can feel the tension in the sub.

Since the men are trying to stay quiet and not move even the smallest sound is accentuated. Be it water dripping, or the creaking of the sub itself. All of the voices are whispers and the only time we actually hear the sound of the sub running is when we are outside the sub. For the most part we don't hear the motors when we are inside with the men.

As the sub slowly descends we hear the effects of the water pressure. The squeaking and creaking and a low pitched groaning of the metal. Then the glass starts cracking and breaking and rivets start popping.

This is punctuated with the sound of the engines of the ship on the surface and the sound of the sonar as it passes overhead. We see the depth charges explode and immediately we cut inside to see the devastation.

Every time it becomes quiet in the sub we can hear the sailors breathing, or whimpering as the camera slowly moves from face to face. It is the quiet time in between the depth charge explosions that builds the tension in the scene. Even the injured are not allowed to speak or scream. They suffer silently.

This is a film that knows how to use the entire dynamic range of a sound track. In this scene it is constantly going from quiet to loud and it is mostly done using dialogue and sound effects. A minimum amount of music is layered in for maximum effect.

The use of silence is a major component of sound design in this film.

I truly believe that if this movie was to be re-made that scene would be wall to wall music and it would still have an impact, just a different one.

The other thing that has always struck me about this film is that they turn the submarine in to a character with its creaks and groans. During the depth charge sequences and when they are stuck on that ledge further down than the sub was designed to go, we hear it sounding human-like, moaning in pain.

Check out the subtitled version. Some amazing sound work in this movie and it's a good story!

TOUCH OF EVIL

I know, I have a thing for older films, I can't help it. It's also why I believe that you need to know your film history to become a better filmmaker.

TOUCH OF EVIL is an innovative film with its use of camera and sound. There are two versions of this film and I think you need to see them both. Orson Welles was fired after the first rough-cut and the studio completed the original version without him. In the late 1990s a fifty-eight page memo was discovered and Walter Murch was brought in to restore the film to Welles' original vision.

Watch the opening of both versions. The original opening is up on YouTube (http://www.youtube.com/watch?v=iAw_3HN_nsE), it is hard to find it on DVD anymore.

The Henry Mancini score is amazing. I think it's one of the best film scores I've ever heard and it perfectly captures the mood and feel of the film.

Now watch the new version (also on YouTube http://www.youtube.com/watch?v=Yg8MqjoFvy4). The first thing you notice is the absence of the Mancini score. As the camera moves you hear music and the sounds from the different clubs that you pass and the different people. The natural sounds of the street come through and there is a variety of music. The sound also seems to travel with you and it is edited and mixed for perspective.

The technique that Welles wanted for the sound of this opening is called "worldizing" and it was something that Walter thought he was pioneering some fifteen years later in AMERICAN GRAFFITI.

Watch these two sequences back to back and think about the different feelings both evoke. Personally, I like them both but I respect the updated version and am thrilled that the memo was found and TOUCH OF EVIL was restored closer to Welles original vision.

FINDING FORRESTER

I figured I should have a scene from a film I did in here so I can tell you how I achieved the sound that I wanted. I have chosen the Madison Square Garden scene from FINDING FORRESTER. In this scene Forrester (Sean Connery) has a panic attack when he goes to a basketball game with Jamal.

When I first saw the scene without the FX it was pretty lame. You see Forrester spinning around, falling; there really wasn't much to it. After a discussion with Gus we decided to do the panic attack from Forrester's point of view. Everything the viewer is hearing is what is going on inside Forrester's head.

Earlier in the script Jamal finds some old photos of a young Forrester and someone else at Yankee Stadium in the late 30s. They look like they are really enjoying themselves. Later on in the film Forrester reveals that he and his brother went to the ballpark all the time when they were growing up and then his brother went off and fought in the war. When he came back he wasn't the same and eventually he died in a car accident after drinking.

I decided to use those two incidents in my sound design in this scene. Since he is having a panic attack everything is occurring in his head so the sounds don't have to be natural, or based in reality.

During the panic attack I included the sounds of a baseball organ and soldiers' marching feet, things that are part of his past, things he remembers that shaped him.

When Forrester gets separated from Jamal in the crowd that's when he starts to panic. I cued the panic attack with a game buzzer on the FX track. We hear the buzzer and then the sound

382

dies out. Forrester looks around and doesn't see Jamal. He starts to panic.

As the panic attack builds I start layering in more sound. Voices sound strange, some are slowed down or we used re-verb. I put in some low-end rumbling and a cold wind, very lightly, I just want you to feel the bottom end of the sound. It sounds like something bad is about to happen. I layer on more sounds that get louder and louder. I am building the track up and that's when you start hearing the baseball organ, it all reaches a climax with Forrester on the floor under some bleachers and the sounds of marching feet are deafening.

The scenes bounce back and forth between Jamal looking for him and Forrester freaking out. Jamal's sound is very natural, everything is normal, but Forrester's sounds are getting more chaotic. Once Jamal finds Forrester the sound becomes normal and natural again.

None of that stuff was in the script. It's what a sound designer adds. I think it really made the scene memorable.

Other films to check out

Rent ALL THAT JAZZ, there's a wonderful scene where the cast is doing a run-through of the new play and the main character (Roy Scheider) can't hear any of the dialogue. We hear his pencil breaking, his heart beating, and other sounds like that. It's an incredible look inside his head for that scene. It helps develop and reinforce his character.

I love AMADEUS. It is a perfect blend of picture and sound editing and the music is placed seamlessly in to the narrative. How can you beat a film that people say "I don't like that kind of music, but I loved that film!" A great sounding film.

Other great sounding films include: AMERICAN GRAFFITI, THE GODFATHER, APOCALYPSE NOW, THE MOSQUITO COAST, MY OWN PRIVATE IDAHO, THE LORD OF THE RINGS Trilogy, the first STAR WARS Trilogy, JURASSIC PARK, THE CONVERSATION, GIMME SHELTER, the Pixar Films, THE ADVENTURES OF MARK TWAIN, THE TALENTED MR. RIPLEY, anything by Walter Murch, Ben Burtt, or Gary Rydstrom, the list goes on and on.

Watch the dental torture scene in MARATHON MAN, if that doesn't make you squirm, nothing will.

Final Thoughts

Well, you've made it this far. Now you have a good idea of the various steps you need to go through to get good sound on your film. One of the things I have learned talking to all of these people and making my own films is that there are no hard and fast rules with anything pertaining to sound.

Always ask yourself, how can I move my story forward using sound? Look at THE CONVERSATION, AMADEUS, APOCALYPSE NOW, DAS BOOT, THEM, SAVING PRIVATE RYAN, BLOW OUT, the list goes on and on.

Gary Rydstrom says that sound is about emotion. Think about ways to add emotion to your stories without using music. Well-placed silence works wonders, or a few subtle effects when trying to get in to a character's mind.

How can you record dialogue on set correctly so that your best performances are useable?

Give your sound people the time they need to get their microphones set. By doing this you should be able to capture that great performance that can't be duplicated in ADR.

Doing sound right is about taking the same time and care that you give to your images. It takes a lot less time to get the microphones in their proper place then it does to get your lighting right. Take the time now and you'll save time and money in post-production and be much happier with your final film.

Well, there you have it, some amazing professionals telling you about sound. It's really not that hard, and it will heighten the experience, if you take the time to learn about it.

If you listen to the people in this book, then maybe the sound in your movie won't suck and you just might get more people to see your work; if you've also paid attention to story and acting. And isn't getting a bigger, wider audience what we, as storytellers, are all about? I think so.

Now, stop bothering me! I don't do sound anymore!

GLOSSARY

16mm mono - 1 mono track recorded on 16mm sprocketed tape (also called magnetic film or mag).

35mm mono - 3 mono tracks recorded on 35mm sprocketed tape (also called magnetic film or mag). This is also known as a DME (Dialogue, Music, Effects). A DME can also be a six-track configuration as well.

Academy leader - See SMPTE Universal Leader

Academy roll-off - Control of the upper frequencies in terms of total response heard by the audience in a cinema, to minimize the effect of unwanted random noise in the system.

ADR or Automated Dialogue Replacement - Also known as looping and formerly known as post sync dialogue. A process of re-recording dialogue in a studio in lip-sync with the image. The actor delivers hers/his line while watching the looped picture thereby creating a clean version of the line.

Aliasing - Distortion in a reproduced sound wave caused by a low sampling rate during the recording of the sound signal as digital information.

Ambiance Track - See Room Tone

Bed - See Music Bed

Binkies - Re-drawn copies of the dubbing charts which are made after pre-mixing is complete. An Americanism, which comes out of Lucasfilm in San Francisco.

Bins - An old film term for when you physically hung pieces of film and magnetic film (audio) in a metal bin while you were working with them. When you were cutting a scene together you would have multiple takes from that scene hanging in a bin that you could grab and physically edit them in to a sequence (yes, with tape and a razor blade or splicer).

Bond Company - An insurance company that you pay to guaranty that should something happen during production they will put up the money to finish the film, or pay off the investors if the film cannot be completed. They issue what is known as a Completion Bond.

Burn-in Time Code - A video tape with a window displaying the time code present on the time code track superimposed over a small portion of the picture, usually with a white or black background. Older burn-in time code displays can be a frame out due to the time taken to generate the burn in.

Buzz Track - An Americanism of Room Tone

CD or Compact Disc - A digitally encoded disc capable of recording more than one hour at a sampling rate of 44.1 k.

Circle Takes - Are the best takes from a specific scene. The director will tell the script supervisor to "circle that take" after they've said cut. The script supervisor draws a circle around the take on their notes/logs. Traditionally in film, only the takes that were circled would be printed at the lab after the film was processed saving time and money. If you don't print the takes they didn't need to be processed and the assistants didn't have to sync them up with the sound. I still use circle takes even in digital. If a take isn't circled, I don't input it in to my editing system. It makes no sense to waste time dealing with material you know you're not going to use.

Clapperboard - (also called a slate) A board, which is used to mark the head sync or tail sync of a take by snapping closed the hinged section on top of the board. This gives a visual and aural head or end mark to the particular take and is used to sync rushes.

Completion Bond - A motion picture completion guaranty is a written contract that guarantees a motion picture will be finished and delivered on schedule and within budget. The majority of films produced and fully financed by the major Hollywood studios are, in effect, self-guaranteed. However, most independently financed films, including many that are released and distributed by the major studios, require a completion guaranty, such as a bond.

Compressor - A piece of audio equipment, either digital or analogue where-by the out-put of the unit can be reduced in a selectable ratio to the input of the unit with the result of reducing the dynamic range of the program. Typical ratios range from 2:1 to 20:1.

Conform - Conforming is an old film term. The editor edits the workprint, and then the lab (or a negative cutter) conforms the original film, meaning they cut the original negative according to the editor's instructions, making the A & B rolls of the negative "conform" to the edited workprint. The phrase is also used to conform all of your sound reels (or tracks) to match the new edit of the picture. (Sound editors hate conforming, but you rarely start the sound work with a "locked or completed" picture.

Control Track - A series of pulses recorded onto a videotape to resolve the playback speed by controlling and syncing the video frames. Also used on DTS sound format films to lock the CD's to the film.

Cross-fades - To fade out (an image or sound) while simultaneously fading in a different image or sound.

Cross-talk - The leakage of one signal into another. There are many examples such as the leakage of phone or communication lines into an audio recording. The leakage between adjacent tracks on a multi-track analogue tape.

Dailies - An Americanism for rushes. The film and audio shot on a particular day sunk up so that the director and the editor can watch them and start to make editorial decsions.

DAT or Digital Audio Tape - Two channel digital audiotape used on a DAT recorder. This was the standard tape format for field recording for a few years. The tapes were usually recorded at 48k sample rate.

DAW or Digital Audio Workstation - A computer-based recording and editing computer used for the non-linear editing of dialogue, music, and effects.

DME Tracks or Dialogue, Music, Effects Tracks - 35mm mono - 3 mono tracks recorded on 35mm sprocketed tape (also called magnetic film or mag). The dialogue is on track 1, the music is on track 2 and the effects are on track 3. It can also be a six track format with one dialogue track two stereo effects tracks, two stereo music tracks and one track left over for reverb or any thing else you may want to keep separate.

Dolby 5.1 - See Mixing formats.

Dolby Stereo - four tracks recorded onto 35mm magnetic tape

(also called magnetic film or mag), in the following order. Left = track 1, Center = track 2, Right = track 3, and surrounds = track 4 and then encoded onto two tracks of 35mm magnetic film sometimes called an LT RT or a printmaster.

Double Head - A system for screening a film, which does not have a married print. The sound is locked in sync with the image using a projector and a separate audio dubber. This is used for screening rushes and also for final mix screenings before a printmaster is made.

DTS or Digital Theater Systems - A six track digital system developed by Universal Pictures for Steven Spielberg. The sound is recorded onto three compact discs and locked to the film image using a control track printed on the film between the normal optical area and the image.

Dub Stage - A film/video audio mixing studio where you do your pre-mixing and final mixes. Term used only in LA.

Dubber - A 16mm or 35mm machine that will playback sprocketed tape (also called magnetic film or mag) in sync with the image. The machines are locked together with the projector using special synchronous motors, which will chase the projector and remain exactly in sync. Some dubbers can record and are usually referred to as master recorders.

Dubbing - The act or process of furnishing a film or tape with a new sound track or adding music, sound effects, etc., to an existing one. This term, only used in LA.

Dummy - An American term for a playback dubber.

EBU - European Broadcasting Union

EBU Time-code - Denotes a twenty-five frame time-code rate

used by the European Broadcasting Union.

EQ-ing or Equalizing - Traditionally it is adding filters to dialogue to make it sound smoother and/or more consistent in the context of a particular scene.

Error Correction - The process whereby digital equipment can overcome errors or drop outs in the data that it is processing, usually by repeating information immediately before and after the interruption to the data.

Faders - A multiple-unit volume control used in changing gradually from one signal source to another, decreasing the volume from the first audio or visual source while increasing the volume from the second.

Fine Cut - Occurs after the rough cut. It is what you are doing as you're getting your picture closer to completion.

Flatbed Editing Machine - A modern film or sound editing system where reels are laid horizontally on "plates" on a mechanized table with sound and picture heads. Brands include, Kem, Moviola, & Steenbeck.

Foley - Formerly known as post sync effects. The creation of footsteps and other effects by walking in sync with a projected image. Hence the terms Foley walkers, Foley artists or Foley dancers. The resultant recording will be free from any background noise and can then be used to support the sync sound in the final mix and also used to fill the M+E mix. The term is an homage to Jack Foley of Warner Studios who was one of their first sound effects creators.

Frame Rate - Frequency at which video frames occur. 29.97HZ in NTSC and 25HZ in PAL

FX - Sound effects.

Group ADR - A group of extras to do background conversations.

Kem - See Flatbed editing machines

L-C-R-S (Left, Center, Right, Surrounds) - See Dolby Stereo.

Line Count - Determining how many lines of the original dialogue you are going to replace with ADR.

Looping - See ADR.

M+E (Music and Effects) - Music & FX master for foreign language films. A copy of the final mix of a movie minus the dialogue. Any resultant loss of effects in the mix that were on the dialogue tracks are replaced by using the Foley to fill out the mix.

Mag or Magnetic Film - Film which is coated with an iron oxide compound on which sound is recorded and from which sound is reproduced.

Magnetic Printmaster (Lt - Rt) - An encoded two track recording of the final mix. The four tracks of the final mix comprising of Left, Center, Right, and Surround tracks are reduced to two encoded tracks using Dolby Stereo equipment called a DS-4. This is known as an Lt - Rt (left total - right total) where all the left information is in the Lt and all the right information is in the Rt. The center information is encoded equally in the left and right tracks at a lower level (-3db) and the surround information is also carried in the left and right tracks equally, at a lower level (-3db) but 180 degrees out of phase.

Mix Stage - Specific room for mixing all of the audio elements (dialogue, music and effects) to picture.

Mixing - To combine all of the audio elements, Dialogue, Music & Sound Effects in to one final collection of tracks.

Mixing Formats - There are many formats films are mixed in and they are changing all the time. See 16mm mono, 35mm mono, Dolby stereo, DTS, SDDS, SRD

MOS - Stands for filming without sound (literally "mit out sound"). It comes from the days when the German directors emigrated to Hollywood. As many of them could not clearly pronounce "with" they said "mit" (which also means "with", in German) the phrase 'mit out sound" stuck and is used to the day, mostly it is just referred to as MOS.

Music Bed - Background music under dialogue or narration. Mostly applied to non-drama films.

MX - Short hand for music tracks

National Television Standards Committee or NTSC - The American format for TV broadcast and video. The standard is 525 lines per frame at 29.97 frames per second. The Australian standard is known as PAL, and the French standard is known as SECAM.

One Light Workprint - An workprint of the original negative without any adjustments for exposure or color correction.

Optical Sound Track Negative - Sound track in which the recording uses variation of a photographic image.

P-FX Tracks - Production sound effects that are separated from the dialogue by the dialogue editors so that you have the option of using them or not in your mix. Sometimes production effects are replaced by sound effects from a sound effects library.

Production Sound FX - The sound effects that were recorded on location often at the same time as the dialogue, like footsteps or car doors.

PAL or Phase Alternating Line - Invented in Germany, it is the TV broadcasting standard for Australia, New Zealand, United Kingdom, Germany and most European countries except France. Based on 625 lines per frame at twenty-five frames per second. The French Standard is known as SECAM.

Phase /Phasing - When using more than one microphone you need to be wary of phasing, or cancellation. Due to the way sound waves interfere with each other, problems can occur when the same sound source is picked up from different mics placed at slightly different distances. A common example is an interview situation in which two people each have a hand-held mic - when one person talks they are picked up by both mics and the resulting interference creates a phasing effect.

Post Sync Dialogue - See ADR

Post Sync Effects - See Foley

Room Tone - An atmosphere track recorded on set for each scene of a film. The mics are positioned exactly as they were in the take or slate so as to record a background as similar as possible to the previously recorded dialogue . It is then transferred along with the selected dialogue takes for that scene and used to fill out any gaps in the dialogue track and then mixed into the dialogue pre-mix so as to achieve a smooth and seamless background to the scene.

Rushes - Also known as dailies. The first print from the film negative screened the day after they are shot. They are played double head with the sound and are used to check technical quality and artistic performance.

Sampling Rate - The number of times per second that a program is sampled to convert from analogue to digital. 44.1k for CDs and 48k for DAT. The higher the rate the greater the quality of recording.

SDDS or Sony Dynamic Digital Sound - A six-track digital system developed by Sony. The mix is printed twice, once each on the two edges of the 35mm print. One side is offset from the other to compensate for print fogging or edge damage and is read separately into ram. The system will switch automatically to the best signal and therefore by-pass any print damage or fogging. If the damage is so great that both signals from each edge of the film are corrupted the equipment will switch to the analogue mix on the optical sound track.

SECAM - The French TV standard based on 825 lines per frame.

Slate - A term used to identify a series of camera positions or angles. Eg; Slate 2 Take 3 would signify the third attempt at shooting the second camera position or angle in the scene. This information is written on a clapper board and contains the scene, slate, and take numbers, and is filmed at the head or end of a shot so as to identify it for printing and editing.

SMPTE Universal Leader - In the mid-1960s, SMPTE replaced the Academy Leader with a newer universal leader, called the "SMPTE Universal Leader", designed for both television and theatrical projection applications (though it did not gain widespread acceptance theatrically). It featured a continuous countdown from eight to two (measured in seconds, rather than feet), with the numbers in the center of a target with two white circles and a rotating "clock arm" animation. At the beginning, before the countdown, it features "16 SOUND START" and then "35 SOUND START" in a circle target. Then "PICTURE START" appears and the countdown begins. During the four count, the letters "C C F F" would appear around the countdown, signifying the use of those frames as "control frames." At two, a quick beep would be heard, sometimes known as the two-pop.

Spot/Spotting Session - When you go through the film looking for things to either add or replace. The ADR supervisor "spots" the movie to see what lines of dialogue need to be replaced. The sound designer "spots" the film to plan out what sound effects they want to use and where they're going to place them. The composer "spots" the film for music. Where do they want it and what style should it be. Spotting sessions usually happen with the director and many times the picture editor and producer as well.

SRD Dolby Digital - A six-track digital system encoded in packets of information between the sprocket holes on a 35mm print. The print also carries the analogue mix encoded in the usual optical position using SR noise reduction. If there is any damage that digital error correction cannot handle the equipment will automatically switch over and read the analogue track until the damaged section has passed.

Sweetening - Is a phrase that should never be used!!! We don't put sugar on audio track's only video people do that. Real Filmmakers mix (See Mixing)

Tail Pop - A one frame burst of tone placed at the end of a sound reel usually two seconds after the last frame of image. May also be called End Pop.

Take - The record of the number of times in a slate, a sequence of lines is filmed. See Slate for more info.

Temp Dubs - Temporarily mixing of dialogue, sound effects, and music. Used mostly for audience test screening.

Two-pop - Sound used to denote the start of a sound recording, which is part of the SMPTE Universal Leader.

Unwinding the Tracks - Going in to the master location recording and pin pointing single or multiple tracks of dialogue for sound editing.

Upright Moviola - A trade name for an upright film-editing machine.

Walla - Background ambiance or noises added to create the illusion of sound taking place outside of the main action in a picture.

Walla Group - The word walla was created in the old radio days when they needed the sound of a crowd in the background. They found if several people simply repeated, "walla, walla, walla, walla," it sounded like people talking. The audience did not really hear the words, just the buzz of voices. (Also See Group ADR)

Wild Lines - Dialogue that is recorded without the camera rolling. These can be the same lines from a scene that you're shooting and the camera or the location was too noisy to get good sounding dialogue. You do extra takes without the camera running or in a quieter part of the location. Wild lines can also be additional dialogue that is recorded after the fact that can be used to make transitions from scene to scene smoother or if you want to add additional information that was not in the original script.

Wild Track - Recordings of audio elements that are not recorded synchronously with the image.

Workprint - Copies of the original film negative used as a reference during the sound and picture editing process.

X-track - When you're editing dialogue and come across production sound effects that you are going to replace (doors, footsteps, etc) but you want to have them available for the mix in case the director would prefer to use them as compared to other effects that have been added. The dialogue editor puts them on to an X-Track, which is usually muted during the mix but all of those sounds are available and in sync should they need to be used.

& Other Points of Interests

I really hate doing a list like this because like video cameras, parts of this list will probably be obsolete by the time this thing is published. So I am going to post this list on my web site as well. Please feel free to drop me lines to update or add to it.

So for what it's worth, here it is …

Websites (and blogs) I like:

www.angryfilmmaker.com - I have to blow my own horn.
www.yourscreenplaysucks.com - This is my buddy William Akers. He's written a wonderful book. Here's his blog (http://yourscreenplaysucks.wordpress.com/)
www.POLLARDdesign.com - Cool titles, logos, and graphics, plus Jeff is a buddy of mine who does all of my design. You better call him!
www.dcshorts.com/ - This is the best damn short film festival out there. Jon Gann truly cares about films and filmmakers.
http://reelplan.com/ - A site Jon Gann runs to help filmmakers and film festivals.
www.zoomcreates.com - They designed and host my website. What can I say.
www.showbizsoftware.com - They have great software for contracts, budgeting, scheduling, you name it!
www.writebrothers.com - The best screenwriting software

http://www.shericandler.com/ - Sheri Candler Marketing and
  Publicity - Really knows independent film marketing.
www.microfilmmaker.com - another good magazine resource
www.independentfilmsdirect.com - Good features and articles
www.marklitwak.com - Entertainment Law Resources - Mark
  writes a lot of good things that we all need to know.
www.warshawski.com - Morrie Warshawski is great when it
  comes to fund raising stuff. Buy his books.
http://documentaries.wordpress.com/sponsorship-info/ -
  Documentary sponsorship site.
www.mediathatmatters.org - Progressive media stuff. We gotta
  support these guys!
www.gailsilva.com - Gail Silva consults on documentaries and
  was the Executive Director of the Film Arts Foundation for
  many years. She is a true champion of Independents.
www.swamp.org - Southwest Alternative Media Project down in
  Houston. These folks are great for workshops and screenings.
www.bavc.org - Bay Area Video Coalition.
www.911media.org - 911 Media Arts Center in Seattle. Good
  screenings and work shops.
www.mewanthorsie.blogspot.com - My favorite film related
  blog.
www.IFP.org - The Independent Feature Project. They host the
  Independent Feature Film Market. A little too main stream for
  my tastes, but they can be a good source for information.
http://groups.yahoo.com/group/Oklahomamoviemakers - Nice
  group of folks.
www.thewritersstore.com - All of your writing needs even if
  they don't stock my books.
www.celtex.com/overview - All sorts of free programs for
  making movies.
www.wga.org - Writer's Guild of America
www.wgaeast.org - Writer's Guild East
www.sag.org - Screen Actors Guild

www.aftra.org - The American Federation of Television and "
Radio Artists
www.ascap.com - The American Society of Composers, Authors
and Publishers (ASCAP)
www.bmi.com - Broadcast Music, Inc
www.filmmaking.net - There are all sorts of things here. Poke
around for a while.

If you want to make movies you have to speak the language.

www.filmsite.org/filmterms1.html - Cinematic Terms
http://homepage.newschool.edu/~schlemoj/film_courses/glossaryof_fil
m_terms/glossary.html - Cinematic Glossary from the New School.
This is a great list.
www.filmterms.com - Film Terms by Tim Moshansky
www.everything2.com/index.pl?node_id=436819 - Filmmaking
Terminology

Books I like, or think you need to read!

The Angry Filmmaker Survival Guide Part One by Kelley Baker
In the Blink of An Eye by Walter Murch
On Directing Film by David Mamet
True and False by David Mamet
Film Technique and Film Acting by V.I. Pudovkin
Film Form (a collection of essays) by Sergei Eisensten
Film Sense (a collection of essays) by Sergei Eisenstein
Your Screenplay Sucks! 100 Ways to Make it Great by William Akers
Save The Cat! by Blake Synder
The Writer's Journey by Christopher Vogler
The Anatomy Of Story by John Truby
Stealing Fire from the Gods by James Bonnet
Producer To Producer by Maureen Ryan - Great book!
*Science Fiction Prototyping: Designing the Future with Science
Fiction* by Brian David Johnson
*Sound for Film and Television and 5.1 Surround Sound Up and
Running* by Tomlinson Holman

Script Supervising and Film Continuity, Third Edition by Pat P Miller
A-Z Guide to Film Terms by Tim Moshansky
Lighting for Digital Video & Television by John Jackman
The Filmmaker's Handbook: A Comprehensive Guide for the Digital Age by Steven Ascher, Edward Pincus
The Complete Independent Movie Marketing Handbook by Mark Bosko - I learned a lot from this book, and Mark is a really nice guy.
Think Outside the Box Office by Jon Reiss
Selling Your Film Without Selling Your Soul by Sheri Candler & Jon Reiss
The Insider's Guide to Independent Film Distribution by Stacey Parks
All I Need to Know about Filmmaking I Learned from the Toxic Avenger by Lloyd Kaufman

And don't forget to check out a few film magazines.

www.filmmakermagazine.com - Filmmaker Magazine
www.moviemaker.com - Moviemaker Magazine
www.Independentmagazine.org - The Independent

If you find mistakes, or want to add more places please check out my web site, www.angryfilmmaker.com, and drop me a line. I want to try and keep some of these things up-to-date.

COOL CRAP TO OWN

You've read about the making of the movies, now own the DVDs:

- **Kicking Bird** (Soundtrack also available)
- **Birddog**
- **The Gas Café**
- **Criminal Justice**
- **Fins Feather & Friends**
- **Kelley Baker Short Films**

Go on, go to the website now and get 'em! You know you want them!

AngryFilmmaker.com

Or tell 'em how you really feel
with an Angry Filmmaker
T-shirt or cap >

You also might want stuff like Mouse Pads,
Clocks, Coasters or Stickers (not shown).

< Whoa Pardner! Don't forget a coffee mug for Mom!

Look, you're not gonna remember everything I told
you so grab a few of these: The Angry Filmmaker's...

- 50 Things You Better Know About **Pre-Production**
  Before You Embarrass Yourself Making Your First Feature

- 38 Things You Better Know About **Production**
  Before You Embarrass Everyone Making Your First Feature

- 40 Things You Better Know About **Post-Production**
  Before You Embarrass Your Family Making Your First Feature

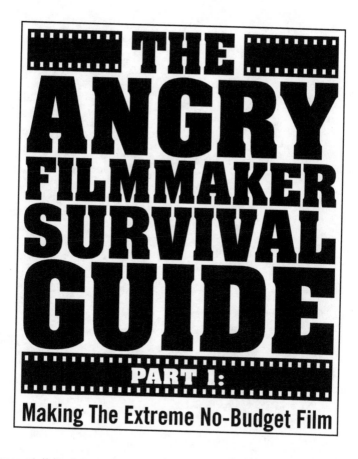

Making The Extreme No-Budget Film

Angry or not, Kelley Baker knows his stuff, and he tells it all in this book that's part indie film war story, part instructional manual for true independents, and part furious rant. It's always entertaining, and it might just tick you off, but – most important – the advice contained within these pages will help you get your film made. Anyone reading this book can tell Baker truly wants to help passionate wannabe filmmakers realize their creative visions without going bankrupt or making the kinds of mistakes they can't afford to make.

– Chris Hansen, writer/director *The Proper Care and Feeding of an American Messiah.*

Order your copy at:
AngryFilmmaker.com